WA 1265388 8

D0230245

Delivering Welfare

Second Edition

Public Policy and Management

Series Editor: Professor R.A.W. Rhodes, Department of Politics, University of Newcastle.

The effectiveness of public policies is a matter of public concern and the efficiency with which policies are put into practice is a continuing problem for governments of all political persuasions. This series contributes to these debates by publishing informed, in-depth and contemporary analyses of public administration, public policy and public management.

The intention is to go beyond the usual textbook approach to the analysis of public policy and management and to encourage authors to move debate about their issue forward. In this sense, each book describes current thinking and research and explores future policy directions. Accessibility is a key feature and, as a result, the series will appeal to academics and their students as well as to the informed practitioner.

Current titles include:

Delivering Welfare

Second Edition

Tony Butcher

Open University Press
Buckingham · Philadelphia

Open University Press
Celtic Court
22 Ballmoor
Buckingham
MK18 1XW

email: enquiries@openup.co.uk
world wide web: www.openup.co.uk

and
325 Chestnut Street
Philadelphia, PA 19106, USA

Learning Resources
Centre

12653888

First published 1995
Reprinted 1997

First published in this second edition 2002

Copyright © Tony Butcher, 2002

All rights reserved. Except for the quotation of short passages for the purpose
of criticism and review, no part of this publication may be reproduced, stored
in a retrieval system, or transmitted, in any form or by any means, electronic,
mechanical, photocopying, recording or otherwise, without the prior written
permission of the publisher or a licence from the Copyright Licensing Agency
Limited. Details of such licences (for reprographic reproduction) may be
obtained from the Copyright Licensing Agency Ltd of 90 Tottenham Court
Road, London, W1P 0LP.

A catalogue record of this book is available from the British Library

ISBN   0 335 21017 1 (hb)   0 335 21016 3 (pb)

Library of Congress Cataloging-in-Publication Data
Butcher, Tony, 1943-
    Delivering welfare / Tony Butcher. – 2nd ed.
       p.   cm. – (Public policy and management)
    Includes bibliographical references and index.
    ISBN 0-335-21017-1 – ISBN 0-335-21016-3 (pbk.)
       1. Public welfare administration–Great Britain.   I. Title.   II. Series.
HV248 .B89 2002
361.6–dc21   2002023849

Typeset by Graphicraft Limited, Hong Kong
Printed in Great Britain by Biddles Limited, Guildford and King's Lynn

Contents

Figures and tables

Preface

The aim of this second edition of *Delivering Welfare* is to provide an introduction to the delivery of welfare for students of British social policy and public administration. It describes and discusses the organization of the 'public face' of welfare delivery at the central and local levels – concentrating on the five core social services of social security, health care, education, housing and the personal social services – and the arrangements for coordination, accountability and public involvement. It also focuses on a number of key issues that have attracted attention since the early 1980s and the new directions that welfare delivery has taken. Although the discussion of the details of changes in the arrangements for the delivery of welfare, and the accompanying legislation, focuses essentially on England and Wales, the issues raised are applicable to the whole of Britain.

The organizational arrangements for the delivery of social services have been a major concern of government since the election of the Thatcher government in 1979. Under the Thatcher and Major governments, a series of radical changes challenged the public administration model of welfare delivery associated with the developments of the immediate post-war period. Local authorities, the traditional front-line delivery agencies of the welfare state, moved towards an 'enabling' role, and privatization, the search for efficiency and the customer orientation all became important features of the arrangements for the delivery of the major social services. The Blair government elected in 1997 has continued many of these initiatives, as well as putting its own stamp on the arrangements for the delivery of welfare.

This second edition retains the original structure of the first edition, but has been completely revised and updated to take account of the impact of the first Blair government, 1997 to 2001. This new edition draws heavily on the work of the many writers who have contributed to current thinking and research in the various areas covered by this wide-ranging and important subject. In examining recent developments, I have also quarried the mine of information that is available on the web sites of government departments, local authorities, the National Health Service (NHS) and other organizations (the UK government web site – www.open.gov.uk – provides access to the web sites of the various public sector organizations). I would like to thank my colleague, Ed Randall, for his advice in helping me to access some of the less well-known sites, and for reading parts of the revised sections of the book. I am also very grateful to my wife, Christine, for her expertise in constructing the tables and figures for this new edition.

I noted in the first edition of this book that one of the consequences of working in higher education in the 1990s was that research and writing had increasingly to be undertaken at times that ate heavily into family life. Unfortunately, nothing has changed in this respect. Accordingly, I would again like to thank my family for their patience and support while I have been preparing this new edition.

Tony Butcher

Abbreviations

ACC	Association of County Councils
AHA	area health authority
BQS	Better Quality Services
CAG	Comptroller and Auditor General
CCT	compulsory competitive tendering
CHC	community health council
CPRS	Central Policy Review Staff
CSA	Child Support Agency
CTC	city technology college
DEmp	Department of Employment
DES	Department of Education and Science
DETR	Department of the Environment, Transport and the Regions
DfE	Department for Education
DfEE	Department for Education and Employment
DfES	Department for Education and Skills
DHA	district health authority
DHSS	Department of Health and Social Security
DoE	Department of the Environment
DoH	Department of Health
DSS	Department of Social Security
DTLR	Department of Transport, Local Government and the Regions
DWP	Department for Work and Pensions
FAS	Funding Agency for Schools
FEFCE	Further Education Funding Council for England

FMI	Financial Management Initiative
GLC	Greater London Council
GP	general practitioner
HA	health authority
HAT	housing action trust
HEFCE	Higher Education Funding Council for England
HMI	Her Majesty's Inspectors of Education
HSC	Health Service Commissioner
ILEA	Inner London Education Authority
JASP	Joint Approach to Social Policy
JCC	joint consultative committee
JCPT	joint care planning team
LEA	local education authority
LMS	local management of schools
LSC	learning and skills council
MNI	Ministry of National Insurance
MoH	Ministry of Health
MP	Member of Parliament
MPNI	Ministry of Pensions and National Insurance
NAB	National Assistance Board
NCT	New Control Total
NHS	National Health Service
ODPM	Office of the Deputy Prime Minister
Ofsted	Office for Standards in Education
OS	Operational Strategy
PAC	Public Accounts Committee
PAR	programme analysis and review
PCA	Parliamentary Commissioner for Administration
PCG	primary care group
PCT	primary care trust
PESC	Public Expenditure Survey Committee
PFI	Private Finance Initiative
PIU	Performance and Innovation Unit
PPP	public–private partnership
PSA	Public Service Agreement
QAP	Quality Assessment Package
RAWP	Resource Allocation Working Party
RHA	regional health authority
RMI	Resource Management Initiative
RSG	Rate Support Grant (now Revenue Support Grant)
TEC	Training and Enterprise Council
UAB	Unemployment Assistance Board
UDC	urban development corporation
VFM	value for money

1

Introduction

The welfare state that was created in the years immediately after the Second World War ended in 1945, and which was consolidated and expanded in the following three decades, was deliberately set up under a form of state organization which placed a great deal of emphasis on the bureaucratic ideal of efficient and impartial administration. It was what has been called an 'administrative model' of welfare delivery characterized by the familiar bureaucratic features of hierarchical structure, clearly defined duties and rule-based procedures, in which tasks which could not easily be controlled by rules were carried out by professionally qualified staff who were given what has been referred to as 'bounded discretion' in the performance of their work (Hadley and Young 1990: 12). Such an approach to the delivery of welfare was a deliberate move away from the provision by voluntary and charitable organizations that had been such an important feature of welfare provision for much of the nineteenth and early twentieth centuries. The Labour government which came into office in 1945 and established the apparatus of the welfare state as part of the post-war settlement, 'turned [their] backs on philanthropy and replaced the do-gooder by highly professional administrators and experts' (Crossman 1976: 278). In the brave new world of post-war Britain the public sector was entrusted with the primary responsibility for the delivery of social welfare. Faith was placed in the public sector as 'a way of guaranteeing provision that was comprehensive and universal, professional and impartial, and subject to democratic control' (Webb et al. 1976: 7).

The post-war Labour government regarded the state and its administrative apparatus as the main instruments of social change (Hadley and Hatch

1981: 15). The institutions of public administration – central government departments, elected local authorities and the newly created National Health Service – were seen as the most effective means of delivering the core social services of social security, health care, education and housing, together with the various local authority health, welfare and children's services which were later to be consolidated as the personal social services in the early 1970s.

What can be described as the public administration model, with its emphasis on the efficient and impartial administration of services, characterized the organization of the delivery of welfare in Britain for most of the post-war period. Not only was the system created in the years immediately following the Second World War based upon this approach, but also, as Hadley and Young (1992: 13) have shown, subsequent reorganizations of local government, local authority personal social services and the NHS in the 1960s and early 1970s took many of the principles of this model for granted. Since the mid-1970s or so, however, the public administration model, and the institutions associated with it, has been the subject of critical debate, particularly following the election of the Conservative Thatcher government in 1979. This debate has been joined by critics on all sides of the political spectrum, ranging from the group of thinkers described as the New Right, through the welfare pluralists with their advocacy of the voluntary sector, to the so-called New Urban Left. But it is the first group who have been particularly influential: indeed one commentator has argued that the general agreement that there is a case against large state welfare bureaucracies is among the New Right's 'most striking intellectual achievements' in the field of social policy (Deakin 1987: 177).

Since the election of the first Thatcher government, the welfare state has been passing through an era in which traditional assumptions about the organizational arrangements for the delivery of welfare have been fundamentally questioned and in which major changes have been made in the organization and management of the delivery agencies concerned. The reforms introduced by Conservative governments in the 1980s and 1990s have been seen as part of the application of the idea and practices of the so-called 'new public management', which has helped to transform the public sector. Although the Labour Party was initially hostile to some of these developments, and the assumptions associated with them, the 1990s saw a growing consensus between the Conservative and Labour parties on the organizational arrangements for the delivery of welfare. By the time of the 1997 general election, Labour had adopted many of the practices of the new public management and the accompanying vocabulary of managerialism and consumerism. These practices and ideas have been reflected in Labour's approach in government.

The organization of welfare delivery, and developments since the early 1980s, will be discussed in greater detail in later chapters. Meanwhile, the aim of this introduction is to outline the main characteristics of the public administration model and to provide a brief review of the major criticisms that have been made of the traditional institutions and processes of welfare delivery.

The public administration model of welfare delivery

The traditional public administration model that underpinned the arrangements for the delivery of welfare in Britain for most of the post-war period had several distinctive characteristics:

- bureaucratic structure
- professional domination
- accountability to the public
- equity of treatment
- self-sufficiency.

These will be described in the following sections.

Bureaucratic structure

A major characteristic of the public administration model of welfare delivery is the emphasis on bureaucratic organization. Associated with the classic account outlined by the German sociologist Max Weber (1964) in the early years of the twentieth century, bureaucracy is a term used to describe a form of organization which in its 'ideal type' exhibits a number of characteristics, such as the hierarchical structure of offices, the clear specification of functions, rule-based procedures, and staff who act impartially without favouritism (see, for instance, Albrow 1970).

Bureaucratic structure has been a major feature of the traditional pattern of organization in the delivery agencies of the welfare state. The traditional organization of the delivery of social services by both central government departments and local authorities has been characterized by the principle of hierarchy, the emphasis upon uniformity of treatment, and the division of responsibilities around particular tasks such as education and housing (see, for example, Stewart 1986: 12–15). Thus the giant social security system operated by the then Department of Social Security (DSS) was described as 'the most bureaucratized, routinized and therefore "clericalized"' of the major social services (Pollitt and Harrison 1992: 10). Writing in the mid-1980s about local authorities, the major delivery agencies of the welfare state, Stewart (1986: 15) argued that the principles of the bureaucratic mode had become 'written into the thought processes' of those who worked in local government. In his view, they had become not principles but assumptions that were rarely challenged. The form of bureaucratic structure traditionally found in the local authority departments concerned with the delivery of welfare has been what has been described as that of a 'professionalised bureaucracy', the professional staff of such organizations being allowed a certain amount of freedom in the way they deliver services (Taylor-Gooby and Dale 1981: 206). As we shall see, this latter form of bureaucracy has also been a characteristic of the organization of the NHS.

The advantages of a bureaucratic system of organization are well documented: they are said to include such virtues as consistency, reliability and susceptibility to political control. A bureaucratic form of organization is also supportive of what we will later identify as two other key features of the public administration model, the values of accountability and equity (see Pitt and Smith 1981: 139). By allowing for the detailed control of subordinate staff within a hierarchical structure, bureaucracy provides a means by which large organizations can carry out their functions in accordance with the requirements of public accountability (Greenwood and Wilson 1989: 25). Bureaucracy's emphasis on the depersonalization of administration also means that the users of a bureaucratic organization's services are subject to 'formal equality of treatment' (Weber 1964: 340).

Professional domination

Another major characteristic of the public administration model of welfare delivery has been the important role played by professionals in the delivery of social services. Although the biggest spending social service, social security, is a clear exception to this general rule, professionals have dominated the delivery agencies of the welfare state. As we shall discuss in Chapter 3, elected local authorities and the institutions of the NHS are dominated by professionals. It is doctors, teachers, social workers and other welfare professionals – described by one writer as the 'trusted instruments' of the welfare state (Donnison 1982: 21) – who deliver welfare and, in many cases, make key decisions about resource allocation and other important issues. As Klein (1973: 4) has observed: 'The Welfare State is, in many respects, also the Professional State'.

The development of welfare professionalism was an inevitable concomitant of the expansion of state social services in the post-war period. As Wilding (1982) puts it in his discussion of the nature of professional power in the field of social welfare:

A commitment to welfare by government means a need for professionals – to advise on the organisation of services, to manage, man and mediate services, to decide questions of eligibility and need, to individualise justice, to raise standards of health and child care.

(Wilding 1982: 14–15)

The three decades following the end of the Second World War represented what has been described as 'the high tide of professionalism' in the welfare state, with professionalism becoming 'the dominant occupational paradigm' (Laffin and Young 1990: 32, 17). The two well-established welfare professions – medicine and education – consolidated their positions: indeed, as we shall discuss in Chapter 3, the medical profession were given substantial representation in the administrative structure of the NHS established in 1948, as well as being allowed to continue to enjoy considerable professional autonomy in the way they delivered health care. Although not enjoying the same degree of influence and autonomy as the medical profession, the teaching profession was also given a substantial amount of freedom in the running of the post-war education system.

Other welfare professions developed within local government as local authorities were given responsibility for those services requiring what has been described as face-to-face 'professional style' involvement with the users of services (Cochrane 1993: 14). Thus, the new welfare responsibilities imposed on local authorities by the post-war legislation dealing with domiciliary and residential care, child care and community care 'pointed the way' for the growth of the social work profession in the 1950s and 1960s (Marwick 1982: 62–3), culminating in the creation of a single professional social work organization, the British Association of Social Workers, in 1970. This particular process of professionalization was reinforced by the setting up of unified local authority social services departments a year or two later. While the development of professionalization in the sphere of local authority housing was not nearly as rapid as in the other two major local authority social services, the commitment of successive post-war governments to municipal housing did result in an acceleration in the development of housing management, which had begun to establish itself as a profession by the late 1970s (Rhodes 1988: 221–2). In the closely related area of town planning, the post-war package of land-use planning established by the Attlee government, and developed by later administrations, increased the power of another professional group – town planners – in decisions about housing and urban problems.

Thus, in the words of one commentator, 'Professional power has marched hand in hand with public welfare' (Wilding 1982: 70). Although it is difficult to generalize about the nature and extent of such power in the delivery of welfare, it is possible, using the typology constructed by Wilding (1982), to identify the different types of power exercised by welfare professionals. First, welfare professionals exercise power in both the making of welfare policy and its administration. Second, the power of welfare professionals is underpinned by their generally accepted right to define the needs and problems of their clients. Third, welfare professionals exercise power and influence in the allocation of resources, not only at the level of general planning decisions by central and local government, but also at the organizational level – hospitals, schools and so on – and in routine decisions affecting the individual client. These last two forms of power both affect the way services are delivered and are examples of the way in which welfare professionals exert power over people – the fourth type of power. Finally, welfare professionals have power to control their area of work, through such devices as self-regulation of the profession.

These powers clearly derive in part from the expertise of welfare professionals and the important role that they play in both the making and implementation of social policy, but, as Wilding (1982: 67) observes, professional power is also buttressed by the bureaucratic nature of welfare delivery agencies. Being part of a bureaucratic organization releases welfare professionals from many of the constraints encountered if they work on their own in the private sector. Thus Wilding usefully quotes Klein (1973: 5): 'To the extent that the professional becomes part of an administrative machine . . . so his command over resources, and his ability to affect the consumer, is magnified'.

Accountability to the public

Another important characteristic of the public administration model of welfare delivery is accountability. The concept of accountability is an elusive one and we shall encounter it, in its various guises, throughout this book. One important aspect of what Day and Klein (1987: 1) describe as this 'chameleon word' is the existence of public accountability to elected representatives, at both the national and local level. As one textbook on public administration put it: 'At its most elementary, public accountability simply requires that public bodies give an account of their activities to other people and provide a justification for what has been done' (Smith and Stanyer 1976: 30–1). Thus the Secretary of State for Work and Pensions is accountable to Parliament for the operations of the Department for Work and Pensions (DWP), while their cabinet colleague, the Secretary of State for Health, is accountable to Parliament for everything that happens in the NHS. At the local government level, local authority cabinet members and officers responsible for the delivery of education, housing and the personal social services appear before scrutiny committees of the elected local authority to explain policy.

The accountability of the delivery agencies of central government, local government and the NHS is not confined to the political dimension. The armies of bureaucrats and professionals employed by the delivery agencies of the welfare state are also subject to what has been referred to as administrative accountability: the duty to account to non-political bodies which examine the fairness and reasonableness of administrative procedures – administrative tribunals and the various ombudsmen who operate at the level of central government, local government and the NHS (Oliver 1991: 27). This particular form of accountability also includes the duty of local authorities and NHS bodies to account to the Audit Commission with regard to efficiency and value for money (VFM). Like other public bodies, the delivery agencies of the welfare state are also accountable to the courts, having to make sure that their activities conform to the requirements of legality.

Thus, as one distinguished writer on post-war social policy, Richard Titmuss (1974: 55), observed, public accountability is a distinguishing feature of the public administration of the social services, the agencies delivering social services being subject to 'quality controls' through Parliament and other procedures. In addition, the welfare professionals employed by local authorities and the NHS, who, as we have seen, play a major role in the delivery of welfare, are also accountable to their peers and professional associations. We shall discuss these various forms of accountability in more detail in Chapter 5.

Equity of treatment

Another characteristic of the public administration model, with its emphasis on impartial administration, is that the personnel responsible for the delivery of social and other public services are, in the words of Greenwood and Wilson (1989: 9), 'expected to treat members of the public fairly without showing partiality to one at the expense of another'. Or as Glennerster (1992a: 32) has put it: 'Public organisations must be seen to be dealing fairly with all those who use the service. Like cases must be treated alike'.

Many of the services and benefits provided by the delivery agencies of the welfare state are specified in detail in legislation and there is a public expectation that delivery agencies and their staff will treat everybody equally and fairly. This value of equity 'puts a premium on stability, consistency and accuracy' in the operation of public bodies (Smith and Stanyer 1976: 31). As we shall discuss in Chapter 5, in parts of the social security system, this expectation is actually institutionalized in the form of the adjudicatory machinery provided by administrative tribunals. A range of ombudsmen also operate in an attempt to ensure that the users of social services are treated reasonably in their dealings with the various delivery agencies of the welfare state.

Self-sufficiency

Finally, another characteristic of the public administration model is what Stewart and Walsh (1992: 509), speaking of the public services in general, refer to as the assumption of self-sufficiency. Where a public organization is responsible for a function, it has normally carried out that function itself and employed those who deliver the service. As Pinker (1992: 273) has observed, it was 'taken for granted' in the years following the creation of the welfare state that the state had a dominant role to play as both the funder and provider of social services.

The two roles were not always combined. Before the emergence of a developed welfare state, government intervention in both education and housing had involved the separation of the funder and provider roles. Thus, in the nineteenth century, central government gave grants to voluntary societies to provide local education, while immediately after the First World War ended in 1918, government subsidies were given to private builders to provide working-class housing. But the need for closer quality control, together with demands for stronger financial and political accountability and equity in service provision, resulted in the fusion of the roles of funder and provider (Glennerster 1992a: 32–3; 1992b: 15–16). The 'accepted way of thinking' about the delivery of welfare in the system that developed in the post-war period was that social services should be both financed and provided by an agency of the state (Glennerster 1992a: 31). Thus welfare delivery agencies fulfilled the role of both funder and provider of most social services. The state provided and financed the core social services of education, housing, the personal social services, social security and health care.

The public administration model under challenge

The public administration model of welfare delivery has long been the subject of criticism, but the traditional methods of delivering welfare, and the key assumptions underpinning them, have been the subject of particular debate since the election of the first Thatcher government in 1979. The debate has revolved around a number of specific, though interrelated, concerns. It is possible to identify four main themes: first, that the delivery agencies of the welfare state are inefficient, wasteful and unbusiness-like, with a lack of concern for efficiency and value for money; second, that welfare delivery agencies are provider dominated and pay insufficient attention to the needs and wants of the users of their services; third, that the institutions of welfare delivery and their personnel are not close enough to their users or customers; and fourth, that the delivery agencies of the welfare state are not sufficiently accountable. The rest of this chapter will discuss these concerns.

Inefficiency and waste

Contrary to the classic Weberian notion of bureaucracy as a form of organization that operates more efficiently than other forms of body, there has long been a popular view that associates public sector bodies with inefficiency and waste. Indeed, Albrow's examination (1970: 89–91) of the various usages of the term includes one definition of bureaucracy as 'organizational inefficiency', and writers on bureaucracy have long pointed to such imperfections as duplication of effort and unnecessary red tape. Since the early 1980s, criticisms about inefficiency and waste in the delivery agencies of the welfare state have been part of a wider debate about the size and efficiency of the public sector, a topic which we shall discuss in greater detail in Chapter 8.

All three major types of delivery agencies of the welfare state have been the subject of concerns of this kind. Central government's administration of what is by far the most expensive part of the welfare delivery system – the huge social security benefits operation – has long been the target of criticism regarding its inefficiency and wasteful procedures. The House of Commons Public Accounts Committee (PAC), charged with the oversight of the spending of government departments, has regularly commented on the overpayment of social security benefits resulting from administrative errors (see, for example, Public Accounts Committee 1971), as well as the high costs of administering the social security system (see, for example, Public Accounts Committee 1978). One survey in 1984 discovered that 40 per cent of social security benefit claimants were not receiving their correct entitlement to benefit because of errors by the then Department of Health and Social Security (DHSS) (McKnight 1985: 35), while, a few years later, evidence on the same department's efficiency indicators showed that over 10 per cent of supplementary benefit payments were wrongly calculated (see MacPherson 1987: 142). In 1987, the National Association of Citizens Advice Bureaux actually sought an action for judicial review against the DHSS for the department's failure to meet its target times for processing benefit claims. There continued to be criticisms throughout the 1990s about the enormous waste of public money arising from wrongly paid social security benefits (see, for example, Public Accounts Committee 2000).

There has also been a widespread belief that local authorities, the major delivery agencies of social services, are inefficient and wasteful, despite the fact that there is little real evidence to prove or disprove such claims (Newton and Karran 1985: 17–18). Concern about value for money in local authorities figured prominently in the evidence given to the Layfield Committee on local government finance in the mid-1970s (Layfield 1976: 90). There has been particular concern about the management of local authority housing. For example, in the early 1980s, the former chief housing officer of one London borough, Alex Henney (1984: 216, 260), argued that local authorities had 'spent a great deal of money producing unpopular housing slowly and expensively, without knowing what it cost'. He further maintained that the problem of waste and the lack of concern for value for money was not confined to local authority housing: it was widespread and also included education and the personal social services.

Neither has the third major welfare delivery agency, the NHS, been immune from such criticisms. A study undertaken for the Royal Commission on the National Health Service in 1979 referred to criticisms about the quality of management in the service, a view supported by research undertaken for the Commission, which concluded that the NHS's system of financial management did little to ensure that resources were efficiently and effectively used (Merrison 1979: para. 4.19). Parliamentary select committees have also charged the NHS with inefficiency in the use of resources, highlighting defects in the financial control exercised by health authorities and stressing the need to increase the commitment to value for money (see, for example, Public Accounts Committee 1976). Criticisms of the lack of efficient management and value for money in the NHS have also come from the right-wing Adam Smith Institute, whose director referred in the late 1980s to the costs of the service being unknown and waste remaining unchecked (Butler 1988).

One critic actually referred to the NHS in the late 1980s as 'the land of waste', alleging that it wasted several billion pounds every year, examples of which ranged from an inefficient use of property to the lack of controls on the purchase of certain types of medical equipment (see Coleman 1989: 122). Evidence of widespread variations in levels of spending on similar services between different health authorities has also raised questions about efficiency and value for money in the NHS. Official figures published in the late 1980s revealed that the average cost of treating acute hospital inpatients in 1986–87 varied by as much as 50 per cent between different health authorities (Department of Health 1989a: 3).

These kinds of complaints about the inefficient and wasteful nature of welfare delivery agencies were given intellectual respectability in the 1980s by the New Right. Thus public choice theory (which we shall examine further in our discussion of provider domination in the next section) argues that the inefficiencies of public sector bureaucracies are located in what has been referred to as the 'property-rights structure' of such organizations, in which there is no incentive to closely monitor organizational slack (Dunsire and Hood 1989: 147).

Criticisms about inefficiency and waste have not been confined to those on the right of the political spectrum. In the run-up to the 1997 general election, 'revulsion at waste' was depicted by two of Tony Blair's advisers as 'a core New Labour instinct' (Mandelson and Liddle 1996: 151). Over four years after the election of the Blair government, there continued to be criticisms about the efficiency of the delivery agencies of the welfare state. The Department of Health (DoH) found that there was still considerable scope for local authority social services departments to improve their efficiency (Department of Health 1998: para. 7.16). In late 2001, a senior DoH official said that at least one-sixth of the NHS's annual budget was being lost through waste and inefficiency (Smith and Cracknell 2001).

Provider domination

Another major theme in the contemporary debate about the traditional arrangements for delivering welfare has been the concern about provider domination. Critics on both the right and the left of the political spectrum have argued that the delivery agencies of the welfare state are provider

dominated and driven by the needs and wants of the providers of services –
welfare bureaucrats and professionals – rather than by the needs and wants
of the users of those services.

There are a number of strands to this particular argument. From the
perspective of the ideology of the New Right, public choice theorists argue
that welfare delivery, and other public sector, organizations promote the
growth of their activities and tend to 'oversupply' their services in an attempt
to maximize their budgets, responsibilities, status and job security (see, for
example, Niskanen 1971). Not only is it argued that what is seen as the
tendency of public bureaucracies to oversupply services results in waste
and lack of value for money, but also it is claimed that it leads to the preferences of the consumers of services being ignored in favour of narrow
sectional interests. Thus, writing in the early 1980s about welfare administrators, Nigel Lawson, then Financial Secretary to the Treasury, argued
that far from being 'the selfless Platonic Guardians of paternalistic mytho-
logy', the providers of social services were 'a major powerful interest group
in their own right' (Lawson 1980: 9). In 1973, one of Lawson's colleagues
in the Thatcher government, Nicholas Ridley (1973: 87), the minister in
charge of the restructuring of council housing in the late 1980s, had described
the work of one leading public choice theorist as 'of devastating importance'.

Twenty years later, another Conservative Cabinet minister, William
Waldegrave (1993), writing about the post-war reforms of the public sector,
argued that:

> it turned out that we had designed public services where the interests
> of the providers systematically outweighed those of the users, and
> which, driven only by the natural tendency of all provider organizations
> to claim that they can only do better with more money, contained an
> overwhelming dynamic for increasing cost which was bound to end
> in conflict with reality.
>
> (Waldegrave 1993: 9–10)

Concerns about provider domination in the welfare state have not, of course,
been confined to critics on the right of the political spectrum. Critics on the
left have expressed similar worries, although, as we shall see in later chapters,
the solutions offered by the two sides have been very different. Thus, a
Fabian pamphlet of the late 1980s claimed that welfare bureaucracies were
unresponsive to public demands, having taken it upon themselves to
'designate what the public needs rather than responding to its demands'. It
argued that the delivery agencies of the welfare state 'see the public as a
passive receiver of services rather than as citizens who have obligations to
and rights over public institutions' (Corrigan et al. 1988: 10).

Arguments of this kind overlap with long-standing criticisms of the
role of welfare professionals in the making and implementation of decisions
about the delivery of welfare. Since the late 1960s, there has been a growing
challenge to the right of welfare professionals to define needs and problems

and to the view that professional solutions are the best responses to the kinds of problems found in such areas as housing and health care. As Pollitt (1984b: 29) has argued, the 'heroic, uncritical image' of welfare professionals as highly educated experts with the interests of their clients and the public good at heart, has come under attack. Thus Wilding (1982) has observed that:

> professional influence means that in many issues the decisions made serve professional interests rather than the public interest . . . it leads to services organized according to professional skills and ideas rather than according to client need.
>
> (Wilding 1982: 23)

The provider domination critique has been applied to a number of welfare delivery agencies. Thus the criticisms of the state education system made by the right-wing Adam Smith Institute (1984: 2–3) in the mid-1980s referred to 'producer capture', arguing that the local authority education system had been 'captured' by producers – the teachers and administrators – whose objective was not to respond to the wishes of the consumers, but to impose their own wishes on the educational system. Ranson and Thomas (1989) encapsulate the issue in their summary of this particular critique:

> The professionals create a technical language which serves only to bamboozle ordinary people and they organize the system for their convenience rather than to respond to the demands of the consumers.
>
> (Ranson and Thomas 1989: 56)

Local authority housing is also an area in which critics have claimed that provider definitions of needs and problems have been accepted by policy-makers rather than the definitions of those directly affected by the outcomes of policies (Wilding 1982: 30). One element of the New Right critique of state housing is that the design and management of post-war housing has been dominated by professional and bureaucratic self-interest, unwilling to adapt to consumer demand (see Cole and Furbey 1994: 192–3).

Such strictures have not been confined to the social services delivered by local authorities. Similar criticisms about provider domination were made about the NHS before the reforms of the early 1990s. Thus Alain Enthoven (1991: 62–3), the North American health economist, whose notion of an internal market was so influential in the debate leading up to the Conservatives' NHS reforms (on which see Chapter 8), argued that: 'Behind the rhetoric of caring for patients, the NHS was provider-dominated', with each district health authority (DHA) being a monopoly supplier of health services to people in its particular area. As Enthoven (1991) observed:

> consultant physicians had lifetime contracts with Regional Health Authorities, with merit pay determined by professional recognition, not service to patients. Nobody was seriously charged with the

responsibility to measure and prioritize patients' needs and wants and then to use resources as effectively as possible in response.

(Enthoven 1991: 63)

Provider domination has also been criticized by the Labour Party, which has 'consistently positioned itself' on the side of the consumer of public services against the provider power of public bureaucracies and professionals (Clarke et al. 2000: 15). The Blair government has made it clear that no vested interests will stand in the way of renewing the public services, Tony Blair arguing that 'Pupils do not exist for state schools, but state schools for pupils. The patient does not exist for the NHS, but the NHS for the patient' (quoted in Morris and Grice 2001).

Consumerism and being closer to the customer

Closely related to criticisms about provider domination has been the growing concern about the relationships of the delivery agencies of the welfare state and their staff with the consumers of services. Writers on private sector management emphasize the importance of listening to the customer: the best run private sector organizations are seen as those who, inter alia, take the customer seriously (see, for example, Peters and Waterman 1982; Osborne and Gaebler 1992). But the period since the early 1980s has been dominated by criticisms that unlike the best run private sector organizations, organizations in the public sector are not 'close' enough to their 'customers'. While the term 'customer' might not be the most appropriate term to describe the users of social services, the gulf between the delivery agencies of the welfare state and the users of their services has been at the forefront of debate since the late 1980s. The importance attached to the users of services was reinforced by the advent of the Major government's Citizen's Charter and the subsequent publication of individual charters for most of the core social services. Consumerism was already on the Labour Party's agenda – its 1987 election manifesto had proposed a Quality Commission to ensure efficient, responsive and high quality local authority services – and was to become a major theme of the Blair government's approach to the delivery of public services.

Writing in 1990, Laffin and Young (1990) described the whole issue of consumerism as a 'major new addition' to the political agenda. Speaking of consumerism within local government, they argued that:

The rise of consumerism . . . challenges the bureaucratic or professional definition of citizens' needs. Consumerism reflects the disillusionment with the paternalistic welfare state which is increasingly seen as large and bureaucratised and as insensitive to individual requirements.

(Laffin and Young 1990: 43)

As we shall discuss in our examination of this issue and developments since the early 1980s in Chapter 9, consumerism and the concept of being 'closer to the customer' have a number of different dimensions. One important dimension is the geographical accessibility of service providers to the users of their services. Another dimension is what has been described as 'social accessibility' (Hambleton and Hoggett 1988: 22) – whether the staff responsible for delivering welfare are sensitive enough to the needs of the users of their services. Getting closer to the customer also involves finding out about the needs of service users, generating consumer feedback on service delivery and providing more information on services. As the Blair government put it in its *Modernising Government* White Paper (Cabinet Office 1999: 25), 'If public services are to serve people better, the Government needs to know more about what people want'.

An excellent example of the way in which the welfare delivery system has been said to demonstrably fail to reflect the principle of being close to the customer has been central government's arrangements for the delivery of social security benefits. The administration of the social security system has long been the target of complaints, critics arguing that high levels of staff turnover, inadequate staff training, poor pay and low levels of staff morale have all combined to create a climate which has not been conducive to giving sufficiently high priority to the 'sympathetic administration' of the benefits system (Alcock 1987: 117). As Metcalfe and Richards (1990: 96) observed of the arrangements for paying benefits to the unemployed: 'Few claimants felt that the system worked in a way that made any concessions to their convenience or their interests'.

The government department responsible for the delivery of social security benefits has long been aware of its poor relations with the public. As long ago as 1983, the then DHSS acknowledged that it was not fully complying with its statutory duty to provide 'a prompt, accurate, courteous and humane income maintenance service'. In a revealing phrase, the permanent secretary in charge of the social security side of the department stated that its staff had to recognize that 'doing business with one of our local offices must often seem a less agreeable experience than approaching many other undertakings' (quoted in MacPherson 1987: 131). In 1988, research comparing 20 organizations providing services to the public showed that although the customers of the social security system rated it as providing a better service than the courts and the police, and on a par with local authorities and some other bodies, it was ranked lower than 14 other organizations with which the public had contact (Moodie et al. 1988: para. 20).

It is not only central government departments that have been criticized for failing to take the consumers of their services seriously. Criticisms have also been made about the gap that exists between the local authority departments responsible for the delivery of local social services and the users of their services. High on the agenda have been concerns about the geographical inaccessibility of the departments responsible for housing and the personal social services. Concern has also been expressed that local authorities have tended to provide services *to* the public rather than *for* the public, with service providers believing that they know what the public wants or needs (Stewart and Clarke 1987: 167). Research conducted for the Association of Metropolitan Authorities in the mid-1980s found that nearly one-third of those members of the public who had attempted to contact a local authority official had experienced difficulty in getting hold of the right person, with a similar proportion finding officials uninterested in their problems (quoted in Gyford et al. 1989: 245).

Concern about the lack of sensitivity to service users has also been an important theme in criticisms of the NHS. Since its inception in the late 1940s, the NHS has been pervaded by the medical model of health, in which the medical profession has a pre-eminent position in matters of health care (see, for example, Ham 1999: 207). The general acceptance of this particular model has been used to justify not only the dominant role of the medical profession in the delivery of health care, but also the profession's failure to take sufficient account of the needs of patients and to involve the public in the running of the NHS (Hogg 1990: 154–5). In the words of one commentator writing in the 1970s, there has been a tendency within the NHS to assume that 'what is good for medicine is also good for the patient' (Brown 1973: 84). As a result, for many years, the NHS was seen as a producer-orientated organization that made little attempt to discover the reactions of the public to its activities. Such arguments were given official respectability in the early 1980s in the critique of the Griffiths Report (1983: 10), which concluded that, unlike the private sector, it was not clear that the NHS was meeting the needs of its customers.

Accountability

Another major strand in the contemporary debate about the delivery agencies of the welfare state and their personnel has been concern about their lack of accountability. This concern has several dimensions, one of which is the accountability of delivery agencies for the money which they spend. Particular concern has been expressed about the financial accountability of the NHS, with the House of Commons Public Accounts Committee during the late 1970s and early 1980s highlighting the lack of financial control exercised by various health authorities over spending from the funds provided through the DHSS (see, for example, Public Accounts Committee 1976, 1977, 1981). The recessionary economic climate of the 1970s and 1980s also saw a growing concern on the part of central government with ensuring that delivery agencies such as the NHS and local authorities – widely viewed, as we saw earlier, as inefficient and wasteful organizations – were answerable for the efficient use of resources.

The debate about accountability has not been confined to concern about the control of spending and the efficient use of resources by welfare delivery agencies. It has also included worries about the professionalization of welfare delivery, which has, in the words of one observer, the potential to become a mechanism for avoiding not only control from the centre, but also accountability to the consumer (Means 1993: 16). In a similar vein, Elcock (1983: 25) has argued that local government professionals are resistant to outside control, suggesting that what he refers to as 'accountability outwards' to colleagues within the professions and relevant local authority departments has been strengthened at the expense of 'accountability upwards' to elected local councillors and 'accountability downwards' to the users of services. Welfare professionals such as social workers, teachers and doctors – who interact with members of the public and exercise a high degree of discretion in their work – are examples of what have been termed 'street-level bureaucrats' (Lipsky 1979: 17). Such groups are difficult to control, especially the medical profession – described as 'the ultimate example' of 'street-level' power (Lowe 1993: 47) – which has traditionally operated on the basis that doctors have 'clinical freedom'.

A key theme in New Right criticisms of the welfare state has been that unless welfare delivery agencies and other public organizations are limited by stronger systems of accountability, they will put their own interests before those of service users (Oliver 1991: 15). This particular argument was an important element in the development of Conservative government policy towards the public sector, it being argued that there was a 'implied mistrust' of traditional forms of public accountability as a means of controlling the performance of public services (Oliver 1991: 14). Consequently, Conservative governments in the 1980s and 1990s introduced a number of initiatives in an attempt to enable the consumers of social services to exercise greater influence over the delivery of welfare. This emphasis on accountability to the consumer has been continued by the Blair government.

Plan of the book

The remainder of this book is divided into two parts. Part I describes and discusses the structure and organization of welfare delivery – the 'public face' of welfare. Chapter 2 focuses on the central government departments responsible for the provision of social services. It identifies the main social service departments and their functions, highlighting the important distinction between those government departments that are directly involved in the delivery of social services and those who perform what is essentially a policymaking, resource allocation and supervisory role. The chapter goes on to explore the work of the DWP – created by the Blair government following the 2001 general election, and the biggest spending government department – and the role of its semi-autonomous executive agencies, operating at arm's length from the policymakers who remain in the core of the department in Whitehall.

The discussion of the organization of welfare delivery is continued in Chapter 3, which examines the other public bodies responsible for the delivery of welfare – elected local authorities, the institutions of the NHS, and various quasi-governmental bodies. This chapter also discusses the problems encountered by central government departments in attempting to ensure that the organizations making up what has been described as 'sub-central government' successfully implement centrally determined welfare policies. An important issue raised by the number and range of bodies involved in the delivery of welfare is that of coordination, which is the subject matter of Chapter 4. The coordination and planning of social services is essential to the delivery of welfare, and the chapter discusses the major obstacles to the successful coordination of social policies and assesses the various mechanisms intended to overcome these barriers. As we shall discuss, the Blair government has attempted to overcome such obstacles by endeavouring to introduce a more holistic approach to the delivery of social, and other, services through its emphasis on 'joined-up government'. In Chapter 5, we turn to a discussion of the procedures for accountability and the redress of individual grievances, as well as discussing the various arrangements for involving the users of social services in the processes of welfare delivery.

Having discussed the framework and institutions of welfare delivery, Part II leads to a discussion of important developments since the early 1980s. Chapter 6 considers the changes that have taken place in the role of elected local authorities as delivery agencies of the welfare state. It begins by looking at the role of local authorities and their relationships with central government in the post-war years before the election of the Thatcher government in 1979. It then considers developments under the Thatcher and Major governments, particularly the transformation of local authorities from front-line delivery agencies of the welfare state into what have been described as enabling authorities. As we shall see, the erosion of local authorities as direct service providers has not been reversed by the Blair government, and service provision continues to be shared with a range of other organizations. Chapter 7 moves on to an examination of the privatization of welfare delivery, focusing in particular on the privatization of council housing under the Conservatives, contracting out, the encouragement of the private sector, and the introduction of quasi-markets into the operation of the NHS and the personal social services under the Thatcher and Major governments. The chapter also examines the expanding role of the voluntary sector in the context of the privatization of welfare delivery, as well as the increasing emphasis on public–private partnerships (PPPs), which has been such a significant development under the Blair government. Closely related to questions of privatization is the whole issue of managerialism and the search for efficiency and value for money in the operations of the delivery agencies of the welfare state, and this is the subject matter of Chapter 8. As we shall see in this chapter, all three main types of welfare delivery agencies – central government's social service departments, local authorities and the NHS – have been greatly affected by attempts to encourage value for money and more business-like methods, a process seen by many observers as conflicting with the traditional values of the public administration model of welfare delivery. Chapter 9 looks at attempts to bring the delivery agencies of the welfare state closer to what are increasingly described as the 'customers' of social services, as manifested in such initiatives as the increasing emphasis on consumerism and customer care in the delivery of welfare and the geographical decentralization of local authority housing and the personal social services to area and neighbourhood offices. This chapter also examines the principles of 'charterism' implemented in the major social services following the introduction of the Major government's Citizen's Charter, relaunched by the Blair government as *Service First*.

The final chapter returns to the public administration model discussed in this introductory chapter and considers how it was affected by developments under the Thatcher and Major governments. It concludes with a discussion of the impact of the Blair government on the arrangements for delivering welfare, and its contribution to the developing governance of welfare.

Further reading

Hadley and Young (1990) provide a useful summary of different critiques of the traditional organization of public services, while different models of governance and organization for delivering public services are discussed in the report of the Commission on Public Private Partnerships (2001). Deakin (1994) examines the origins of the ideas that underpinned the challenge to the welfare state under the Thatcher and Major governments.

Part I

The public face of welfare

2

Central government and welfare

A key feature of the organization of the major social services in Britain – the 'public face of welfare' – and a theme which will run throughout this chapter and Chapter 3, is that most of these services are not delivered by central government departments, but by other forms of public sector organization. Apart from the social security benefits system, the delivery of the major social services is the responsibility of non-departmental organizations. It is the organizations making up what Rhodes (1988) refers to as the 'sub-central governments' of Britain – elected local authorities in their various forms, the institutions of the NHS and a range of quasi-governmental bodies operating on the fringes of both central and local government – that are the major executants of welfare policy. As we shall see later, this gap between the making of welfare policy and its delivery has important implications for central government's control of the implementation of its welfare policies.

Thus there are two 'public faces' of the government of welfare in Britain. One face is made up of a small number of central government social service departments which are not normally delivery agencies of welfare, but are, as we shall see later, primarily concerned with the functions of policymaking, resource allocation and supervision. The other public face of welfare consists of a range of non-departmental organizations, notably local authorities and NHS bodies. This latter face of welfare – the world of welfare delivery outside the Whitehall departments – will be the subject of Chapter 3. The purpose of this chapter is to examine the organization and role of central government departments in the delivery of welfare.

Central government's social service departments

When discussing the central government departments responsible for the social services in Britain, one immediately comes up against problems of classification. Which central government departments are concerned with the social services? Where does one draw the line between social service departments and the rest?

Writing about central government in the late 1950s, Chester and Willson (1957: 139–40) maintained that what they referred to as the 'social services' formed what had come to be thought of as a coherent group of governmental functions. This 'coherent group' consisted of four major service areas: education, health, 'cash payments' (that is, pensions, health and unemployment benefits, family allowances and assistance) and environmental conditions such as public housing. Since the late 1950s, there has, of course, been a rapid expansion and consolidation of local authority personal social services, sometimes described as 'the fifth social service'. Thus, a useful starting point nearly half a century after Chester and Willson's analysis is to take the government departments responsible for the five core social services – education, health care, social security, housing and the personal social services – which most commentators agree make up what has been called the 'welfare state' in Britain (see, for example, Lowe 1993).

On this basis, the major Whitehall social service departments today are the Department for Education and Skills (DfES), the Department of Health – responsible for the personal social services as well as the NHS – the Department for Work and Pensions and the Office of the Deputy Prime Minister (ODPM), which has responsibility for social housing. The pattern of social service departments is based upon the functional principle enunciated by the Haldane Report in 1918, whereby the responsibilities of government are allocated between departments according to the services to be performed rather than the clientele to be dealt with. A departmental structure built upon this 'philosophically ambiguous' concept (Pollitt 1980: 95) has – as we shall see in Chapter 4 – important implications for the coordination and planning of related services.

Another approach to the classification of social service departments is to update the scheme drawn up in 1970 by the then head of the home civil service (Armstrong 1970). This categorization divided the major government departments into five segments: overseas and defence; financial, economic and industrial; physical; social; and law and order (see Table 2.1). The DfES, the DoH and the DWP clearly fall within the 'social' sector. The fourth major social service department, the ODPM, with its responsibility for social housing, can be placed on the dividing line between the 'social' and the 'physical' sectors.

One other major government department also has 'social' responsibilities. The Home Office, with its responsibility for coordinating government action affecting the voluntary sector, can be placed on the dividing line between the 'social' and the 'law and order' sectors.

Table 2.1   Main central government departments 2002

Overseas and defence	Ministry of Defence
	Foreign and Commonwealth Office
Financial, economic and industrial	Department of Trade and Industry
	Treasury
	Department of the Environment, Food and Rural Affairs
Physical	Department for Transport
	Office of the Deputy Prime Minister
Social	Department for Education and Skills
	Department for Work and Pensions
	Department of Health
Law and order	Home Office
	Lord Chancellor's Department

Source: Adapted from Diagram 3 in Armstrong 1970

Although our discussion of central government's arrangements for the delivery of welfare will concentrate on the four major social service departments of the DWP, DoH, DfES and ODPM, we should also note the special cases of Scotland and Wales. With the exception of social security, responsibility for the delivery of the major social services in both these parts of Britain is not the responsibility of functional departments such as the DoH and DfES, with headquarters in Whitehall, but is in the hands of the devolved administrations established in 1999 by the Blair government following the first elections to the Scottish Parliament and the Welsh Assembly. The Scottish Executive took over the responsibilities of the Scottish Office and has four departments involved with the major social services – the Development Department, which has responsibility for social housing; the Education Department, which is responsible for pre-school and school education; the Enterprise and Life-Long Learning Department, which is responsible for further and higher education; and the Health Department, which has responsibility for the NHS in Scotland and social work. The Scottish Parliament has primary and secondary legislative powers

Table 2.2   Central government social service departments and responsibilities

• Department for Work and Pensions	Social security system; employment services; employment training
• Department of Health	National Health Service; personal social services provided by local authorities
• Department for Education and Skills	Pre-school education; schools; further and higher education; developing skills for the workforce
• Office of the Deputy Prime Minister	Policies for local government; housing; urban policy
• Home Office	Voluntary services

over these devolved matters. The Welsh Assembly does not have such wide-ranging responsibilities for social services as its Scottish counterpart, but its Social Policy and Local Government Affairs grouping is responsible for education, housing, health and personal social services, which are organized into various directorates and groups. The Assembly has only secondary legislative powers. By contrast, the Northern Ireland Assembly has full primary legislative and executive authority over education, housing, health care and personal social services, day-to-day responsibility for which is in the hands of departments staffed by the Northern Ireland Civil Service.

Having identified the social service departments of central government, let us look at each of them in more detail (see Table 2.2).

Department for Work and Pensions

The DWP is Whitehall's biggest spending department, disposing of about one-third of total government spending. Its major executive responsibilities are in the hands of a number of semi-autonomous agencies. The most important of these agencies, Jobcentre Plus, is responsible, through its nationwide network of district offices, for providing help in finding jobs and paying benefits to people of working age. One of the DPW's predecessors, the Ministry of National Insurance, was responsible for only 6 major social security benefits when it was set up in 1948: its modern-day equivalent has responsibility for over 20 such benefits. We shall examine the history and structure of this key department in more detail later (pp. 29–32).

Department of Health

The DoH originated in 1919 as the Ministry of Health, a department which absorbed the Local Government Board, as well as taking over the powers exercised by a number of other bodies. It started life concerned with local government, housing and public health, together with the supervision of health insurance and some pensions work. Although it lost its insurance and pensions responsibilities to the newly formed Ministry of National Insurance in 1945, it retained its responsibility for housing until 1951. In 1948 it became responsible for the newly created NHS.

The Ministry of Health was amalgamated with the then Ministry of Social Security in 1968 to form the giant DHSS, although it regained its separate status in 1988. In addition to its responsibility for the NHS, the DoH is also responsible, through its Social Care Directorate, for the oversight of the personal social services delivered by local authorities.

Department for Education and Skills

The third major Whitehall social service department, the DfES, originated in 1899 as the Board of Education, although its origins can be traced back to a Privy Council committee set up in 1839 to administer the government grants made to the voluntary church societies which provided elementary schools. Following the pioneering Education Act 1944, the Board of Education became a ministry; 20 years later, the Ministry of Education became the Department of Education and Science (DES), its responsibilities being enlarged to include the financing of the universities and various aspects of civil science. It kept this new title up until the aftermath of the Conservative victory in the 1992 general election, when its responsibilities for sport and science were transferred to other departments, and it was renamed the Department for Education (DfE). In 1995, it took over the employment responsibilities – including the payment of unemployment benefit and the running of the jobcentre network – of the Department of Employment (DEmp) to form the new Department for Education and Employment (DfEE). Following the re-election of the Labour government in 2001, the DfEE lost its employment responsibilities to the newly created DWP, and was renamed the DfES. Although long regarded, in its various guises, as a 'Cinderella' department (Hennessy 1990: 428), the DfES is one of the largest spending Whitehall departments. It has, however, very little direct involvement in the day-to-day spending of these vast amounts of money, state education being delivered by local education authorities and other non-departmental organizations.

Office of the Deputy Prime Minister

Central government responsibility for the key social service of housing, along with the associated area of urban policy, lies with central government's fourth major social service department, the ODPM. The ODPM had originally been established as part of the Cabinet Office following the 2001 general election, and contained the Social Exclusion Unit (see p. 71) and the Government Offices for the Regions. In 2002, the ODPM was established as a department in its own right, and expanded to include housing, urban policy and planning, local government and regional policy, taking over many of the responsibilities of the former Department of Transport, Local Government and the Regions (DTLR). A new Department for Transport concentrates solely on transport issues. The DLTR had been created in 2001 from parts of the Department of the Environment and the Regions (DETR), which had been established by the Blair government in 1997 as the result of the merger of the Department of the Environment (DoE) and the Department of Transport. The DLTR could trace its antecedents back to the Ministry of Housing and Local Government formed in 1951 as a result of the hiving off of certain functions from the Ministry of Health, and later merged with the Ministry of Public Building and Works in 1970 to create the original DoE.

Home Office

The other central government department involved with aspects of the social services is the Home Office. One of the oldest government departments, dating from 1782, the Home Office is what one commentator has referred to as the 'ragbag of Whitehall' (Fowler 1967), being responsible for a variety of domestic functions of government which have not been given to other departments. Although it lost its responsibilities for childcare to the former DHSS following the implementation of the Seebohm Report (1968) on the reorganization of local authority social services in the early 1970s, it is still involved in the welfare sphere through its Community Policy Directorate, which is responsible for the coordination of central government policy towards the voluntary sector.

A federation of departments

Thus central government responsibility for the social services is distributed among a variety of departments. Why are welfare responsibilities distributed in the way summarized in Table 2.2? Why, for example, does the list of social service departments not include a Ministry of Social Welfare, as discussed by some observers in the late 1960s (see, for example, Lapping 1968), instead of related functions being distributed between separate departments like Health, Work and Pensions, Education and Skills, and the Office of the Deputy Prime Minister? Why are the organizational arrangements for the payment of social security benefits not linked with the Inland Revenue to form a new department (see, for example, Wicks 1987: 242)? Why does Britain not have a single government department to deal with the needs of elderly people (shared mainly between the DWP, the DoH and the ODPM)? The answer to these questions can be found in the fact that the pattern of social service departments owes more to political considerations and changing needs than to administrative theory (see, for example, Pollitt 1984a). In the words of two commentators on this issue, the process of distributing responsibilities between central government departments has been 'a continuous process of creation, fission, fusion and transfer, rapid at some times, slower at others' (Hanson and Walles 1984: 139). As we shall see in the next section of this chapter, one clear expression of the ad-hoc nature of this process has been the changing arrangements for the distribution of functions relating to social security.

One of the consequences of this essentially incremental process of allocating departmental functions is that the boundaries of central government's social service departments are arbitrary. We have already noted that government policy for elderly people is shared between at least three social service departments (the DWP, the DoH and the ODPM). As we shall see in Chapter 4, such overlap creates serious problems for the coordination and planning of welfare delivery.

Within this collection of departments, there is no such thing as a 'typical' Whitehall social service department. The size, functions and characteristics of social service departments differ enormously. Social service departments vary considerably in their size, ranging from a very large department like the DWP, with some 125,000 staff, to very small departments like the DoH and DfES, each with about 5000 civil servants. The small size of these two departments reflects the fact that they are not directly responsible for the delivery of major services. The former DTLR, most of whose officials were involved with transport, had some 17,000 staff, although the ODPM is much smaller. The Home Office has about 60,000 staff, although most of these are not engaged in work affecting the delivery of welfare.

Social service departments vary not only in size, but also in the extent to which they are concerned with the direct administration of welfare policies. Dunleavy's analysis of the British central state (1989: 254–5) includes three major types of government departments: delivery agencies, transfer agencies and control agencies. Delivery agencies are departments that directly undertake the delivery of public services to citizens using their own staff to implement policies. Transfer agencies are 'money-moving' organizations, handling payments of some kind made by government to private individuals. Finally, central government includes control agencies, whose primary role is to pass government funds to other public sector organizations in the form of grants and to supervise the activities of those organizations, while having no major responsibilities for service delivery of their own.

The DWP, in Dunleavy's terminology, is a transfer agency, whose staff are responsible for the administration of the huge social security benefits system. It is Whitehall's biggest spender, with a budget of over £100 billion per year, equivalent to about 30 per cent of total government spending. The DWP also acts as a delivery agency for the provision of the range of employment services to jobseekers through its network of local jobcentres.

The other three major social service departments are control agencies, whose core budgets absorb only a very small proportion of their programme budgets. Spending on their own activities is small. Thus, the DfES spends only a fraction of its budget on its own activities – administration, research and miscellaneous services – the remainder going to such delivery agencies as local education authorities, city technology colleges (CTCs), further education corporations in charge of sixth form colleges and further education colleges, and universities. The DoH is also primarily a control agency. It is the institutions of the NHS that deliver health care services. The department's core health budget – spent on the cost of administration and other central services – is only just over 2 per cent of its total NHS budget, the bulk of its expenditure on health care being spent by hospitals and family practitioners – family doctors, dentists, opticians and pharmacists. The DoH also acts as a control organization – through its Social Care Directorate – for the personal social services provided by local authorities. The ODPM is also primarily a control agency, operating through local authorities and quasi-governmental bodies such as the Housing Corporation and housing action trusts (HATs) in the implementation of its social housing policies.

Thus the only central government social service department directly involved with the delivery of major services is the DWP, and day-to-day responsibility for the delivery of its main executive services is actually in the hands of semi-autonomous agencies operating at arm's length from departmental headquarters – notably Jobcentre Plus. Such agencies operate under the direction of chief executives who work within the parameters of policy and resources frameworks set by their parent departments. Although the creation of executive agencies was a key feature of the development of central government in the late 1980s and 1990s, the process proceeded very much further in the then DSS – which had responsibility for the direct provision of services – than in traditional control departments responsible for education and health care, where the scope for hiving-off was limited. Thus Jobcentre Plus is fundamental to the mainstream policy and operations of what is now the DWP. The agencies that have been established within the other major social service departments, however, are not concerned with mainstream policy and operations, but with providing services to their departments using particular specialist skills. Thus, although the DoH has five executive agencies, they all deal with technical activities – such as controlling the standards of medicines (Medicines Control Agency) and managing NHS estate and property (NHS Estates). With the transfer of the Teachers' Pensions Agency – responsible for the administration of teachers' superannuation scheme – to a private sector organ-ization in 1996, what is now the DfES has no executive agencies. We now turn to a fuller discussion of the impact of the agency concept on central government's largest social service department, the DWP.

The changing face of the Department for Work and Pensions

As we have seen, in terms of both spending and numbers of staff, the major social service department is the DWP, which has a chequered history. A brief examination of the history of the DPW, and its predecessor departments, will throw further light upon the changing arrangements for the grouping of departmental responsibilities for the social services.

The antecedents of the DPW are complicated, but its origins can be traced back at least as far as 1916 and the establishment of the Ministry of Pensions, which was set up to administer the war pensions scheme introduced during the First World War. However, the administrative arrangements for the delivery of income maintenance in the inter-war period were complicated by the fact that contributory pensions were administered by the Ministry of Health, non-contributory pensions by the Board of Customs and Excise, the workers' compensation scheme for industrial injuries by the Home Office, and the unemployment insurance scheme by the Ministry of Labour. In 1934 the Unemployment Assistance Board (UAB), under the direction of the Ministry of Labour, was set up to administer a means-tested unemployment assistance scheme. In the early 1940s, the UAB was renamed the Assistance Board and also took over responsibility for supplementing the income of old age pensioners.

Thus by the time of the publication of the influential Beveridge Report on social insurance in 1942, a number of government departments were involved in the delivery of income maintenance. The beginnings of the administrative rationalization of the system emerged soon after Beveridge, with the establishment in 1944 of a Ministry of National Insurance (MNI) to superintend the administration of the new system of social security adopted by the wartime coalition government. The Ministry of Labour continued to administer unemployment insurance on an agency basis and in 1948 the renamed National Assistance Board (NAB) took over responsibility for administering the national assistance scheme. The reasoning behind this particular division of functions was the importance attached by the government to preserving the distinction between insurance and assistance (Minister of Reconstruction 1944: para. 161).

Although the creation of the MNI helped to rationalize the administrative arrangements for the delivery of social security, the government did not merge the Ministry of Pensions with the new department, as had been recommended by the Beveridge Report, probably because it was thought politically important to treat war pensioners as a separate group (Chester and Willson 1957: 180). But the Beveridge proposals did not disappear, and in 1953 the Ministry of Pensions was dissolved and its functions amalgamated with the MNI to form the Ministry of Pensions and National Insurance (MPNI). The rationale behind the merger of the two departments was to eliminate the duplication of administrative arrangements for the payment of pensions and national insurance benefits.

Thirteen years later, in 1966, the Labour government decided that a merger of the MPNI and the NAB would make for even greater adminis-trative simplification, as well as the elimination of stigma, in the delivery of benefits (Brown and Steel 1979: 283). Described by one writer as 'a piece of obvious administrative streamlining' (Pollitt 1984a: 69), the merger of the two departments resulted in the creation of the Ministry of Social Security.

The fusion process asserted itself again in 1968, when the recently formed Ministry of Social Security was amalgamated with the Ministry of Health to form the giant DHSS. The unification of the two departments was part of a wider trend towards the establishment of giant departments, the creation of the DoE – another social service department – in 1970 being another example of the process. The reasoning behind the establishment of the DHSS was the potential advantages offered by the wider application of resources and a more coherent approach to the priorities of social care (Nairne 1983: 247). In the event, however, as we shall discuss in Chapter 4, health and social security were administered in the new giant department in two separate wings, the two sets of activities having little in common (Brown 1975: 285). In due course, the forces of fission reasserted themselves. In 1988, as part of the Thatcher government's attempts to demonstrate its commitment to the NHS, the DHSS was split into two separate depart-ments, with the Department of Social Security emerging as a separate department.

During the 1990s, the newly created DSS underwent a major upheaval, with most of its functions being transferred to semi-autonomous Next Steps agencies, operating within the terms of framework documents defining goals and setting targets. The decision to adopt the agency model for most of the executive functions of the DSS followed a study initiated in 1988 which concluded that virtually all the operational tasks of the DSS could be run more effectively as executive agencies. The Resettlement Agency was subsequently established soon afterwards to administer the DSS's hostels for single homeless people without a settled way of life. In April 1990, the department established the Information Technology Services Agency to develop and support the computing and communication technology services required by the DSS and its agencies. The main work of the agency involved the calculation, recording and payment of social security benefits, with links to terminals in local social security offices and the local offices of the Employment Service (see p. 31). But the jewel in the crown of the establishment of executive agencies in the DSS was the setting up in April 1991 of the Benefits Agency, which by the 2001 general election employed over 68,000 staff, nearly one-seventh of the total non-industrial civil service, and was responsible for the efficient and effective delivery of the government's social security benefits scheme through a nationwide network of local offices. The same month saw the establishment of the Contributions Agency to operate the National Insurance scheme. In April 1993, the department set up the Child Support Agency (CSA), which is responsible for the operation of the child support maintenance system. A sixth executive agency followed a year later, with the establishment of the War Pensions Agency responsible for the delivery of services to war pensioners. In 1996, the Resettlement Agency ceased to exist, having disengaged central government from the direct management of hostels.

As a result of these developments, by the election of the Labour government in 1997, 97 per cent of DSS staff were working in five executive agencies, with only a small number of officials located in headquarters offices in Whitehall. Several changes in the DSS's agency profile took place during the first term of the Blair administration. In April 1999 the Contributions Agency was transferred to the Inland Revenue, and a year later the Information Technology Services Agency ceased to be an agency, being reabsorbed by the DSS. The department acquired another executive agency in April 2000, with the launching of the Appeals Service, which is responsible for the administration of appeals on decisions made by the central and local offices of the DWP (see Chapter 5).

Following the re-election of the Labour government in 2001, much more fundamental changes took place in the configuration of the DSS with the incorporation of those parts of the DfEE dealing with employment policy, along with the Employment Service, to form the DWP. Staff of the Employment Service – a semi-autonomous executive agency – were responsible for the jobsearch aspects of claims for jobseeker's allowance, with Benefits Agency staff administering benefit payments. The Employment Service also had day-to-day responsibility for the jobcentre network.

The newly created DWP inherited five executive agencies, reduced to a total of four after the War Pensions Agency was transferred to the Ministry of Defence in the summer of 2001. The transformation of the DWP continued in April 2002, when the Benefits Agency and the Employment Service were replaced by two new executive agencies. Jobcentre Plus incorporated the Employment Service and those parts of the Benefits Agency that provided services for people of working age. The new agency offers a single point of contact for people of working age who are looking for work and claiming benefits. It has been described by the prime minister as representing 'the face of 21st century government' (*Hansard* 2000). Another new executive agency – the Pension Service – took over all pensions-related business from the Benefits Agency, providing an integrated service designed to meet the needs of pensioners. The creation of executive agencies such as those found in the DWP (see Figure 2.1) raises important questions and we shall return to this key development in Chapters 8 and 9.

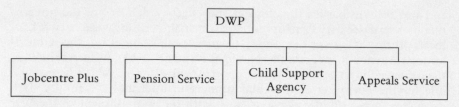

Figure 2.1   The Department for Work and Pensions and its executive agencies 2002.

The role of government departments

Despite the fact that most social services are delivered by non-departmental agencies like local authorities and NHS bodies, and, in the case of the DWP, by semi-autonomous executive agencies, central government departments carry out important functions affecting the delivery of welfare. These are the development of policy, the securing and allocation of resources, and the monitoring and supervision of the activities of delivery agencies.

Policymaking is central to the role of central government departments. Indeed, Webb and Wistow (1987: 131) maintain that the 'primary significance' of central government is that it 'shapes and elaborates the legal framework, created by Act of Parliament, in which local authorities, voluntary organizations and private services operate'. Although they were writing specifically about the personal social services, Webb and Wistow's argument also applies to the other major social services of education, housing and health care. Delivery agencies like local authorities and NHS bodies may retain a fair degree of discretion in the implementation of central government's welfare policies, but the legislative framework clearly lays down the parameters for their activities.

A second important role undertaken by central government departments is the securing of resources, which they then allocate to the various delivery agencies for which they are responsible. By far the bulk of the money spent by the delivery agencies of the welfare state is acquired by their parent departments in Whitehall through the system of public expenditure allocation. About one-half of local authority revenue spending is financed by grants from central government, and the NHS is almost entirely financed from Exchequer funds. As we shall discuss in Chapter 4, government decisions about the total level of public spending and the allocation of funds between different spending programmes are taken in the context of the government's public expenditure allocation system, which is superintended by the Treasury.

The third major role of central departments is monitoring and supervising the agencies that deliver welfare. Whitehall's social service departments possess a range of instruments enabling them not only to monitor and supervise the activities of local authorities and NHS bodies, but also to intervene in their operations. We discuss these instruments, and the relationship between the two sides, in the rest of this chapter.

Controlling the delivery agencies

Before we come to discuss the instruments available to central government departments in their dealings with the major delivery agencies of the welfare state, we first need to examine the justifications for central intervention.

One important justification given for central intervention is the major role played by local authorities and NHS bodies as delivery agencies of the welfare state and the enormous amounts of money involved in their operations. Local authority spending in England on the three major social services delivered by local government – education, housing and the personal social services – amounted to something in the order of £51 billion in the financial year 1998–99. Government spending on the NHS in the UK in the same financial year was just over £45 billion. This level of spending, allied to the importance of the services involved, helps to account for what Smith and Stanyer (1976: 124) refer to as the demand for 'efficient and honest government', a demand which has been reflected in the attempts by governments since the early 1980s to encourage a greater emphasis on efficiency and value for money in the public sector (see Chapter 8).

A second factor in the case for central intervention in the affairs of local authorities and NHS bodies is the need to promote what has been described as 'territorial justice' – the notion that the users of a particular service in one area of the UK should receive the same standard of service as people in another area (see, for example, Davies 1968; Byrne 1990: 248). As the Labour government stated in 1977, one of the roles of central government is to ensure that local services such as education, housing and personal social services 'are provided at broadly comparable standards' (Department of the Environment 1977: para. 2.2). Similar arguments were used in the context of the attempts to ensure a more equitable distribution of resources between the various regions in the NHS, based on the Resource Allocation Working Party (RAWP) formula introduced in the late 1970s. The RAWP system allocated resources based on such factors as population size, population profile and morbidity patterns. Although RAWP was replaced by a new approach to resource allocation with the NHS reforms of the early 1990s, its underlying principles were retained (Ham 1999: 192).

A third important factor in the case for central government intervention arises from the undeniable fact – however unpleasant it may be to many localists – that the social services provided by local authorities often have a party political dimension. Central governments, of both major political parties, periodically commit themselves to national policies in fields where the delivery of services lies in the hands of elected local authorities, many of which are often under the control of a political party of a different persuasion. Thus, for example, as we shall discuss in more detail in Chapter 6, Labour governments in the 1960s attempted to promote the concept of comprehensive education through the famous Circular 10/65, while the Conservative government in the 1980s attempted to privatize local authority housing through the introduction of the controversial Housing Act 1980, which gave council house tenants the right to buy their homes. Governments also attempt to promote particular lines of service development in the NHS. Thus, for example, the 1974–79 Labour government attempted to fulfil its objective of giving priority to spending on services for client groups like mentally ill and mentally handicapped people by publishing guidance to health authorities on priorities for service development (Department of Health and Social Security 1976). It is hardly surprising that central government will attempt to ensure that such policies – invariably included in election manifestos – are successfully implemented by delivery agencies at the local and sub-national level.

Finally, and crucially in the context of developments during the period of the Conservative governments from 1979 to 1997, there has been the economic case for central intervention in the affairs of local government. Successive post-war governments have argued that no central government, with its responsibility for macro-economic policy, can allow local government spending to remain completely free from central control or influence. Thus, in 1977, the Labour government argued in a Green Paper that because of its responsibilities for the management of the economy, central government had to concern itself with total local government expenditure and taxation. Consequently, the role of central government was to 'ensure that, in aggregate, local government's spending plans are compatible with the Government's economic objectives' (Department of the Environment 1977: para. 2.2). The economic case for central intervention became even more significant with the election in 1979 of the Conservative government, which argued that 'overspending' local authorities damage the health of the national economy. It further stated in 1986: 'Because Governments are responsible for the overall management of the economy they have to be concerned with the amount of local authority expenditure, borrowing and taxation' (Department of the Environment 1986: para. 1.13). Such a view has not been without its critics, it being argued that the case for central government control of local government spending is 'built on shaky theory and lacks empirical support', and that local government current spending has little impact on national aggregate demand (Newton and Karran 1985: 124; see also Jackman 1982). The Blair government has continued to keep a firm hold on local government spending, stating that central government has a strong interest in local government spending, partly because such a large proportion of that spending is financed by the centre (Department of the Environment, Transport and the Regions 1998: para. 5.3).

The instruments of central intervention

Using the typology developed by Stanyer (1976: 221), it is possible to discuss the relationships between central government and the delivery agencies of local government and the NHS in terms of two main types of central intervention – methods of influence and methods of control. Whereas the latter methods presume a confrontation between central government and its delivery agencies and allow for any conflict to be resolved in favour of central government, methods of influence are intended to prevent such a conflict arising in the first place by encouraging consensus between the two sides. We first look at the weapons enabling central government departments to intervene in the affairs of local authorities, before turning to an examination of central government's controls and influences over NHS bodies.

At the heart of the apparatus for controlling the welfare delivery agencies of local government is legislative and judicial control. Local authorities are creatures of legislation, deriving their powers from Acts of Parliament. The limits of a local authority's powers in education, housing and the personal social services are set by the doctrine of ultra vires, according to which no local authority is allowed to carry out any activity unless permitted to do so by an Act of Parliament. The doctrine is enforced by the courts, and a local authority which attempts to exceed its legal powers may be prevented from doing so by a court order. Legislation also imposes certain statutory duties upon local authorities – for example, the Housing Act 1980 requires local housing authorities to sell council houses to tenants who request it. Such duties are often reinforced by provisions which give government ministers the power to issue a directive ordering a local authority to carry out, or refrain from carrying out, a particular action. Legislation sometimes also contains default powers enabling the relevant minister to take over the responsibilities of recalcitrant local authorities or transfer responsibilities to other bodies. This 'big stick' of default power was used in the famous Clay Cross affair in 1974 (see Chapter 6) and in the early 1980s over Norwich City Council's slow progress in selling council houses. More recently, such powers have been used by the Blair government to intervene in the affairs of individual local education authorities (see Chapter 6).

What Byrne (2000: 422) describes as the 'closest and most continuous form of control' over local authorities is the range of specific administrative controls given to government ministers by various statutes. Thus the Secretary of State for Health must approve the appointment of local authority directors of social services. The same minister can also issue regulations prescribing how local authorities should perform duties as various as the arrangements for the fostering of children or charges in old people's homes. Government ministers can require local authorities to prepare plans for the development of a particular service: thus, under the School Standards and Framework Act 1998, local education authorities have to submit education development plans to the Secretary of State for Education and Skills. These, and other types of administrative controls, have been described by one commentator as setting up 'gates' or 'bottlenecks' through which individual local authorities must pass certain proposals before they can be implemented (Dunsire 1981: 176).

Each of the methods of intervention described so far has a statutory basis and is therefore, in the terminology used by Stanyer (1976: 221), a form of 'control'. In addition, central government departments possess a range of other methods whereby they can attempt to 'influence' the affairs of local authorities. One major form of administrative influence is the use of departmental circulars, described in the mid-1970s by the then DES as 'the main instrument of formal communication with local authorities' (Central Policy Review Staff 1977: para. 2.7). The content of circulars varies from technical advice to such major policy pronouncements as DES Circular 10/65, which requested local education authorities to submit plans for the reorganization of secondary schools in their areas on comprehensive lines.

In two of the major social services, education and the personal social services, the central government department charged with responsibility for the oversight of these services maintains an inspectorate whose duties are to visit local authorities and report on standards of efficiency. The use of such inspectorates is one of the oldest forms of central government intervention, going back at least to the Poor Law Inspectorate of the mid-nineteenth century, and make up what one writer has called a system of central government 'quality control' (Glennerster 1992a: 80). The Education Act 1944 imposed a duty on ministers to ensure inspection of every educational establishment, and Her Majesty's Inspectors of Education (HMIs) were given responsibility for monitoring and advising local education authorities. Following the establishment of the Office for Standards in Education (Ofsted) in 1992, the number of HMIs was reduced and private teams led by registered inspectors tender for school inspection work. The DoH's Social Services Inspectorate, which monitors the efficiency and effectiveness of local authority social services departments, was established in 1983. A much more recent innovation is the Housing Inspectorate, established by the Blair government in 2000 as part of its Best Value initiative, and located in the Best Value Inspectorate under the auspices of the Audit Commission (see Chapter 8).

A third form of central government influence over the activities of local authorities is through finance. As we saw earlier, the bulk of local authority revenue comes from central government grants. Although a significant proportion of central support is given through specific grants – which must be spent on a particular service or project – since 1958 most central government financial support has been distributed to local authorities in the form of a general grant which is not allocated to specific services – formerly Rate Support Grant (RSG), now Revenue Support Grant. As Byrne (2000: 429) points out, both forms of grant enable central government to exercise a form of influence. Specific grants help to encourage the provision of a particular service. General grant brings with it the power to exercise a general 'influence', since local authorities can be encouraged or discouraged from spending by changes in central government grant. Thus an increase in the amount of central grant can be used to encourage local authorities to increase spending, while, conversely, a government wishing to encourage a decrease in local government spending can reduce the amount of central grant. Since local taxation – whether it be in the form of local authority rates, community charge or council tax – is unpopular with those who have to pay it, it is argued that local councils would probably be reluctant to impose extra costs on local taxpayers in order to maintain spending levels. As we shall see in Chapter 6, large increases in central government grants played a major part in influencing the rapid expansion of the various local authority social services during the post-war development of the local government welfare state.

Thus central government departments have a variety of methods through which they may attempt to control or influence the activities of local authorities. It is, however, difficult to generalize about the relationship between the two sides. As Griffith (1966: 528) has pointed out, each government department has its own philosophy about the way in which local authorities should be treated. The balance of power between the two sides has also varied over time. Thus, historically, local housing authorities have been used to a higher degree of autonomy than other local social services (Karn 1985: 163), although the situation has changed since the early 1960s. Writing in the mid-1980s, Karn (1985: 163–5) identified three main phases in the central–local relationship in this particular area: a period of laissez-faire from 1919 to the 1960s, where local authorities were left to define the extent of local housing need and how far it should be met; the period from the 1960s to the late 1970s, which was characterized by a more intervention-ist concern with the quality, scope and cost of local authority housing; and the period following the election of the Thatcher government, which was characterized by financial cuts, privatization and increased centralization. The relationship between central government and local education authorities has also been marked by change, in this case a movement away from a period of local dominance in the late 1960s and early 1970s to one of increasing centralization (see Ranson 1985). In the words of two other commentators, 'the "live and let live" relationship of the 1960s and early 1970s gave way to increasingly forceful attempts by national governments of both parties to impose their influence' (Wilson and Game 1998: 107). We shall discuss developments in central government–local government rela-tions since 1979 in more detail in Chapter 6.

Like its sister departments in their relations with local authorities, the DoH also has a range of influences and controls available to it in its relations with NHS bodies. Thus the DoH provides guidelines through circulars (such as the circular on competitive tendering issued in 1983) and consultative documents and White Papers spelling out priorities for the development of particular health services (for example, the 1981 White Paper *Care in Action*: Department of Health and Social Security 1981). The Commission for Health Improvement, reporting to the Secretary of State for Health, inspects NHS trusts and primary care trusts.

The DoH also exercises administrative influence within the NHS through its power to issue regulations on a range of matters. In addition, the secretary of state has the power to appoint, and to dismiss, the chairs and non-executive members of NHS bodies. Ultimately, as in the case of the relationship between central government departments and local authorities, the Secretary of State for Health has the power to direct NHS bodies to comply with the department's wishes, and has the ultimate power to suspend individual NHS bodies. Although Brown (1979: 10–11) has argued that these drastic powers 'are about as usable in practice as nuclear weapons', they were used in 1979 when, after threatening to overspend its budget, the Lambeth, Southwark and Lewisham Area Health Authority was suspended and replaced by a team of centrally appointed commissioners. The powers were also used in 1999, when, following concern over management, the secretary of state removed the non-executive directors of the Guild Community Health Care NHS Trust in Lancashire (Ham 1999: 165). The Blair government has introduced mechanisms whereby the secretary of state can impose special measures on failing NHS bodies.

A study of central–local relations in the mid-1960s concluded that the Ministry of Health had a laissez-faire attitude towards local health authorities (Griffith 1966: 515), but since the creation of the giant DHSS in 1968 central government has developed a more interventionist approach (Hunter and Wistow 1987: 49). In particular, as we shall see in Chapter 8, the NHS has witnessed a marked change in central–local relations since the early 1980s.

Given the battery of weapons available to central government departments in their relations with local authorities and the institutions of the NHS, it is not surprising that some observers have characterized the relationship between the centre and both these types of welfare delivery agencies as that of principal and agent (see, for example, Robson 1966 on local government and Powell 1966 on the NHS). As we shall see in later chapters, however, this view is a misleading one. Both types of welfare delivery agencies – elected local authorities and appointed NHS bodies – possess important resources and central government is dependent on them for the implementation of centrally determined social policies (see Rhodes 1979; Ham 1999: 166).

Further reading

The historical development of central government's social services departments up to the late 1980s can be traced through a reading of the second edition of Chester and Wilson (1968), Pollitt (1984a) and Hennessy (1990). There are no equivalent histories of the 1990s, but a discussion of the impact of the Benefits Agency can be found in James (2001). Readers should consult the DWP web site, www.dwp@gov.uk for up-to-date information on developments in the DWP executive agency structure. Information on the role of the ODPM can be found at www.odpm@gov.uk. For more detail on the role of central government departments in controlling the activities of local authorities and NHS bodies, see Wilson and Game (1998) and Ham (1999).

3

The government of welfare outside Whitehall

As we saw in Chapter 2, the social service departments of central government are mainly concerned with the functions of policymaking, resource allocation and supervision. With the exception of the DWP, government departments are not usually involved in the day-to-day delivery of welfare, and, even in the case of the DWP, the delivery of services has been hived off to semi-autonomous agencies operating at arm's length from the policy-making core in Whitehall. Leaving aside executive agencies like Jobcentre Plus and the Pension Service, for most people what might be termed the 'public face' of the statutory social services consists of the organizations which make up the system of 'sub-central government', consisting of local authorities, the institutions of the NHS, and the various quasi-governmental bodies associated with the delivery of welfare (Rhodes 1988; Stoker 1990). It is these non-departmental organizations, and the part that they play in the delivery of welfare, that form the subject matter of this chapter.

The local government welfare state: from the cradle to the grave

The major delivery agencies of the welfare state are local authorities, consisting of unpaid, locally elected councillors who are accountable to their local electorates. The fact that local authorities are elected is an important part of the traditional case for local government, the localist tradition arguing that this particular delivery agency of the welfare state contributes to local

Table 3.1   Local authority social services total gross expenditure and staff, England 1998–99

Sector	Spending (£m)	Staff
Education	25,018	707,000
Housing (includes housing benefit)	13,689	65,000
Personal social services	12,392	216,000
Total local authorities	81,431	1,613,000

Source: Department of the Environment, Transport and the Regions (2000c), Table 2.2; Office for National Statistics (2001), Table 7.8

democracy by enabling people not only to express the views of the local community, but also to participate in the delivery of local services through election as local councillors. Localists also claim that local government helps to spread political power, thereby contributing to a pluralistic system of government (see, for example, Jones and Stewart 1983: 5–8; Widdicombe 1986: 47–52). For many, however, the major justification for local government is that it is an efficient means of providing for the welfare of the population (Hampton 1991: 5). As multifunctional bodies, local authorities can respond to local needs and conditions and coordinate the provision of such services as education, housing and the personal social services (see, for example, Sharpe 1970: 166).

Although local authorities are responsible for a wide range of services, the major category, in terms of both expenditure and staff, is what has been termed the 'personal' group – education, housing and the personal social services – defined by Byrne (2000: 96) as the services which seek to enhance personal welfare. In the financial year 1998–99, this group of services accounted for 63 per cent of local government total gross expenditure in England and over 61 per cent of local authority staff (see Table 3.1). These three services are sometimes referred to as 'collective consumption' services – those services which are used by people in order to live and bring up their families (Kingdom 1991: 480). Consequently, local government has often been described as influencing people's lives 'from the cradle to the grave' or 'from womb to tomb' (Redcliffe-Maud and Wood 1974: 15; Chandler 1991: 32), although this description has been slightly less applicable since the transfer of local authorities' health functions to the NHS in 1974.

The most important of these three services, education, was brought under local authority control in England and Wales following the Education Act 1902. This Act abolished the elected local school boards established under the Education Act 1870 to superintend the provision of elementary (what would now be called primary) education and transferred their powers to the counties and county boroughs set up as part of the restructuring of local government at the end of the nineteenth century. These newly designated local education authorities were also given powers to provide secondary or 'higher' education beyond the elementary level. The larger county districts were also given powers to provide elementary education. Local school boards in Scotland were not abolished until 1918, when counties and the largest burghs became local education authorities.

Further important changes followed the Education Act 1944, a piece of pioneering legislation which was to form the basis of the local authority education system until the Education Reform Act 1988. As a result of the 1944 Act, the counties and the county boroughs were made the sole local education authorities, with responsibility for ensuring the provision of primary and secondary school education in their areas. Local education authorities were also given responsibility for the provision of further education, an area of activity which included some of the colleges which were later transformed into polytechnics during the rapid expansion of higher education in the late 1960s and 1970s and which later became the 'new' universities in the early 1990s. The 1944 Act created what has been described as a 'partnership' between central and local government, with central government having the duty to 'promote' the education of school children, while local education authorities provided and operated the schools.

Education is by far the costliest local authority service, accounting for almost one-third of total local authority spending. It is little wonder that it has been regarded by many as being a semi-autonomous local authority service (Jennings 1977: 124), with one writer on local government describing it as constituting 'almost an authority within each council' (Elcock 1986a: 119). As we shall discuss in Chapter 6, the position of local education authorities as monopolistic providers of state education in their areas was transformed following legislation in the late 1980s and early 1990s which had the effect of removing a large number of schools from local education control, together with polytechnics, colleges of higher education and further education institutions. Significant initiatives affecting the role of local education authorities have also been introduced by the Blair government.

Local authority involvement in the second major social service, the provision of housing, dates back to the end of the nineteenth century when local authorities were given powers by the Housing of the Working Classes Act 1890 to build housing for general needs. Local authorities, however, were not obliged to build such housing, and this limitation, together with the absence of central government subsidies, meant that only a few local authorities, notably London County Council, built houses under this legislation. It was not until the Housing and Town Planning Act 1919 (the Addison Act), which followed Lloyd George's famous promise to build 'homes fit for heroes' for the service personnel returning from the First World War, that central government provided local authorities with subsidies encouraging them to build housing to let at affordable rents.

During the inter-war period, 1.5 million council homes were built. In the post-war period, local government involvement in housing increased substantially with the extension of the policy of government subsidies, notably by the post-war Labour Attlee government through the Housing Act 1946, which trebled the monetary value of subsidies compared with 1939 (Malpass and Murie 1990: 74). The Attlee government saw local authorities as the main means of meeting the serious housing shortage created by the bomb damage of the Second World War, and the majority of building licences in the immediate post-war years were given to local authorities rather than to private builders, a decision which was justified on the grounds that local authorities could be trusted to honour planning agreements (Lowe 1993: 245). In the words of Aneurin Bevan, the minister responsible for the Attlee government's housing programme: 'If we are to plan, we have to plan with plannable instruments, and the speculative builder, by his very nature, is not a plannable instrument' (quoted in Hamnett 1993: 151). As a result, over 80 per cent of all new dwellings constructed between 1945 and 1951 were built by local authorities.

Local authorities continued to play an important role in the provision of social housing after 1951. By 1979, the zenith of local authority housing, some 31 per cent of all dwellings in Britain were in the local authority sector. Like local authority education, local authority housing has been the subject of much criticism since the election of the first Thatcher government in 1979, with council tenants being encouraged to purchase their homes and much of the local authority housing stock being transferred to housing associations.

The third major social service delivered by local government, the personal social services, is much more recent, dating, in its present form, from the Local Authority Social Services Act 1970. The antecedents of the modern-day personal social services, however, go back much further. Some of the personal social services – those dealing with elderly people, children and mentally ill people, for example – have their roots in the nineteenth-century Poor Law, while others – the home help service, for instance – developed as offshoots of other local services such as health, education and housing (Seebohm 1968: paras 52–3). What Hill (1993: 38) describes as 'the foundations' of the development of the personal social services were laid in the late 1940s by the Attlee government. With the dismantling of the Poor Law, local authorities were given responsibility for providing services for elderly and handicapped people by the National Assistance Act 1948. They were also given significantly increased responsibilities in the field of childcare by the Children Act of the same year, and, as part of the tripartite structure set up to run the new NHS, were given charge of community health services. Until 1970, administrative responsibility for these various services was divided between separate local authority departments for welfare, children's and local health services.

It was not until the late 1960s and the early 1970s that the personal social services really 'leapt from the margins to the centre' of social welfare (Younghusband 1978: 35), and it was the fastest growing of the five major social services in the 1960s (Gould and Roweth 1980: 349–50). Following legislation in 1970, which closely followed the proposals of the Seebohm Committee two years earlier, the three separately organized services of welfare, care for deprived children and local health care were brought together under the wing of self-contained local authority social services departments.

The new social services departments' responsibilities for local health services were later transferred to area health authorities in 1974, as part of the unification of the NHS (see p. 50). Despite this loss of functions, local authority social services departments are still responsible for a variety of important services, notably the provision of residential care for elderly people, children, mentally ill and handicapped and physically disabled people, but also including the protection of children and various forms of social work. Like the other two major social services provided by local authorities, the organization and management of local authority social services departments was the subject of substantial change during the period of the Thatcher and Major governments, with the separation of the roles of purchaser and provider in the area of community care (see Chapters 6 and 7).

The development of the local government welfare state

As we saw in the last section, education and housing emerged as major functions of local government well before the Second World War. During the inter-war years, as a result of the abolition of the boards of guardians and the transfer of their duties to counties and county boroughs in 1929, local authorities also played a key role in poor relief and in the running of the majority of hospitals. Such was the growing importance of local government in the provision of social welfare during this period that in 1935 one eminent authority wrote that local government was firmly established as 'the most effective instrument of social welfare in our national life' (Robson 1935: 464). But, despite its involvement in welfare delivery in the immediate pre-war years, local government during this period was mainly concerned with what have been described as 'production-orientated' services – trading services, such as gas and electricity, and public goods, such as highways and street lighting, that benefited all local residents (Loughlin 1986: 6). In 1935, spending on the collective consumption services of education, housing, poor relief and hospitals totalled only just over 40 per cent of total local government current expenditure in England and Wales (see Table 3.2).

The local government welfare state only really took off in the postwar period, with the launching of the welfare state by the Labour government after the 1945 general election. Although the late 1940s saw the handing over of local authority hospitals to the newly established NHS and the transfer of poor relief to the new National Assistance Board as part of the

Table 3.2 Local authority current expenditure on social services in England and Wales 1935 and 1980 (percentage of total current expenditure)

Sector	1935	1980
Education	19.1%	36.1%
Housing	9.8%	21.8%
Poor relief	8.0%	—
Hospitals	5.0%	—
Personal social services	—	6.9%

Source: Jackman 1985: 151

establishment of a national social security system, local government was given new responsibilities in the field of social welfare, while some existing responsibilities were expanded. As we have seen, local authorities were given wider powers in the area of childcare, as well as being given responsibility for providing services for elderly and handicapped people. The role of local education authorities was expanded by the introduction of universal free state secondary education up to the age of 15 in the Education Act 1944. Local authorities were also given a major responsibility for implementing the state's policy of housing reconstruction.

As a result of these developments, local government became what Stoker (1991: 5) has called a 'prime vehicle' in the post-war drive to create the welfare state. The thirty years following the end of the Second World War witnessed a substantial development of the local authority education service in the 1950s and 1960s, a massive growth – fuelled by central government subsidies – in the rate of council house building, and a major expansion of the personal social services in the 1960s and early 1970s. By 1980, the three major social services of education, housing and the personal social services made up nearly two-thirds of local government current expenditure in England and Wales (see Table 3.2).

The welfare state character of local government was also manifested in the redistributive nature of central government's grant aid to local authorities, whereby the general grant (later renamed Rate Support Grant and then Revenue Support Grant) which made up the bulk of central government's financial support to local government took account of the needs and resources of individual local authorities (Pickvance 1991: 52). To use Pickvance's terminology (1991: 49), the post-war period saw the creation of a 'welfare state' model of local government, in which local authorities were responsible for the delivery of a range of services and relied on a mixture of central and local finance, supported by a grant equalization system, which paid grant to those authorities whose financial means were below the national average. This latter component was specifically intended to secure a degree of territorial justice, uniformity between local authority service provision being, as we saw in Chapter 2, a key part of central government's concern with the activities of local government.

The structure of the local government welfare state

The structure of the local government welfare state in Britain is a complex one. Responsibility for providing local government's three core social services rests with 386 main local authorities. In the non-metropolitan counties of England, responsibility for social services is split between two tiers, a system that was established with the reorganization of local government structure in 1974. In the upper tier, 34 county councils, ranging in population from 283,000 (Shropshire) to just over 1.3 million (Kent), have responsibility for the provision of education and personal social services. At the lower tier, 238 district councils, ranging in population from just under 25,000 (Teesdale, County Durham) to just over 198,000 (Northampton), are responsible for housing. It had been argued in the reform process of the early 1970s that the accurate assessment of housing requirements and the provision of housing and housing advice to individuals is of such 'paramount importance' that the housing service should be operated as close to the citizen as possible (Department of the Environment 1971: para. 23).

The local government system in Greater London and the six metropolitan counties of the West Midlands, Greater Manchester, Merseyside, West Yorkshire, South Yorkshire and Tyne and Wear is very different from that of the non-metropolitan counties. Before 1986, responsibility for education in Greater London was divided between the 20 Outer London boroughs and the Inner London Education Authority (ILEA), which provided education for the 12 Inner London boroughs. Responsibility for housing was divided between the Greater London Council (GLC) and the 32 London boroughs. Of the three major social services, only the personal social services were the unfettered responsibility of each of the London boroughs. This division of functions had been in place since the reform of London government in 1965. With the abolition of the GLC in 1986, and the winding up of the ILEA two years later, each of the London boroughs is now responsible for all three major social services in its area. (The City of London also has responsibilities for the three major social services in its area, but, with a population of only about 6000 people, it is not one of the main local authorities.) A similar single-tier system exists in the six metropolitan counties, where, since the abolition of the metropolitan county councils in 1986, 36 metropolitan districts serve as multipurpose authorities with responsibility for the provision of all three social services.

In 46 areas in England outside Greater London and the metropolitan counties, there is a system of unitary (that is, single-tier) local authorities, which are responsible for education, housing and personal social services

Table 3.3 Local authorities and the social services

Function	NMC	NMD	MD	LB	UA
Education	x		x	x	x
Housing		x	x	x	x
Personal social services	x		x	x	x

Key: NMC: non-metropolitan counties; NMD: non-metropolitan districts; MD: metropolitan districts; LB: London boroughs; UA: unitary authorities

in their areas. There are 22 unitary authorities operating in Wales, and 32 unitary authorities providing local government services in Scotland (see Table 3.3).

Thus, throughout a great deal of England, responsibility for the three local authority social services is divided between two tiers of local government. This two-tier system, which dates from 1974, is the product of many years of debate, and conflicts with the principle put forward by various official bodies in the 1960s that all three major local government social services should be provided by the same local authority. The shortcomings of the two-tier system were recognized in 1991 by the Conservative government, which initiated a process to reshape the structure of local government in England outside Greater London and the metropolitan counties, the underlying assumption being that unitary authorities could often be the best form of structure (Department of the Environment 1991a). In 1992, a Local Government Boundary Commission embarked upon a review of the structure of local government areas in England and made a series of proposals advocating the creation of unitary authorities in many parts of the country. In the event, however, although the Conservative government replaced the two-tier system in Scotland and Wales with a system of unitary authorities, it introduced only 46 unitary authorities in England. We shall return to this issue in Chapter 4.

Managing the local government welfare state

Responsibility for decisions about local authority social services traditionally rested with the full council, made up of all the elected members. In practice, however, the full council met infrequently and generally ratified decisions made elsewhere, its functions and powers having been traditionally devolved to committees (such as education and social services) covering the main responsibilities of the authority. This traditional system is currently in a process of transition, the local authority committee system having been criticized by the Blair government as leading to 'inefficient and opaque decision making' (Department of the Environment, Transport and the Regions 1998: para. 3.4). From June 2002, most local authorities have been required to introduce new political structures, involving some form of executive leadership taking the leading role in local authority decision making. With the exception of the smallest non-metropolitan districts, most local authorities will operate through a cabinet with a leader elected by the council, or through an elected major, with scrutiny committees of backbench councillors reviewing decisions taken by the executive, and making policy proposals to the executive.

The staff responsible for the planning and delivery of local authority services are organized hierarchically in departments which, like those of central government, are organized on the functional principle – departments of education, housing and personal social services. Most of the senior positions in local authority departments are held by professionally qualified staff. Unlike their central government counterparts, local authority education and social services departments are what Stanyer (1976: 157) refers to as 'professional organizations', in which the most senior positions are held by those who have qualifications in the activity being undertaken by the organization, while those staff who have general educational qualifications occupy positions lower down the departmental hierarchy. Thus a local authority social services department will be headed by a director of social services, one or two deputy directors and up to five assistant directors, all of whom are generally qualified social workers. Local authority administrators generally work as 'subordinates of the specialist', relieving the professionals of those tasks which do not require specialist experience and qualifications (Poole 1978: 43). Most local education authorities expect their directors of education to have considerable experience of teaching and a high proportion of education officers begin their careers in the teaching profession: indeed, it has been suggested that those who do not are hindered in their career in educational administration (Regan 1977: 28). As we saw in Chapter 1, the development of professionalism has not been nearly as rapid in the local authority housing service as it has been in education and the personal social services, and membership of the appropriate professional organization is not as important in housing departments as in the other two local authority social services (Laffin 1986).

As Laffin and Young (1990: 21) observe, professionalism has been the dominant organizational principle within local authorities since the end of the Second World War. But the role of local government professionals has come under serious challenge since the late 1960s, when questions began to be asked about the compartmentalized way in which local authority services had developed (Laffin and Young 1990: 21). While welfare professionalism within local government has undoubted strengths, it can result in tunnel vision, with the compartmentalization of professionals into separately organized departments leading not only to problems in the coordination and integration of related activities, but also to allegations that individual local authority services, such as education, promote themselves with the purpose of satisfying the aspirations of particular local authority professionals rather than meeting the needs of the local community (Poole 1978: 44). As a consequence, there has been an increasing emphasis on the importance of viewing local government as being responsible for the social, economic and physical well-being of its community as a whole (Bains 1972). We shall turn to these important issues in Chapter 4.

Delivering health care

Collective consumption services are not only delivered by elected local authorities. Another major delivery agency of the welfare state is the National Health Service. The second most expensive of the social services, after social security, the NHS spent £59 billion in 2000–01, nearly 15 per cent of total public expenditure, and employed nearly 1 million staff.

The structure of the NHS is very different from that of central government departments and local authorities. Indeed, the service has been aptly described as 'an administrative oddity' (Carter et al. 1992: 103). Although overall policy and the allocation of funds are the responsibility of the DoH in Whitehall, the day-to-day administration of the NHS is in the hands of health authorities (HAs), special health authorities, NHS trusts and primary care trusts (PCTs) acting on behalf of the Secretary of State for Health. The various NHS bodies are governed by appointed boards and employ non-civil service staff.

The NHS has a unique organizational form. In the words of one writer, it was the first large public sector organization concerned with a universally available welfare service in which 'a different kind of democracy from that traditionally understood was introduced by a form of direct delegation from a Minister to chosen individuals representing a wide sweep of special and professional interests' (McLachlan 1979: x). This particular form of organization was the result of a deliberate decision taken by the post-war Labour government not to entrust responsibility for the day-to-day administration of the NHS either to a central government department or to elected local authorities.

The decision not to place responsibility for the day-to-day running of the NHS in the hands of a central government department with its own regional and local structure staffed by civil servants, and with clear lines of accountability between the responsible minister and NHS staff, was based on the desire to avoid a centralized service run directly by the then Ministry of Health. As one commentator on these events has observed, the ministry lacked both 'the experience and the inclination' for operating the new service – as we saw in Chapter 2, the ministry's major functions involved housing and local government. It was a department 'with a tradition of regulatory rather than executive functions, reluctant to take on direct administrative responsibilities for a complex service' (Klein 1989: 12, 9). Although responsibility for the running of the majority of hospitals was already in the hands of elected local authorities – the Poor Law hospitals having been transferred to county councils and county boroughs in 1929 – and a municipally controlled health service had originally been favoured by the Ministry of Health, the suggestion that the new system of health care delivery be entrusted to local government was also rejected. Concern was expressed about the suitability of existing local authority areas for the administration of the new service, but the main reason for the rejection of this particular alternative was the fierce opposition of the medical profession to local government control of hospital and general practitioner (GP) services. The medical profession has always been hostile to the idea of local government control of its activities, fearing that this would somehow encroach upon its cherished clinical freedom. One study of the creation of the NHS actually referred to the medical profession's 'hatred' of local government control of their services (Willcocks 1967: 95), and the medical profession has repeated its opposition to the possibility of local government control ever since.

Thus, when the NHS was launched in 1948, responsibility for the administration of the new service was decentralized to regional and local bodies. In what became known as the tripartite structure, one set of institutions – appointed regional hospital boards and hospital management committees – were responsible for hospital services; another set of institutions – executive councils, responsible to the minister – ran the services provided by GPs, dentists, pharmacists and opticians; and local authority medical officers of health and their departments provided a range of local community health services, thereby ensuring that some health responsibilities remained with local government. Representatives of local authorities, together with members of the medical profession, were also included in the membership of the first two sets of institutions.

As with so many areas of the British administrative system, the NHS structure that emerged in 1948 was the result of compromise, in this case between the Cabinet minister involved, Aneurin Bevan, and the medical profession (see, for example, Willcocks 1967). As one senior official involved in the early planning of the NHS was later to observe, the structure set up in 1948 'was as far as we could reasonably expect to go at the time' (Godber 1975: 61). Or as Brown (1973: 120) put it, it was an administrative structure 'which seemed to combine the best prospects for success with the minimum of disturbance to existing arrangements'.

It was over a quarter of a century before a unified administrative structure was created for the NHS. In 1974, following criticisms of the tripartite structure – the lack of a single body with overall responsibility for the provision of health services; the difficulty of securing coordination in a system deliberately built upon fragmentation; and the absence of proper machinery for local medical planning (Brown 1975: 142) – it was replaced by a unified structure which brought the whole of the NHS under regional health authorities (RHAs) and area health authorities (AHAs). Despite the emphasis upon integration, however, GPs retained the freedom to work as independent contractors that had been awarded to them in 1948. Nor did the 1974 reorganization go nearly as far as the reforms introduced the year before in Northern Ireland, where responsibility for the delivery and management of both health and personal social services was given to area health and social services boards.

Important changes took place in the structure of the NHS under the Thatcher and Major governments. In 1982, AHAs, which were seen as being too large for the proper delivery of services, were abolished and replaced by district health authorities as part of the Conservative government's wider attempts to create a 'slimmer and fitter' public sector (see Chapter 8). Following the recommendations of the Griffiths Report in 1983 (see Chapter 8), changes also took place in the central management of the service, with the establishment of a NHS Management Board (later to become the NHS Executive), responsible for the central management of the NHS (see Klein 1990). Even more radical changes to the machinery for the delivery of health care were introduced in 1991, with the creation of NHS trusts as part of the newly created internal market (see Chapters 7 and 8).

A further round of streamlining followed in the last years of the Major government. In 1996, DHAs and family health service authorities – responsible for the management of family practitioner services – were merged to form unified health authorities (HAs), whose responsibilities included commissioning health care services from NHS trusts or other providers. The functions of RHAs and the regional outposts of the DOH were merged to form eight regional offices of the NHS Executive.

This 'bewilderingly complex' structure (Greenwood et al. 2001: 206) underwent even further reorganization in 1999 following the election of the Blair government, with a new tier – primary care groups (PCGs), comprising local GPs and community nurses – being added to the NHS structure. Covering localities of about 100,000 people, the PCGs were run by boards including GPs and representatives of the HA and the local authority. They were responsible for commissioning hospital and community services for the local community. In April 2002, the 481 PCGs, along with the NHS Executive, the eight regional offices of the DoH and the 95 HAs were replaced by a new structure. According to the government, the 1948 model of the NHS was 'simply inadequate' for the needs of the twenty-first century. It was time to 'move towards beyond the 1940s monolithic topdown centralised NHS towards a devolved health service' (Department. of Health 2002: 3).

The new National Health Service

At the top of the new NHS structure in England (see Figure 3.1) is the DoH, which is responsible for developing policy, managing the overall

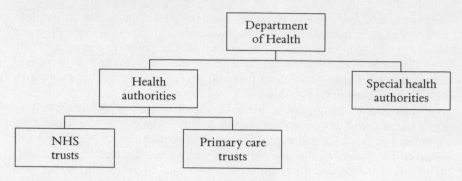

Figure 3.1   Structure of the NHS in England 2002.

health care system, regulating and inspecting the NHS, and intervening should problems occur. Within the DoH, four Directors of Health and Social Care, covering geographical areas, oversee the development of the NHS.

In the middle of the NHS structure are 28 HAs, each covering a population of around 1.5 million people. Run by boards consisting of non-executive directors appointed by the secretary of state and executive directors appointed by the chair of the authority, HAs monitor the performance and standards of local NHS trusts and PCTs. They are due to become strategic health authorities in late 2002, with responsibility for strategically developing the local NHS services in their areas.

The NHS organizational jigsaw is completed by three other main types of bodies. NHS trusts are self-governing units – mainly hospitals or groups of hospitals – that provide acute and specialized hospital services or community services. They are run by boards of directors consisting of a chair, up to five executive directors appointed by the secretary of state and an equal number of non-executive directors. Most of their income is derived through service agreements that they, as health providers, negotiate to provide services for the purchasers of health care – the PCTs, which evolved from the PCGs. In 2002, the Blair government announced that it intended to establish the best hospitals as foundation trusts, which would be freed from excessive central government control.

There are 302 PCTs, each covering populations of about 170,000 people, and made up of the GPs and nurse practitioners in their area. The chairs and lay members of the boards of PCTs are appointed by the Secretary of State for Health. The boards also include professional members. Described as the 'cornerstones' of the new NHS (Department of Health 2001b: 13), they combine the provision of primary care with the commissioning of hospital and community care from NHS hospitals or the private sector. They are also able to provide community health services themselves. It is envisaged that PCTs will become 'the lead NHS organisation' in assessing need, planning and securing all health services and improving health (Department of Health 2001b: 5). When they were established, PCTs were responsible for 50 per cent of the NHS budget in England and Wales. By 2004, this will have risen to 75 per cent.

The NHS also includes a number of special health authorities. These are bodies that provide health services to the whole of Britain, such as the National Blood Authority and the National Institute for Clinical Excellence.

Thus the NHS is characterized by what has been described as a 'baroque administrative structure' (Carter et al. 1992: 103). In the words of another observer, from the top it resembles 'a mountain range rather than a pyramid' (Rose 1989: 325). Within this complicated organizational structure, the medical profession has traditionally played a dominant role. Indeed, writing in the late 1980s, Rhodes (1988: 78) stated that the NHS was the most cited example of a 'professionalized policy network', in which professional, rather than managerial or political, influences had been dominant. The creation of the NHS in 1948 was underpinned by the establishment of what has been described as an 'underlying concordat' between the state and the medical profession, an agreement which gave doctors not only power over the allocation of resources within the NHS, but also representation as of right on policymaking bodies at all levels of the service (Elston 1991: 67). As we shall discuss in later chapters, the development of managerialist and consumerist challenges within the NHS by Conservative governments in the 1980s and 1990s brought this concordat into question, and what has been referred to as 'the frontier of control' between doctors and managers was shifted in favour of the latter (Harrison 1988).

The arm's-length administration of welfare

In addition to the NHS and local authorities, there are a number of quasi-governmental bodies that perform important tasks at arm's length from central government departments and local authorities. Quasi-governmental bodies are not elected and have a certain degree of independence from central and local government control. They play an important part in the organization of the welfare state and the delivery of its services.

The use of such bodies outside the traditional structures of central government departments and local authorities has been an important feature of the development of the welfare state in the post-war period. Indeed, one writer has referred to the post-war period as the 'era of quangocracy' (Rhodes 1988: 54). Quasi-governmental bodies are, of course, not new. Such bodies, in their various guises, have been a feature of the British administrative landscape since the nineteenth century: for example, the Poor Law Commission, which supervised the activities of the Poor Law Guardians, played an important part in the delivery of welfare in the nineteenth century. However, the importance of quasi-governmental bodies has grown markedly in the post-war period.

The whole area of quasi-governmental bodies is surrounded by definitional uncertainty. Various terms have been used to describe such organizations, including non-departmental public bodies, independent public bodies, fringe bodies, arm's-length agencies, extra-governmental organizations and quasi-autonomous non-governmental bodies – popularly known as quangos. Attempts to classify such bodies are difficult because of the wide variety of functions, methods of financing and degree of independence accorded to them. According to Rhodes (1988: 180), the only real generalization that can be made about such bodies is that 'there is no uniformity'.

Some quasi-governmental bodies are promotional bodies that channel funds to other organizations. One such promotional body in the field of welfare is the Housing Corporation, which was established by the Housing Act 1964 to promote the development of housing associations as a 'third force' in the housing market (Harden and Lewis 1986: 169). Following the Housing Act 1974, there was a major expansion of the Housing Corporation, and in the 1980s it came to play a major role as Conservative governments saw housing associations as an alternative to local authorities in the delivery of social housing.

Another example of a promotional body in the field of the social services is the Higher Education Funding Council for England (HEFCE), the successor body to the University Funding Council (itself a succesor to the University Grants Committee) and the Polytechnics and Colleges Funding Council, which is responsible for the channelling of public funds to the universities and other institutions of higher education. (There are also Higher Education Funding Councils for Scotland and Wales.) The Major government established a Further Education Funding Council for England (FEFCE) with responsibility for the channelling of public funds to further education colleges and sixth form colleges, which have the status of further education corporations and are independent of local education authority control. The Blair government replaced the FEFCE with the Learning and Skills Council (LSC) in 2001.

Other quasi-governmental bodies carry out important managerial functions. An example is the housing action trusts set up in the 1980s to manage the refurbishment of local authority housing in designated areas (see Chapter 6). In the 1980s, the Thatcher government also established urban development corporations (UDCs) to oversee the economic and physical regeneration of certain inner-city areas. They were based upon another form of quasi-governmental body, the new town development corporations, the first generation of which were set up in the early post-war years to plan and develop the new towns that were part of the reconstruction plans of the Attlee government. Funded by central government and controlled by government-nominated boards, the UDCs played an important role in the revival of the inner cities under the Conservative governments.

The reasons for the creation of quasi-governmental bodies are several (Hague 1971). In some cases, this kind of body is set up in an attempt to take a particular policy area 'out of politics' – thus the Housing Corporation has been seen as a way of channelling money directly to housing associations rather than government subsidy becoming enmeshed in what has been described as 'the politically sensitive morass of central–local government relations and financial controls' (Cole and Furbey 1994: 216). Quasi-governmental bodies are also often used to bypass existing public sector organizations, government department or local authority procedures being seen as inappropriate. The need to avoid the perceived pathologies of public sector organizations – the 'escape theory' – was an important consideration in Conservative government initiatives of the 1980s in the inner cities, where UDCs were established to escape the constraints associated with local authorities, especially those controlled by the Labour Party. The creation of grant-maintained schools and city technology colleges are other examples of the use of a form of quasi-governmental body by Conservative governments to bypass local government. Another important reason for the creation of such bodies has been to draw upon expertise and experience that would not normally be available in a government department or local authority. The Housing Corporation has been seen as a quasi-governmental body with some of these characteristics (Lewis 1985: 206).

The use of quasi-governmental bodies in the post-war period has been the subject of much debate, with concern being expressed over their alleged lack of democratic accountability and control (see Skelcher 1998). The Conservative government elected in 1979 was especially critical of such bodies, and the early 1980s saw a cull of quasi-governmental bodies – described by one commentator as the blood-sport of 'quango-hunting' (Dunsire 1982: 15). But, although originally hostile towards this arm's-length approach to the delivery of public services, the potential benefits of quasi-governmental bodies as vehicles of welfare delivery were soon recognized by Conservative governments, notably in the fields of education, housing and health care. The creation of quasi-governmental bodies was a major feature of reforms in the delivery of welfare in the late 1980s and early 1990s.

As we shall discuss in more detail in Chapter 6, a central plank of the Conservative government's policy during this period was the creation of grant-maintained schools managed by governing bodies free from local education authority control. Although such bodies included a small number of elected parent governors, they consisted mainly of non-elected governors, including representatives of the local business community. The payment and monitoring of grants to grant-maintained schools was in the hands of another quasi-governmental body, the Funding Agency for Schools. Under the Conservatives, further education colleges and sixth form colleges in England were transferred from local education authorities to appointed further education corporations funded by a quasi-governmental body, the

FEFCE. The Conservative government also established a number of CTCs, managed by appointed governing boards, in parts of England.

In a related area, 82 Training and Enterprise Councils (TECs) were set up in the early 1990s in England and Wales with responsibility for the development of training – including arrangements for the delivery of Youth Training and work-related further education – in their local areas. Two-thirds of their membership was reserved for business people. In 2001, these bodies were replaced by the Learning and Skills Council, a quasi-governmental body that also took over the functions of the FEFCE, and is responsible for the planning and coordination of all post-16 education and training, excluding higher education. National priorities are delivered at the local level by a network of 47 local learning and skills councils, which are business-led, with 40 per cent of their membership drawn from the commercial sector.

The Conservatives also introduced the concept of the quasi-governmental body into the field of local housing. Following the Housing Act 1988, HATs, consisting of boards appointed by the Secretary of State for the Environment, were set up in parts of England to take over and renovate designated run-down local authority council estates. As we saw earlier in the chapter, reforms in the delivery of health care included the creation of independent NHS trusts, run by appointed boards of directors and accountable directly to the Secretary of State for Health. One consequence of the growth of these kinds of non-elected bodies in the NHS, housing, education and elsewhere – what some observers refer to as 'the quango state' – was to revive the debate about their democratic accountability and control (see, for example, Weir and Hall 1994).

The sub-central government of welfare delivery

Our survey of the government of welfare in this and the previous chapter shows that most government policies involving the social services in Britain are not delivered by central government departments but by organizations outside the Whitehall department system – by a system of sub-central government. There is a clear distinction between the small groups of social policymakers in Whitehall and the delivery agencies of the welfare state. This division clearly has important consequences for the social service departments of central government. In the words of Stoker (1990):

> central government may legislate, regulate and exhort but it does so in the context of a system of sub-central government in which day-to-day control and the scope for innovation and initiative is in the hands of a range of other elected representatives, appointees and full-time officials and managers.
>
> (Stoker 1990: 127)

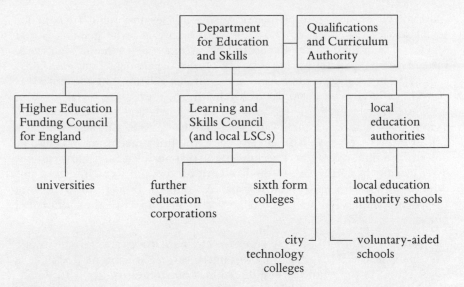

Figure 3.2 The pattern of education delivery in England 2002.

Source: Adapted and updated from figure in Weir and Hall 1994: 50

Thus the organization of the British welfare state is characterized by a complex pattern of delivery agencies. As Hood (1982: 66) has observed, government departments, local authorities and other governmental bodies are increasingly operating in 'complex and dense networks or cross-cutting territorial, functional and hierarchical organizational relationships' and within the context of an increasingly 'money-moving' style of administration – government by grants and by indirect administration. The delivery of education provision in England is a particularly good example of this complex pattern, with its complicated network of local education authorities, further education corporations and CTCs, together with the bodies responsible for funding (HEFCE and LSC), not to mention the Qualifications and Curriculum Authority and other quasi-governmental bodies (Figure 3.2).

One obvious issue created by the existence of what has been described as a system of 'multi-bureaucratic' government (Hood 1982: 67) is the weakening of central government's ability to ensure the successful implementation of centrally determined welfare policies. The literature on policy implementation describes several preconditions for 'perfect implementation', one of which is the requirement that the dependency relationships involved in the implementation process are minimal:

> that there is a single implementing agency which need not depend on other agencies for success, or if other agencies must be involved, that the dependency relationships are minimal in both number and importance.
>
> (Hogwood and Gunn 1984: 202)

As we have seen, the implementation of policies involving such major social services as education, housing, health care and the personal social services do not involve just the central government department concerned. Instead, there is an interlocking network of non-departmental organizations.

The history of central–local government relations in the post-war period is littered with examples of local authority resistance or tardiness in implementing centrally determined social policies, and we shall examine a couple of well-known episodes in Chapter 6. One of these concerns education, where, as we have already seen, the implementation of centrally determined policy is not in the hands of the responsible central government department, the DfES, but in the hands of local education authorities and other non-departmental organizations. As one ex-minister who became Minister of Education after having served as First Lord of the Admiralty, put it:

> In the Admiralty you are a person having authority. You say to one person 'Come' and he cometh, and another 'Go' and he goeth. It is not so in the Ministry of Education. You suggest rather than direct. You say to one man 'Come' and he cometh not and to another 'Go' and he stays where he is.
>
> (Lord Hailsham, quoted in Kogan 1971: 31)

It is not only the delivery agencies of local government that are beyond the day-to-day control of central government. There have also been occasions when the institutions of the other major delivery arm of the welfare state, the NHS, have frustrated the implementation of central policies. As Ham (1992) observes:

> The fact that NHS authorities actually provide service and have day-to-day management and planning responsibilities means that the [DoH] has to work through and with those authorities to achieve its goals.
>
> (Ham 1992: 172)

According to Haywood and Elcock (1982: 139), the history of the NHS shows that NHS bodies have not been 'particularly zestful' in applying central government policies. Indeed, there has been resistance to the implementation of central policies that 'challenge established professional hierarchies and priorities' (Elcock 1986a: 283). For example, central government attempts in the 1960s and 1970s to draw up health service priorities were often frustrated by the opposition of the medical profession, a well-documented example being the inability of central government to shift resources away from the 'glamour' areas of acute hospital medicine to such 'Cinderella' services as those for mentally handicapped people (see, for example, Ham 1992: 208–11). Writing in the early 1980s, Day and Klein (1983: 1813) described the NHS as being rather like a 'feudal society' in which independent authority was exercised by a number of groups, notably the medical profession. As we shall discuss in more detail in Chapter 8, in the early 1990s, organizational reforms in the NHS were introduced in an attempt to reduce what has been described as 'the risk of organizational anarchy' by strengthening lines of accountability and imposing checks and balances within the service (Levitt and Wall 1992: 319).

Another major issue raised by the number and range of organizations responsible for the delivery of welfare is that of coordination. The problem of departmentalism and its implications for coordination and planning at the national level are well documented. Thus Whitehall has been described as 'a seething mass of discrete departmental interests' where ministers are expected to fight their corners in the battle for scarce resources (Drewry and Butcher 1991: 84). Problems of coordination and social planning are also a feature of the world of welfare delivery beyond Whitehall. We have referred earlier in this chapter to the fragmented nature of local government throughout most of England, with responsibilities for the delivery of social services being divided between different types of local authorities. This particular feature of the local government system, together with the division of the related functions of the personal social services and health care, makes a coordinated approach to the local management of welfare delivery difficult. We turn to a discussion of these problems, and to some of the arrangements that have been set up in an attempt to resolve them, in Chapter 4.

Further reading

Wilson and Game (1998) and Byrne (2000) provide the most up-to-date surveys of local government, while Baggott (1998) and Ham (1999) discuss the changing organization of the NHS. Developments in the changing structure of the NHS can be followed on the DoH and NHS web sites – www.doh.gov.uk and www.nhs.gov.uk. Skelcher (1998) is a comprehensive study of the world of quasi-governmental bodies. Leach and Percy-Smith (2001) survey the new world of local governance.

4

The coordination and planning of welfare

It has long been recognized that there is a need for a coordinated approach to social policy and the delivery of welfare. The fact that the people affected by welfare policies are often vulnerable and poorly informed about social services places a 'heavy responsibility' on those involved in delivering these services to produce coordinated outcomes (Webb 1991: 239). Thus the coordination and planning of social services is central to welfare delivery. A group of academic researchers who undertook a study of the practice of coordination in welfare policy in the late 1980s saw effective coordination as an essential part of a collective, rational approach to the making of policy, with an emphasis on the existence of a systems-wide viewpoint, a well-developed capacity for policy analysis, and organizational arrangements appropriate to the analysis of problems and the implementation of solutions (Challis et al. 1988: 33).

A major problem arising from the arrangements for delivering welfare is that social problems and client groups do not always fit conveniently within the organizational and professional boundaries of the welfare state. As Webb (1991: 229) has pointed out, the public services are all too often 'a jumble of services fractionalized by professional, cultural and organizational boundaries and by tiers of governance'. Many social problems cut across the boundaries of the public bodies responsible for welfare policy and its delivery. Examples of such 'cross-cutting issues' include the needs of one-parent families, the care of elderly people and other dependent groups, the problems of homeless people, and the social conditions of the inner cities. Professional defensiveness and cultural differences may also be barriers to effective coordination.

A lot of time and effort has been spent since the early 1960s in attempts to construct structures and procedures designed to improve the coordination and planning of welfare delivery. But before we discuss these arrangements and their impact, we need to look more closely at some of the obstacles to coordination.

Agency fragmentation and welfare delivery

A major characteristic of the structure of both central and local government in Britain is the fragmentation of the agencies responsible for welfare delivery and its planning. This is particularly the case at the level of central government, which has been described as being plural and not singular (Central Policy Review Staff 1977: 21).

As we saw in Chapter 2, the activities of central government have been generally grouped together according to the services performed rather than according to the particular client groups dealt with. The organization of central government departments on the basis of what is known as the functional principle – affirmed by the Haldane Report as long ago as 1918 – is reflected in the major social service departments responsible for social security, education, and health, which are responsible for providing particular services to the community as a whole rather than a range of services limited to particular groups in the community. As Haldane (1918: para. 19) recognized, one disadvantage of such a pattern of departmental organization is the inevitable overlapping between departments. Many client groups cut across the boundaries of government departments. For example, policies for the care and support of elderly people are served by three different social service departments, the DWP, DoH and ODPM, with the result that it is sometimes unclear which particular government department is actually responsible for certain policy issues of importance to this client group.

Uncertainty about which department has the major responsibility for a welfare problem or particular client group has not been confined to policy issues affecting elderly people. Critics of housing policy in the post-war period have highlighted the inadequacy of organizational arrangements for dealing with the problem of homeless people. Thus, up to the enactment of the Housing (Homeless Persons) Act 1977, the legislative powers for providing temporary accommodation for the homeless were not in the hands of the government department responsible for housing, but in those of the department responsible for social security. As a result, there was what has been described as an 'uncertain division of responsibility' between the then DoE and the then DHSS, and their predecessor departments (Raynsford 1986: 37).

The lack of coordination in Whitehall is not confined to the problem of drawing together the activities of different social service departments. On occasions the separate divisions of individual departments may fail to harmonize their policies. A good example of such a failure of interdepartmental collaboration occurred in the DHSS in the 1980s, when the department's policy of financing places in private sector residential and nursing homes through the supplementary benefit system clearly conflicted with its other policy of attempting to persuade elderly people to stay in the community by continuing to live in their own homes. There was inevitably criticism that the social security, health and personal social services divisions of the DHSS had failed to coordinate their policies, with the result that they were 'pulling against each other' (Challis et al. 1984: 32).

The problems created by overlapping functions and departmental fragmentation are compounded by the notorious departmentalism of Whitehall. British central government is characterized by a culture in which the loyalty of departments is upwards to the minister and departmental interests rather than outwards to the government as a whole. The now defunct Central Policy Review Staff (CPRS) – itself set up in an attempt to overcome the problems engendered by departmentalism in British central government (see pp. 69–70) – accurately described central government as 'a federation of separate departments with their own Ministers and their own policies' (Central Policy Review Staff 1977: para. 5.1).

As a result, competition between departments is a major characteristic of the Whitehall system. Central government departments are in competition with each other for scarce resources, and ministers are expected to fight their departmental corners, either in seeking additional financial resources or keeping what they already have under the pressure to make cuts. Thus social service ministers come to Cabinet to fight for their departmental budgets, and not as Cabinet ministers with a collective view about spending priorities. In the words of two American observers of the process, 'The minister who appears to give up without a fight loses credibility all around'; Margaret Thatcher is cited as a classic example of a minister who fought hard for more money when she was in charge of the DES in the early 1970s (Heclo and Wildavsky 1981: 135–7).

Competition between social service departments is not confined to rivalry over their share of the public expenditure cake. Each central government department has a notion of its own territory – what has been described as 'policy ownership' (Challis et al. 1988: 109), with departments fiercely resisting any invasion of their territories by other departments. Thus an attempt to transfer the then Children's Department of the Home Office to the newly created DHSS in 1968 led to a strong and successful protest by the then Home Secretary, James Callaghan (Crossman 1977: 146–8, 150; Callaghan 1987: 235). The DES strongly resisted the threatened invasion of its territory by the Department of Trade and Industry in the mid-1980s, when the latter department attempted to acquire more influence over education policy (Jordan and Richardson 1987: 167–8). It was reported in early 1994 that the DSS and the DEmp were at loggerheads over which of their two departments should administer the jobseeker's allowance due to replace unemployment benefit in 1996. The DSS argued that as unemployed individuals often receive other social security benefits, it would be more efficient for it to administer the new benefit, an argument that was opposed by the DEmp, which was concerned to protect jobs in its department (Grice 1994).

These examples show that, in the words of a former senior civil servant:

> Much of the work of Whitehall is institutionalised conflict between the competing interests of different departments. Each department will defend its own position and resist a line that, while it might be beneficial to the government as a whole or in the wider public interest, would work against the interests of the department.
>
> (Ponting 1986: 102)

Thus the concept of 'central government' is 'an abstraction which conceals reality' (Central Policy Review Staff 1977: para. 5.1). Central government is, in fact, a collection of separate departments, with unfortunate consequences for the coordination and the planning of social services.

The fragmentation of welfare delivery at the local level

The fragmentation of responsibilities for welfare provision and the phenomenon of departmentalism are also features of welfare delivery at the local level. Like their central government counterparts, local authority departments are organized on the basis of the functional principle, with separate departments for such services as education, housing and the personal social services (although the dramatic decline of local authority housing since the early 1980s has meant that some local authorities have amalgamated their housing and social services departments). The fact that there used to be a legal requirement for local authorities to set up separate committees for both education and personal social services – the requirement to have education committees was abolished in 1993, and that for social services committees in 2000 – has also helped to create barriers between the two closely related services.

Within the London boroughs, the metropolitan districts and the unitary authorities – which are most-purpose authorities – coordination between the different departments responsible for education, housing and the personal social services takes place within the individual authorities. In much of England, however, responsibility for the three services is divided between two tiers of local government, with education and the personal social services being a county responsibility and the housing service being administered by the districts. This division has been the subject of much criticism, and as long ago as 1968 the Seebohm Committee argued (1968: paras 676, 681) that an effective 'family service' could be fully effective only if education, housing and the personal social services were the undivided responsibility of the same local authority.

The same conclusions were reached a year later by the majority report of the Redcliffe-Maud Commission on local government in England and Wales (1969: para. 249). After endorsing Seebohm's view that it would be wrong to divide responsibility for education and the personal social services between different local authorities, the report went on to say that the ties between housing and the personal social services were equally strong. Housing was an 'essential part of social policy' and much of the work of the personal social services stemmed directly from housing conditions, with the people and families most likely to make the greatest demands on the personal social services also being those most likely to suffer from severe housing problems. In the report's opinion:

> An authority responsible for the personal social services but not for housing lacks an essential means of dealing with the difficulties of those people and families who need its help; and a housing authority which does not administer the personal social services will not be aware at first hand of the social needs that should receive priority in its management policies and building programmes.
>
> (Redcliffe-Maud 1969: para. 250)

The interdependence of the two services were also stressed by the Wheatley Commission on local government in Scotland, which also reported in 1969, its report arguing that the personal social services were 'linked intimately' with house building, allocation and management (Wheatley 1969: para. 472).

The division of responsibility for housing and the personal social services in many parts of England has been seen as a major barrier to the efficient delivery of welfare, professionals on both sides arguing that it is difficult to separate the 'social' and 'housing' parts of individual cases (Alexander 1982b: 69). There are many areas in which the two services are linked, including the allocation of housing, the problem of tenants with rent arrears and the needs of disabled people. One major area of shared concern which has been a particular problem is the issue of homelessness – what one writer has described as a personal social services 'condition' with a housing 'remedy' (Alexander 1982b: 59). According to Alexander (1982a: 55), in metropolitan districts – where housing and the personal social services are both departments of the same local authority – local councillors and officers have not seen any financial advantage in attempting to pass responsibility for tackling the problem of homelessness from one department to the other. However, he suggests that the situation seems to have been the reverse in the non-metropolitan counties – where the two services are the responsibility of different local authorities – because there has been seen to be some advantage in shifting part of the responsibility from one local authority to the other, particularly when the local authorities concerned are controlled by different political parties.

It was partly to deal with these kinds of problems that Redcliffe-Maud recommended the establishment of unitary (that is, all-purpose) local authorities for the whole of England and Wales outside the Greater London area (1969: paras 252–3). According to Redcliffe-Maud (1969: para. 253), a major strength of the unitary authority is that it can see the full extent of the relationships between different services, the developments in the services needed to meet people's needs, and the gaps between services that need to be filled. Its Scottish counterpart, the Wheatley Commission, also recognized the value of integrating the major local authority social services, recommending that the three key services of education, housing and social work should be the responsibility of the same local authorities (Wheatley 1969: paras 419, 453). Nearly a quarter of a century later, in 1992, the Conservative government established a Local Government Commission to recommend changes in the structure of English local government, believing that there should be a move towards unitary authorities in the non-metropolitan counties. The government argued that one benefit of such a development would be better coordination of services, which would not only improve quality but also reduce costs (Department of the Environment 1991a: para. 25). As we saw in Chapter 3, unitary authorities have been introduced in only some parts of England, although both Scotland and Wales have a system of unitary authorities.

Despite these developments, it would be naive to believe that the creation of unitary authorities across the whole of England would automatically result in the better coordination of local social services, particularly between housing and the personal social services. Like their Whitehall counterparts, local authorities are afflicted by the phenomenon of departmentalism, with local authority officials perceiving that they are in competition with other local authority departments for scarce resources. According to Stoker (1991: 102), such perceptions have three main sources: the 'bureaucratic rivalry' stemming from the wish of officials to protect and extend their departmental empires, the 'professional jealousies' which exist between rival departments over such issues as 'territory' and the 'value clashes' between different departments.

Examples of such competition can be readily found in the field of local authority welfare. Thus Stoker's study of the politics of a housing renewal programme in a Manchester suburb in the mid-1970s found that, in an attempt to pacify departmental interests, responsibility for the programme was divided between three departments – housing, environmental health and architects (Stoker 1991: 101). Other studies of local authority housing have provided examples of interdepartmental conflict (see, for example, Paris and Blackaby 1979), while Challis et al. (1988: 214) found rivalry between local authority education and social services departments over policy for the under-fives, with social services departments being regarded as 'empire builders'. As we shall see in a later section of the chapter, collaboration between housing and the personal social services within the same local authorities is restricted by the problem of conflicting professional attitudes and priorities.

The delivery of welfare at the local level has been characterized not only by the fragmentation of services within local government, but also by the separation of related services between local authorities and the NHS. There is a clear interdependence between the personal social services provided by local authorities and those services provided by the NHS (see, for example, Merrison 1979: para. 16.2). Patients discharged from hospital, particularly elderly ones, often need to be referred to local authority social services departments for such support services as domiciliary care. The provision of such services might even help to support certain people in the community and thereby keep them out of hospital. The increasing attention given to the policy of community care since the late 1980s has helped to emphasize the links between the two groups of services. We shall discuss the arrangements for collaboration between local authorities and the NHS later in this chapter.

The Treasury and social planning

The centrepiece of attempts to improve coordination and social planning at the level of central government is the public expenditure system. Before 1961, central government decisions on public spending were taken for a single year only, with little attention being paid to the long term. Following the famous Plowden Report of 1961 (Plowden 1961), the Conservative government set up the PESC system – an acronym for the interdepartmental Public Expenditure Survey Committee – presided over by the Treasury, the department responsible for coordinating and overseeing the whole public expenditure process. The aim of the system was to provide government ministers with a projection of departmental spending commitments in the medium term (originally five years, but later three years), together with a forecast of economic prospects. The idea was that this information would then enable ministers collectively to take spending decisions and determine priorities. PESC was based on what Jordan and Richardson (1987: 206) have referred to as the notion of 'a rational, considered, collective allocation' of public expenditure. Between 1970 and 1979, the PESC exercise was reinforced by a system of programme analysis and review (PAR), enabling spending departments to assess the effectiveness of current departmental programmes in achieving their objectives and to review other available options. Spending programmes which were evaluated under this system included higher education and school building, but, in the absence of ministerial backing and a strong central organization, PAR was abandoned in 1979 (see Gray and Jenkins 1982).

The PESC system, however, survived and remained the basis for decisions on the spending programmes of central government's social service, and other, departments. Nevertheless, the system had its problems. First, what Glennerster (1992a: 55) refers to as 'the rules of the game' changed. When it was first set up in the early 1960s, PESC was based on volume planning rather than cash planning. This approach meant, for example, that the governmental spending programme for the NHS provided for a volume of so many hospitals, doctors, nurses, equipment and so on, which were costed in constant prices and thus insulated from the effects of inflation. Thus the spending programmes for education, housing, the NHS and the other major social services were protected from any rises in pay and prices for four years ahead, thereby allowing social service managers a degree of confidence in the short term (Glennerster 1992a: 57).

Although this system worked well in a period of low inflation, in the early 1970s underestimations of costs, together with increases in pay and prices, meant that the actual cost of a particular volume of services turned out to be far greater than had originally been planned. The turning point in the PESC system came in 1975, when inflation reached 25 per cent. The out-turn for the 1974–75 financial year was some £6.5 billion more than had been planned – what became known as the 'missing billions'.

The response of the Labour government to what has been called the 'crisis of control' (Wright 1977) was to change the whole basis of the PESC system. In 1976, cash limits (which included an allowance for inflation) were placed on the amount spent on certain programmes for the coming financial year, which meant that, whatever the volume of services provided for in their spending plans, departments could not spend above the limit specified. (The social security programme, which is determined by demand, and therefore difficult to forecast, was not covered by this new system.) Further changes to the system were introduced by the Thatcher government in the early 1980s. The planning period was reduced from five to three years and, in 1982, volume planning was replaced by cash planning, with spending programmes being laid down in terms of the cash that would actually be available for the next three years. Cash plans included an allowance for estimated inflation.

Cash planning clearly had significant implications for spending on social services. If the Treasury underestimated the level of inflation, then spending programmes would effectively be cut in real terms. Thus the spending plans announced each year by the government were 'unhelpful for long-term planning purposes' (Glennerster 1992a: 60), as social service departments were uncertain about the cash that they would be able to actually spend on doctors and hospital equipment, teachers and school equipment, and so on. The result of the introduction of cash planning and other changes was that the emphasis of the PESC exercise shifted from its original concern with medium-term planning to an emphasis on short-term control.

The framework provided by PESC also did not appear to have persuaded spending ministers to adopt 'a rational, considered and collective' approach in their discussions about public spending. Indeed, as Challis et al. (1988: 75) observe, the main determinant of public spending decisions was often 'the relative political weight and forensic skill of the individual ministers struggling to defend their departmental budgets against the Chancellor'. This was confirmed by a former insider, Joel Barnett (1982: 59) – Chief Secretary to the Treasury in the Labour government of the late 1970s – who stated that public spending decisions were never thought through as to their relative priority in either economic or social terms. Instead, they were often made 'on the strength of a particular spending minister and the extent of the support he or she could get from the Prime Minister'. Clearly, the politics of the public expenditure process were more important than the procedures of the PESC exercise (Jordan and Richardson 1987: 209).

Former secretaries of state for the social services have recorded their battles to defend departmental spending. The flavour of the process has been nicely captured by Barbara Castle, secretary of state in the Labour government of the mid-1970s, who was particularly astute at 'fighting her corner'. Thus she records in her *Diaries* (Castle 1980: 641) how the 1976 public expenditure White Paper 'demonstrated vividly how much more successful I have been than some of my colleagues in defending my programmes'. Castle's successor at the then DHSS, David Ennals, appears to have been less successful in his battles with the Treasury, and was apparently actually prevented from arguing the case against a cut in the health programme because the prime minister was annoyed with the way in which Ennals had handled an NHS dispute (Barnett 1982: 59–60). A former Conservative Secretary of State for the Social Services during the 1980s, Norman Fowler, has also referred to his 'battles' with the Treasury (Fowler 1991: 206–7).

Important changes in the PESC system were introduced in 1992. What has been described as the bottom-up approach – in which the total level of public expenditure tended to be the consequence of the compromises negotiated between the Treasury and spending ministers – was replaced by a new top-down approach in which the total level of public expenditure was limited in advance by setting annual ceilings for the New Control Total (NCT). The revised system involved the allocation of resources from within the NCT, the hope being that this would allow for a more collective approach to the setting of spending priorities, with a Cabinet committee making recommendations to the full Cabinet on its preferred allocation of resources (HM Treasury 1993: 6–7). In 1998, the Blair government introduced what was described as 'the most ambitious re-engineering of the public expenditure system' for several decades – the Comprehensive Spending Review (James 1999: 195). This requires individual departments to scrutinize their spending plans from a zero base and to ask how they contribute to the government's priorities. Each departmental allocation is based on a Public Service Agreement (PSA), setting out objectives, aims and performance targets for improving services over a three-year period, between the department and the Treasury. This new system is seen as enabling government decisions about public spending priorities to be 'seen through more objective criteria' than the traditional bartering between ministers (McEldowney 2000: 208).

The search for joined-up government

In addition to the introduction of the system of public expenditure planning, governments have experimented with various other measures in an attempt to achieve better coordination of welfare delivery and the policy planning which underpins it. Developments at the level of central government in the 1960s and 1970s included the creation of giant departments such as the DHSS and the DoE, the setting up of the Central Policy Review Staff, and the Joint Approach to Social Policy (JASP) initiative. As we shall see in the later sections of this chapter, there have also been some important developments at the local level, both within local authorities and between them and the NHS.

One approach to improving coordination at the level of central government's social service departments involved the amalgamation of the separate Ministries of Social Security and Health to form the giant DHSS in 1968. The rationale behind the merger was that the new department could develop a more coherent approach to dealing with social care and apply resources on a larger scale (Nairne 1983: 247). In the event, however, coordination and planning within the DHSS was fragmented and ad hoc. The different parts of the new department had little in common. As a former permanent secretary to the DHSS was later to point out, the tasks of the two main sides of the department were very different: whereas the social security side was derived from legislation and was directly under the control of the department, the health side was concerned with allocating resources to health authorities which exercised a great deal of discretion (Expenditure Committee 1977: Q.897). The department remained 'a conglomerate' (Nairne 1983: 255), being divided essentially along the lines of its three main responsibilities – health, social security and the personal social services. There was little strategic planning and the department was criticized for its failure to adopt a coherent policy strategy across it (see, for example, Social Services Committee 1980). In 1988, on its twentieth anniversary, the DHSS was split into its two former departments, Health and Social Security.

However, as Wicks (1983) has pointed out, social planning is far too important to be left to spending departments alone or to the Treasury. An important attempt to overcome the departmentalism of central government and strengthen its capacity for collective strategic policy planning was the creation of the Central Policy Review Staff by the Conservative government of Edward Heath in 1970. A small, multidisciplinary unit located in the Cabinet Office, the CPRS's major purpose was to tackle problems that crossed departmental boundaries and to extend the perspective of individual spending ministers beyond their narrow departmental briefs. Like PAR, which was introduced at the same time, the CPRS was a deliberate attempt to break down the notorious departmentalism of Whitehall.

From the very beginning, the CPRS invested a great deal of time and attention to social policy, the authors of one history of the unit maintaining that its main contribution in this particular area was in seeing 'the interrelationship between different parts of the jigsaw' (Blackstone and Plowden 1988: 199). Reports were published on such subjects as population and the social services, services for young children with working mothers, and the interactions between housing and social services (see Blackstone and Plowden 1988: Appendix I). But probably the most important initiative in this area was the CPRS's attempt in 1975 to introduce a joint approach to social policy. Fully aware that the most intractable problems of social policy are often the concern of more than one government department and that there existed no framework within which to effectively formulate coherent and consistent social priorities, the CPRS advocated a Joint Approach to Social Policy. JASP promised better coordination between related social services, improved analysis of (and prescriptions for) complex problems – especially where these were the concern of more than one government department – and the development of collective views on policy priorities (Central Policy Review Staff 1975: para. 8).

Although JASP made a promising start, with six-monthly meetings of ministers in the major social service departments and follow-up studies by CPRS staff (including a report which recommended that central government departments should act more interdepartmentally in their dealings with local authorities: Central Policy Review Staff 1977), the exercise fizzled out in 1977. Perhaps its demise was inevitable: as Drewry (1988: 178) has observed, its failure could have been predicted from the outset – as we saw earlier, fighting one's departmental corner is one of 'the most deeply engrained features of the Whitehall culture'.

Disappointment with the lack of coordination within government was expressed by the Labour government on its election in 1997. According to the government, too little effort had gone into making sure that policies were 'devised and delivered in a consistent and effective way across institutional boundaries' (Cabinet Office 1999: 15). In the words of the prime minister: 'Joined-up problems need joined-up solutions' (Blair 1998b). Thus, the *Modernising Government* White Paper published in 1999 declared that one of the keystones of the Labour government's operations was integration, with policies and programmes tackling issues in 'a joined up way, regardless of the organisational structure of government' (Cabinet Office 1999: 10).

As part of this new approach, the Labour government launched a number of initiatives designed to improve cross-cutting working, notably in the area of social policy. These included the setting up in 1997 of the

Social Exclusion Unit – initially based in the cabinet office and now in the ODPM – to tackle in a 'joined-up' way policies to combat poverty and deprivation. There was also the transfer of the Contributions Agency from the then DSS to the Inland Revenue (see Chapter 2). The creation of the DWP in 2001 brought together work and benefit-related services. Another initiative was the establishment in 1998 of the Performance and Innovation Unit (PIU). Located in the Cabinet Office, and described as like 'a latter day CPRS' (Kavanagh and Richards 2001: 11), the PIU was given the task of improving the capacity of government to address strategic, cross-cutting issues. Other initiatives introduced by the Blair government included the creation of task forces with remits that crossed departmental boundaries (see Barker et al. 2000). Located outside 'the embrace of formal departmental structures', task forces – which have included such areas as schools standards and health inequalities – are intended to 'think holistically' (Greenwood et al. 2001: 78).

Other examples of 'joined-up' initiatives have involved the local delivery of services. Thus, the Blair government has set up area-based initiatives such as education action zones (see Chapter 6) and health action zones. The *Sure Start* initiative – involving cooperation between local authority education and social services departments and NHS agencies – is designed to support pre-school children.

Despite the development of joined-up government, sceptics have argued that organizational change is not sufficient to produce integrated policy development or service delivery, and that it requires new cultural values to persuade ministers and officials to move their focus from purely departmental business to a more corporate approach (see, for example, Cabinet Office 2000: 45–6). In the words of one senior official, the proof of the success of joined-up government will be that it enters 'Whitehall's blood-stream' and joining-up 'becomes natural' (quoted in Kavanagh and Richards 2001: 17).

Coordinating welfare delivery at the local level

The importance of coordinating welfare delivery is not confined to the central government level. Criticism of the traditional separatist approach of local authorities has led to a growing recognition of what has been described as an 'integral' view of local authorities. This approach emphasizes the close relations between local authority services and argues that they should be planned as a programme rather than as a combination of separate activities (Greenwood et al. 1980: 15). A series of official reports in the late 1960s emphasized the interdependence between the various social services delivered by local authorities and the consequent need for a more integrated approach to their planning and provision. Thus, the Plowden Report of 1967 on primary schools highlighted the impact of the local environment upon schools and educational standards (Central Advisory Council for Education 1967), while, a year later, the Seebohm Report on local authority personal social services pointed to the complexity of social problems and the need for a more coordinated approach by interdependent local authority departments (Seebohm 1968).

The turning point in the development of structures for a more coordinated and planned approach to local authority services was the report of the Maud Committee in 1967. Highly critical of the absence of coordination and what it referred to as the 'loose confederation of disparate activities' that existed within local authorities, the report concluded that while there might be unity in the different parts of individual local authorities, there was 'disunity in the whole' (Maud 1967: paras 130, 97). A key recommendation in Maud's proposals for a more integrated approach to the management of local services was a reduction in the number of local authority departments and committees and the creation of a management board, which would serve as the focal point for the management of the affairs of each local authority and oversee the work of the authority as a whole. Although the overall reaction to Maud has been described as negative (Haynes 1980: 48), many local authorities did streamline their departmental and committee structures. Notable changes took place in the personal social services, which, following the Seebohm (1968) recommendations, have been administered since the early 1970s by unified social services departments, rather than by the fragmented system developed in the late 1940s. Subsequently, with the decline in local authority housing stock since the early 1980s, some local authorities have amalgamated their social services and housing departments.

However, despite the developments following Maud, the importance of coordination really found expression in the Bains Report of 1972, which argued that the traditional departmental attitude found within many local authorities had to give way to a wider-ranging corporate outlook (Bains 1972: para. 2.11), underpinned by policy and resources committees, chief executives and management teams of chief officers. There was widespread adoption of the structures of corporate planning within local authorities following the reorganization of local government in 1974 (see Greenwood et al. 1980: 50).

Despite such developments, however, there was criticism that although local authorities had adopted the structures of corporate planning, not all had embraced its processes, and that there had been little real impact on departmentalism in many local authorities. In the words of two observers, the structural innovations following Bains were '"corporate icing" on a traditional cake' (Wilson and Game 1998: 327). Thus, research by Challis et al. (1988) into the coordination by local authorities of policies for elderly people and the under-fives found that while each local authority studied had established corporate machinery, a few had never even attempted to develop corporate processes, and what enthusiasm there was for such processes in the other local authorities studied had disappeared. As with central government, departmentalism was a dominant phenomenon and local authority departments 'largely went their own way with little apparent regard to the wider local authority context' (Challis et al. 1988: 160). One issue highlighted by the study was the defensiveness of local education authorities as an obstacle to coordination. Education departments regarded themselves as being more 'professional' than other services, with their own 'professional territory' (Challis et al. 1988: 240, 214). The researchers referred to the 'paranoia' about the effects of service integrity being diluted, a concern which outweighed any estimation of wider benefits (1988: 240).

What has been termed 'strategic collaboration' over the development of local services and the allocation of resources (Sargeant 1979: 173) is seen as being particularly necessary in the case of local authority housing and social services departments. As Hudson (1986: 56) – echoing Seebohm (1968) – states, 'clearly many clients of [social services departments] have housing problems, and many tenants of housing authorities have social problems'. As we saw earlier in the chapter, the problems of housing allocation, rent arrears and homelessness have been identified as particular candidates for collaborative activity (Hudson 1986: 54). Observers, however, have criticized the tradition of limited collaboration between housing and social services departments (see, for example, Challis et al. 1988: 162–3).

An important example of the need for better collaboration is in the area of community care, where local authority housing departments, and other providers of social housing, have a crucial role to play in making policy work at the local level. A report by the Audit Commission (1998) in the late 1990s found that collaboration between local authority housing and social services departments was weak. The full potential of the contribution that local authority housing departments could make in community care was not being met, with joint working between the two sides needing to be improved.

Housing and social services departments have been characterized not only by the absence of strategic collaboration, but also by the absence of what has been termed ad-hoc case coordination regarding the treatment of individual clients (Sargeant 1979: 173). Effective coordination of this kind between the two services has been hindered by their different professional ideologies, one group of writers on housing policy pointing out that while the major concern of housing management is with the administration of standardized procedures, social work has a much more client-based perspective (Clapham et al. 1990: 220). It has also been suggested that communication between the two sides has been inhibited by the existence of a hierarchical structure in which social workers have often found that their opposite numbers in the housing service are at different levels of seniority (Barclay 1982, quoted in Hudson 1986: 58).

Although such problems might be alleviated by the merger of the housing service and the personal social services into single departments – as has occurred in some single-tier local authorities – there is still the problem of the non-metropolitan counties, where the two services are delivered by different types of local authorities. The creation of unitary authorities in many areas has brought responsibility for housing and social services in the non-metropolitan counties under the same authorities, but, as we saw earlier, attitudinal obstacles are still an important barrier to successful coordination.

Notwithstanding the difficulties involved in achieving effective strategic collaboration, and the problems associated with ad-hoc coordination, there have been several examples of what Sargeant (1979: 173) has termed operational coordination between housing and social services departments, whereby formal structures have been up in an attempt to integrate complementary services. Thus some local authorities have decentralized the delivery of both services to neighbourhood and area offices, part of a process that has replaced what has been described as the 'top-heavy' system of corporate management in many local authorities (Hudson 1986: 63; see also Clapham et al. 1990: 218–20). We shall describe this particular development in the local delivery of welfare in our discussion of local authority decentralization in Chapter 9.

Collaboration between local authorities and the NHS

The need to coordinate the delivery of social services within local authorities is only one variable in securing the efficient delivery of social services within a local community. The other major delivery agency of the welfare state at the local level – the NHS – is also responsible for the provision of key services. It is therefore important to develop collaboration between local authorities and NHS bodies.

Although the NHS was deliberately set up to operate outside local government control, there are, as we saw earlier, clear interdependencies between the services delivered by NHS bodies and local authorities. Since the mid-1970s, the growing importance attached to the policy of community care has emphasized the interrelationships between the two types of authorities. In the words of one writer on local government: 'It is clearly unsatisfactory if the right hand of the welfare state does not know what the left is doing' (Kingdom 1991: 61). The importance of collaboration between local authority social services departments and NHS bodies was explicitly recognized when local government and the NHS were both reorganized in 1974 and a formal system of 'strategic collaboration' over service development and resource allocation between the two sides was introduced (see Sargeant 1979).

Legislation imposed a duty on the NHS and local authorities to cooperate in the planning and operation of health and related social services. Collaboration between the two sides was facilitated by the drawing up of common boundaries between the operational tiers of the NHS – the then AHAs – and those local authorities responsible for providing personal social services. Joint consultative committees (JCCs), made up of members of the matching authorities, were established to advise on cooperation and planning. In order to develop detailed planning arrangements, the two sides were required to establish joint care planning teams (JCPTs) of senior officers – a development described as the 'keystone' of joint strategic planning (Challis et al. 1988: 172). In 1976, joint planning was encouraged by the introduction of a system of joint finance enabling NHS funds to be used on projects of benefit to both sides.

However, despite the various structural arrangements introduced to facilitate strategic collaboration, the progress of joint planning was 'limited and uneven' (Hunter and Wistow 1987: 130). Criticisms were made that the whole concept was based upon unrealistic assumptions. In the event, JCCs tended to be 'talking shops' and JCPTs were criticized as 'clumsy and ineffectual' (Challis et al. 1988: 181). The experience of joint planning was described as at best a form of 'parallel planning' based on consultation and the exchange of information (Hunter and Wistow 1987: 113). Various reasons were suggested for the limited impact of joint planning. Writing in the early 1980s, Allsop (1984: 114) stated that both local authorities and health authorities were 'micropolitical systems' which operated in different environments with 'their own organizational imperatives, system of financing and professional and political perceptions of priorities'. An official report in the late 1980s pointed to the major differences of planning timescale, management structure and geographical boundaries between the two types of authority, coterminosity having disappeared with the NHS reorganization of 1982 (National Audit Office 1987: para. 3.7). One academic study concluded that joint planning bore little resemblance to the official model, but 'was essentially a local professional power game' (Glennerster et al. 1983: 90).

The need for coordination between local authorities and the NHS was a central theme of the Griffiths Report (1988a) on the arrangements for community care in the late 1980s. As we shall discuss in greater detail in Chapter 6, Griffiths recommended that local authorities should take the leading role in the development of community care, but as enablers and not necessarily as direct providers of services. The government's response to Griffiths was contained in the National Health Service and Community Care Act 1990, which spelt out the new arrangements for community care. Under these arrangements, local authorities were required to prepare and publish plans for the provision of community care services. District health authorities were also expected to prepare plans laying out the arrangements they proposed for securing community care. If these new planning arrangements were to work, joint planning between the different types of authorities was essential, and the DoH recommended that, wherever possible, there should be planning agreements which included agreed policies on such areas as hospital discharge arrangements and care management. Even where joint planning was difficult – as, for example, in areas where authorities had different boundaries – the two sides were expected to ensure that their separate plans were complementary (Department of Health 1990: paras 2.3, 2.12).

Despite these reforms, problems of poor coordination persisted. In the words of one commentator, 'the boundary between health and social care still threatened to be a focus for competition and conflict between agencies and professions, rather than for cooperation and collaboration' (Hudson 1999: 191). The Blair government promised to foster 'a new spirit of flexible partnership working' between local authority social services and the NHS, which 'moves away from sterile debates over boundaries' to an approach where time and effort is directed towards working across them (Department of Health 1998: para. 6.3). In order to help develop this partnership approach, the Blair government made one of its top priorities the dismantling of what it described as the 'Berlin Wall' that can divide health and personal social services. Thus, the Health Act 1999 gave health authorities and NHS trusts a duty to work more closely with local authorities, and introduced a number of flexibilities to enable joint working. These flexibilities included the use of pooled budgets to fund care services, and lead commissioning, whereby either the health authority or the local authority can take the lead in commissioning services on behalf of both bodies. Building upon the establishment of PCTs as part of the modernization of the NHS (see Chapter 3), the Blair government has also proposed the establishment of care trusts which will be able to commission and deliver primary and community health care, as well as social care, for certain client groups. The first four care trusts were established in April 2002.

The Blair government's concern with improved coordination and joint working has also been reflected in the establishment of health action zones. Established in areas with particular health problems, health action zones are an attempt to improve collaboration between NHS bodies, local authorities and other local service providers. Under the Blair government, legislation has also given local authorities the power 'to promote the economic, social and environmental well-being of their areas'. The intention is that local authorities should stop thinking in terms of departmental functions and start thinking more corporately about what will benefit their citizens, cutting across traditional service boundaries not only within local authorities, such as housing, education and the personal social services, but also those with the NHS and other agencies.

However, as the Blair government's PIU has stated, simply removing barriers to better coordination is not enough (Performance and Innovation Unit 2000: 5). As we have already seen, the attitudes and behaviour of those involved in these kind of arrangements are crucial. The experience of earlier attempts to achieve coordination between local authority personal social services and health services – not to mention the difficulties in securing corporate links between the different social services delivered by local authorities – shows only too clearly that the personnel of welfare delivery agencies do not easily change their behaviour and perceptions when required to develop new approaches to the delivery of welfare.

Further reading

Although now dated in the details, Challis et al. (1988) discuss the barriers to coordination, and include an account of the CPRS and JASP. Deakin and Parry (1999) examine the Treasury and social policy. Some of the problems involved in securing effective collaboration at the local level are discussed in Hudson (1999). On the Blair government's approach to joined-up government, see Performance and Innovation Unit (2000).

5

Accountability and the public

We turn in this chapter to a discussion of the relationship between the delivery agencies of the welfare state and the users of their services. What are the arrangements for ensuring that the providers of social services are held accountable? What mechanisms exist to enable the users of social services – now increasingly described as 'customers' – to participate in decisions about the delivery of those services?

At the heart of the traditional framework of public accountability is the accountability of service providers to democratically elected representatives. But, as we shall discover, accountability upwards to elected representatives is only one part of a complex system through which the delivery agencies of the welfare state are held accountable and controlled. Welfare delivery agencies are also accountable downwards to the consumers of their services. In addition, the welfare professionals involved in the delivery of social services are also accountable outwards to their colleagues (Elcock 1991: 16): indeed it has been argued that the growth of professionalism in the welfare state has resulted in what has been termed the 'privatization of accountability' (Day and Klein 1987: 1), with welfare professionals claiming that their work can be judged only by their peers. The delivery agencies of the welfare state are also subject to legal and financial accountability. A further dimension to accountability has been introduced by demands for user participation in the making of decisions about, and the delivery of, social services.

The accountability of the delivery agencies of the welfare state has been the subject of much political debate since the early 1990s, symbolized by the publication in 1991 of the Conservative government's Citizen's Charter, a document which was followed by the issue of a series of individual charters for such groups as NHS patients, parents of school children, council house tenants and those receiving benefits from the social security system. The Citizen's Charter programme was relaunched with a new focus by the Blair government in 1998. The development of 'charterism' and other initiatives has emphasized the importance of consumer accountability in the arrangements for delivering the social services. We shall turn to a discussion of these more recent developments in Chapter 9. Meanwhile, the focus of this chapter is on traditional methods of accountability and user participation in the social services.

Holding welfare delivery agencies accountable

Traditionally, the delivery agencies of the welfare state have been held accountable through the mechanisms of political accountability. There is a line of accountability running from service deliverers to elected representatives at both the national and local levels, who are responsible to elected assemblies. To paraphrase the description of the situation given by one writer (Brown 1975), there is a chain of command leading from the local social security office and the hospital bed to the relevant ministers in the House of Commons. In the case of the three major social services provided by local authorities, the chain leads first to the relevant committee room in the county hall or town hall and then, because of the overall responsibility of government ministers for the development of these services, to the appropriate minister in Whitehall (Brown 1975: 247).

Through its elected representatives, the public is given the opportunity to question the working of the delivery agencies of the welfare state. Thus the government ministers in charge of a department like the DWP can be questioned by Members of Parliament (MPs) at Question Time and during adjournment debates in the House of Commons. Ministers and their senior civil servants – including the chief executives of Jobcentre Plus and other executive agencies – appear before the House of Commons Public Accounts Committee and the various departmental select committees, such as the Work and Pensions Committee, where they can be questioned about their policies and actions. These parliamentary mechanisms are supplemented by less formal procedures, such as ministerial replies to letters from MPs on behalf of aggrieved constituents. In certain circumstances, an MP might also pass a constituent's grievance to the Parliamentary Commissioner for Administration.

But although the constitutional theory of ministerial accountability might be clear cut, its practice is not. Although ministers have to accept responsibility for all the work that is done in their name, given the size and scale of government departments – especially a giant department like the

DWP – it is impossible for them to be aware of everything that goes on. In the case of the delivery of social security, the problem has been compounded by the hiving-off of responsibility for the delivery of benefits to Jobcentre Plus and other executive agencies, all operating at arm's length from their parent departments in Whitehall and given certain freedoms in the way that they deliver services.

Complaints concerning social security benefits have long formed a major part of what has been described as the 'welfare officer' role performed by individual MPs (Richards 1972: 164). Indeed, research in the late 1970s revealed that the then DHSS received more letters from MPs than any other government department, the bulk of them being case-related and involving social security matters (see Norton 1982: 62). One consequence of the hiving-off of responsibility for the delivery of social security benefits to executive agencies such as Jobcentre Plus and the CSA is that letters from MPs to DWP ministers concerning constituents' complaints about social security matters are now passed on to agency chief executives, who deal with the matter. Although it can be argued that, being involved with the day-to-day delivery of services, the agency is best placed to deal with such complaints, concern has been expressed that this procedure undermines the right of direct access to ministers traditionally enjoyed by MPs.

At the local government level, education, the housing service and the personal social services all conform to the traditional model of political accountability. All three services are controlled by elected local councillors directly accountable to the public at the polls. But the whole concept of local authority accountability is undermined by the detailed controls exercised by central government departments (see Chapter 3): as Day and Klein (1987: 164) put it in their discussion of accountability and the local education service, the members of local education authority committees operated in 'conditions of constrained freedom'. There are also problems in attempting to control services delivered by welfare professionals, who, as we have seen, exercise discretionary powers in the delivery of services. Thus the elected members of the local authority education committee interviewed by Day and Klein (1987: 188) expressed serious doubts about their ability to control the education service, seeing themselves as being 'enmeshed in a web of powerlessness spun by the professionals actually running the service'.

The constitutional position on accountability is also clear cut in the case of the third major delivery agency of the welfare state, the NHS. The Secretary of State for Health is supposed to be accountable to Parliament for everything that happens in the service. In the words of Aneurin Bevan, the Cabinet minister responsible for the setting up of the NHS, 'when a bedpan is dropped on a hospital floor, its noise should resound in the Palace of Westminister' (quoted in Day and Klein 1987: 76). Like his counterpart at the DWP, the Secretary of State for Health is held accountable to Parliament through such traditional parliamentary processes as Question Time and adjournment debates, as well as having to appear before the Public

Accounts Committee and the Health Committee. But, despite this well-developed institutional apparatus of parliamentary control, as the Royal Commission on the National Health Service (Merrison 1979: para. 19.2) noted in 1979, 'detailed ministerial accountability for the NHS is largely a constitutional fiction'. As with government departments like the DWP, the sheer size and complexity of the NHS makes any degree of detailed ministerial supervision impossible.

Responsibility for the day-to-day running of the NHS is in the hands of appointed HAs, NHS trusts and PCTs. Studies in the 1980s found that members of the old-style health authorities appeared 'not to be accountable to anyone' (Hunter 1984: 44), and that they saw accountability upwards to the secretary of state as a low priority, their primary concern being their accountability downwards to the local community (Day and Klein 1987: 101). But in attempting to fulfil this latter responsibility, health authority members felt a sense of powerlessness, being too dependent on the managers of the authority for information (Day and Klein 1987: 97). The removal of local authority representatives from the new-style health authorities set up in 1991 led to criticisms that health authorities were less accountable to the local community (Ashburner and Cairncross 1993: 371). With the election of the Blair government, NHS trusts have been required to ensure a more representative membership of the local community, and local authority scrutiny committees have the power to report on matters relating to NHS provision in their areas.

The traditional framework of accountability in the public sector also includes procedures for enforcing legal and financial accountability. Thus the delivery agencies of the welfare state are duty bound to obey the law and not act ultra vires, and can be required by the courts to fulfil their statutory obligations and to refrain from acting in a manner which is beyond their powers. The development of the welfare state in the post-war period has witnessed a number of cases where the courts have become involved: the Norwich case in 1982, where the Court of Appeal agreed that the Secretary of State for the Environment could invoke powers contained in the Housing Act 1980 enabling his department to take over the running of the city council's sale of council houses, is just one well-known example. Aggrieved members of the public also occasionally resort to the use of judicial review, one notable example being the case of the controversial regulations made in 1985 by the Secretary of State for Social Services, concerning board and lodgings allowances payable to unemployed people, which were declared ultra vires by the courts.

Although changes in the system of judicial review have made the courts more accessible to members of the public wishing to question the legality of the actions of welfare delivery agencies, the courts are generally of limited value for individuals attempting to require public bodies to conform to their legal obligations. Judicial proceedings are not only complex, but also time consuming and expensive. In the view of one writer on public law, judicial review has done nothing for the management of local authority housing waiting lists, the treatment of NHS patients, or claimants in local social security offices (McAuslan 1983: 5). The use of the courts by individuals who are in dispute with welfare delivery agencies is also very much a last resort, disputes over many social services being entrusted, as we shall see in the next section, to internal review procedures and administrative tribunals.

Welfare delivery agencies are also constrained by the requirements of financial accountability. The accounts of central government departments are audited by the Comptroller and Auditor General (CAG), whose findings are reported to the prestigious Public Accounts Committee of the House of Commons, which summons the permanent secretaries of departments, and the chief executives of executive agencies, to answer points raised in the reports. The original concept of audit concentrated on the narrow technical concern of legality and regularity, ensuring that departmental expenditure had been upon approved services and in accordance with statutory authority. Encouraged by the Public Accounts Committee, the CAG extended their investigations to broader questions of efficiency, effectiveness and value for money, a process reinforced by the transformation of the CAG's department, the Exchequer and Audit Department, into the National Audit Office in the early 1980s. As we shall see in Chapter 8, this increasing concern with efficiency and value for money is part of a wider search for efficiency in central government departments.

Financial regularity has also been a major concern of local authorities. Evolving out of the system set up to check the Poor Law accounts in the nineteenth century (Keith-Lucas and Richards 1978: 153), the local government audit system requires the accounts of local authorities to be audited on an annual basis by either the district auditor or an approved auditor from the private sector. Overlapping with the doctrine of ultra vires, local government audit has traditionally been concerned with ensuring that local authorities are able to show legal authority for all their expenditure. Like audit at the national level, however, local government audit has progressed from its traditional concern with regularity and legality to include a far greater concern with value for money and effectiveness.

Financial accountability is, of course, part of a framework of accountability which was established long before the development of the post-war welfare state. As Johnson (1974: 7) has observed, what really matters to the consumer of social services is the quality of those services, the way in which they are delivered, and the accessibility of the agencies which deliver them. It is not surprising, therefore, that it has been suggested that traditional approaches to accountability have become less relevant. Political accountability, in particular, has been seen as 'too blunt an instrument' in the context of the kinds of services delivered by the welfare or service state (Johnson 1974: 7). Traditional approaches to accountability are now supplemented by a number of other methods through which members of the public can attempt to control the social services. An important aspect of these methods are mechanisms that help to enhance user participation. Before we turn to these, however, we need to discuss the procedures for the handling of complaints and enabling individuals to obtain redress for grievances, all of which help to make up what has been described as 'accountability downwards' (Elcock 1991: 16).

Complaining if things go wrong

Most delivery agencies of the welfare state have internal procedures for dealing with formal complaints before such external mechanisms as administrative tribunals and ombudsmen are brought into action. Thus complaints against decisions on social security benefits and child support maintenance are reviewed by officers of the relevant executive agency before being heard by a tribunal run by the DWP's Appeals Service. Complaints about the refusal of a local office of Jobcentre Plus to provide a discretionary grant or loan under the Social Fund are the subject of an internal review, with a further review by a Social Fund inspector. All local offices of Jobcentre Plus have customer service managers to deal with complaints, as do the centres of the Child Support Agency.

Internal complaints procedures also exist within the NHS. Following concern about the high level of complaints about NHS services, the Major government accepted the recommendations of the Wilson Report of 1994 (Department of Health 1994) and, in 1996, introduced a two-stage process for dealing with complaints about family health services, hospital services and community health services. This process involves a relatively informal internal procedure, followed by appeal to an independent panel. A complainant dissatisfied with the response to the report of the independent panel may refer the complaint to the Health Service Commissioner (see p. 88). A number of problems with the two-stage procedure, including poor communication and the time taken to resolve complaints, were identified by an evaluation study in 2001. The DoH is committed to reforming the system so as to build a fast and effective complaints service (Department of Health 2001c).

At the local authority level, individuals who are unhappy with the delivery of a particular service can ask a local councillor to pursue their complaint. Local authorities also have their own internal complaints procedures. Thus, social services departments are required to establish complaints procedures. Since 1978 local authorities have also had a voluntary code of practice for handling complaints from the public, produced jointly by the local authority associations and the Commission for Local Administration (the local ombudsmen), and the Commission has continued to produce guidance and codes on complaints systems. It has been argued that, since the 1970s, local authorities' internal complaints systems, and their responsiveness to complaints, 'have improved immeasurably' (Wilson and Game 1998: 145), as local authorities have developed the customer orientation (see Chapter 9).

Challenging the delivery agencies: the tribunals of the welfare state

In addition to internal complaints procedures, there are also external mechanisms through which the users of social services can make complaints about the delivery of welfare. At the heart of these arrangements are the various administrative tribunals which can sometimes determine disputes if individuals feel that they have been the victims of unfair decisions by a welfare delivery agency. The creation of such bodies has been an important by-product of the many social services and benefits introduced by the postwar welfare state, the delivery of which often give rise to disagreement.

This particular form of redress procedure can be found in all three types of delivery agencies of the welfare state (see Table 5.1). Thus mental health review tribunals hear appeals against cases of compulsory detention of mentally ill individuals. Local education authorities – in the case of all community and voluntary controlled schools – and school governing bodies – in the case of foundation and voluntary aided schools – are required to set up admission appeal panels giving dissatisfied parents the opportunity to appeal against decisions on the allocation of secondary school places.

But the area of the welfare state which gives rise to most complaints is social security, where a number of tribunals adjudicate on the application of – often very complex – rules to individual cases. Thus, pensions appeal tribunals determine appeals from ministerial decisions on war and military service pensions. Cases involving decisions about income support, contributory benefits, disability benefits, decisions of the CSA, and housing benefit are dealt with by the Appeals Service. Launched in 2000 as an executive agency of the DSS, the Appeals Service is a single unified jurisdiction that replaced five separate tribunal jurisdictions – social security

Table 5.1   The main tribunals of the welfare state (numbers of cases decided in 2000)*

Appeals Service	178,521
Admission appeals panels	62,655
Mental health review tribunals	11,833
Social security and child support commissioners	4,754
Pensions appeal tribunals	3,416

Note: * Figures refer to tribunals under the direct supervision of the Council of Tribunals
Source: Council on Tribunals 2001

appeal tribunals, child support appeal tribunals, disability appeal tribunals, medical appeal tribunals and vaccine damage tribunals. In 2000, the Appeals Service received over 270,000 appeals. Appeals against housing benefit decisions were added to the Appeal Service's jurisdiction in 2001.

Modern-day arrangements for dealing with social security appeals have their origins in the tribunals established to settle disputes arising out of the health and unemployment insurance schemes introduced by the National Insurance Act 1911. Formed in 1984, from the merger of the separate supplementary benefit appeal tribunals and national insurance local tribunals, the social security appeal tribunals replaced by the Appeals Service were described as 'one of the most important forms of civil justice in the modern legal system' (Wikeley and Young 1992: 242–3).

The delivery of social security benefits is dependent on those claiming benefit meeting certain rules. Thus adjudication officers working in the local offices of the DWP's Jobcentre Plus take millions of decisions each year concerning the entitlement of claimants to income support and contributory benefits – there were nearly 4 million people receiving income support in 2001. If appeals against benefit decisions are not upheld by an internal review, claimants may appeal to the Appeals Service, which refers the case to a tribunal consisting of one to three persons drawn from a panel appointed by the Lord Chancellor. There is the right of an appeal on a point of law to a social security commissioner and, beyond that, to the Court of Appeal and the House of Lords.

For many people, the tribunals of the welfare state form 'the immediate point of legal contact': they have been described as 'poor people's courts' (Fulbrook et al. 1973: 14). It is generally agreed that tribunals have several advantages over ordinary courts of law, being quicker, cheaper and more informal. Given the types of cases involved, these advantages are particularly important. Individuals claiming social security benefit, in particular, require 'informal, cheap, and speedy adjudication' (Greenwood and Wilson 1989: 305).

There has been a long-running debate about the procedures of such bodies. Following the criticisms made in 1957 by the Franks Report concerning the lack of independence from departmental control and the procedural deficiencies of many tribunals, especially those involved with the adjudication of appeals involving social security benefits, successive governments attempted to judicialize the procedures of these particular tribunals in an attempt to make them more 'open, fair and impartial'. In the words of Franks (1957: para. 64): 'Informality without rules of procedure may be positively inimical to right adjudication'. Thus tribunals dealing with social security appeals were normally chaired by lawyers and were characterized by more formal approaches towards points of law and the admissibility of evidence. Some observers maintained that this process should be supplemented by the extension of legal aid to tribunal proceedings (see, for example, the discussion in Justice-All Souls 1988).

But as social security tribunals became more like the courts, many of the advantages that they were claimed to have over the courts became less obvious (Greenwood and Wilson 1989: 307). The involvement of lawyers in tribunal procedures was seen as a threat to the informality that was supposed to be one of the major benefits of this form of adjudicatory body (see, for example, Fulbrook et al. 1973: 11). The report of the Leggatt Review on tribunals published in 2001 stressed the importance of keeping tribunals accessible and user-friendly (Leggatt 2001: para. 4.17).

Despite some criticisms, the tribunals of the welfare state provide an independent method of resolving grievances, as well as ensuring that the agencies responsible for the delivery of social services and benefits are accountable. The former social security appeal tribunals, in particular, are said to have 'cast a long shadow' over the work carried out in the local offices of the Benefits Agency and the Employment Service (Wikeley and Young 1992: 260). Researchers referred to a 'tribunal effect', the existence of tribunals having a clear impact on the quality of the initial decision-making and the review process in local agency offices (Wikeley and Young 1992: 257).

Despite the existence of the Appeals Service, grievances against decisions involving one of the most important social security benefits – claims for assistance from the Social Fund – are the responsibility of internal reviews and not independent tribunals. Thus applicants dissatisfied with the decision of a local Social Fund officer have the right of appeal to a system of internal review and, ultimately, to a Social Fund inspector. The operation of this set of arrangements has been the subject of much criticism. Thus the absence of an independent appeal against decisions made about payments and loans from the Social Fund has been described by the Council on Tribunals, the watchdog of the working of tribunals, as 'a highly retrograde step' (1985: para. 2.36), the Council pointing out that the discretionary nature of Social Fund decisions is no different in principle from the system in operation before the new arrangements were introduced (Council on Tribunals 1986: para. 11). Another observer has described the exclusion of such appeals from a tribunal as 'a significant and sinister breach of the general principle that disputed claims to State benefits should be subjected to independent arbitration' (Elcock 1990: 36–7).

Welfare delivery and maladministration: the role of ombudsmen

Complaints about the delivery of social services can also be investigated by the ombudsmen institutions that cover all three major types of welfare delivery agency. The British public sector ombudsmen – although only pale shadows of their west European namesakes – are generally concerned with investigating whether decision-making procedures conform to the standard of reasonableness – what one commentator has referred to as 'procedural accountability' (Smith 1981: 1168). Since 1996, the public sector ombudsman systems have been supplemented by an Independent Housing Ombudsman, who investigates complaints from tenants living in accommodation provided by the housing association sector, an increasingly significant part of the delivery of welfare (see Giddings and Gregory 1996).

Complaints alleging injustice caused to individuals as a result of maladministration in central government's social service departments and its agencies can be referred through an MP to the Parliamentary Commissioner for Administration (PCA). Although the concept of maladministration is not defined in the relevant legislation, it is generally agreed that it includes such bureaucratic lapses as bias, delay, incompetence and arbitrariness. Given the numbers of people in receipt of social security benefits, it is not surprising that the PCA's annual reports have revealed that the major central government department directly responsible for the delivery of welfare – what is now the DWP – has consistently been at the top of the complaints league table, accounting for some 42 per cent of the total number of complaints received in 2000–01. Eighteen per cent of the complaints involving the then DSS concluded in 2000–01 were found to be justified or partly justified (Parliamentary Ombudsman 2001). A theme of many complaints against the former Benefits Agency concerned misdirection or incorrect or inadequate advice, while a large number of complaints against the CSA involve failures in enforcement against non-resident parents.

The impact of the PCA on the procedures of what is now the DWP is difficult to assess. Former holders of the office have argued that the mere presence of the PCA has a 'tonic effect' upon government departments in improving the quality of administration, and that there has been evidence of a 'healthy regard' on the part of officials for the need to avoid the PCA's attentions (Compton 1970: 6; Clothier 1986: 207). Other commentators, however, maintain that the presence of the PCA encourages a play-safe attitude among civil servants.

At the local government level, there are a number of local commissioners for administration – three for England, one for Wales and one for Scotland – popularly known as the local ombudsmen. Closely modelled on the PCA – although they can receive complaints directly from members of the public – the local ombudsmen are also confined to investigating injustice caused by maladministration. Thus, although the local ombudsmen may investigate the administrative procedures of a local authority's education service, they are not allowed to investigate complaints about the internal affairs of schools. The main subject of complaints received has been housing (including housing benefit) which has accounted for about 40 per cent of all complaints since the late 1990s, with education and the personal social services – each generating between 6 and 9 per cent of complaints each year – a long way behind. Recent examples of cases where maladministration causing injustice has been found include a council's failure to inform one of its tenants in writing about his statutory rights as a secure tenant; a state school failing to administer its admissions and appeals procedure properly, causing a parent difficulty in preparing her appeal against the school's decision not to offer her son a place; and a complaint about the care received in a local authority residential home (Commission for Local Administration in England 2001).

The ombudsman responsible for the third major delivery agency of the welfare state – the Health Service Commissioner (HSC) – is also modelled on the PCA. The HSC can investigate allegations that hardship or injustice has been caused by the NHS's failure to provide a service, or by the failure of a service, or by maladministration. Examples of recent cases include complaints about poor communications and about poor nursing and medical care (Health Service Commissioner 2001).

Unlike their central government counterpart, the HSC can receive complaints directly from members of the public, although the NHS body concerned is expected to have been given a reasonable opportunity to in- vestigate and respond to the complaint. The original legislation excluded complaints involving solely the exercise of clinical judgement from the HSC's jurisdiction, an important and controversial manifestation of the medical profession's success in blocking the introduction of any changes that would adversely affect their position. Family practitioner services, provided by GPs, general dental practitioners, opticians and pharmacists, were also excluded from the HSC's original jurisdiction. Following the recommendation of the Wilson Report of 1994 on hospital complaints pro- cedures (Department of Health 1994), the HSC's powers were extended in 1996 to allow the investigation of clinical complaints and family practitioner services (see Giddings 1999). Of the completed investigations by the HSC in 2000–01, just over three-quarters involved matters of clinical judgement (Health Service Commissioner 2001).

The public sector ombudsmen have been described as 'the most developed independent grievance-remedial devices'' found in the field of British public administration (Birkinshaw 1985: 127–8) and as a 'success story' (Seneviratne 2000: 591). They also have the advantages, unlike administrative tribunals, of not requiring complainants to present their evidence in court-like proceedings. But, as a study of complaints procedures concludes, 'it is doubtful if their full potential is being tapped' (Lewis and Birkinshaw 1993: 139).

One obvious obstacle to the full realization of this potential is that none of the British ombudsmen have the power to initiate investigations, a limitation which is seen as restricting the investigation of cases involving those users of social services unable to complain in their own interests, such as the residents of local authority nursing homes and long-stay patients in NHS hospitals (Lewis and Birkinshaw 1993: 129). Neither are any of the ombudsmen able to directly enforce their recommendations, although the absence of such powers appears to have been more of a problem with the local ombudsmen than with the others (Giddings 1993: 386, 390).

Another problem is the poor public awareness and understanding of the role of the various public sector ombudsmen. One way in which this is manifested is the high percentage of complaints that do not fall within jurisdiction or cannot be handled for another reason (Cabinet Office 2000: para. 3.3). The PCA has always received significant numbers of complaints that are outside their jurisdiction. The situation is the same with the two other ombudsmen. In 2000–01, 68 per cent of the complaints received by the HSC were either outside the HSC's jurisdiction, could not be accepted because they had not gone through the two-stage NHS complaints procedure, or were not otherwise eligible for investigation. In the case of the local government ombudsmen, nearly 36 per cent of complaints received were either premature or outside jurisdiction. Another issue relating to awareness is the high proportion of people who have not heard of the public sector ombudsmen. A Consumers' Association survey in 1996 found that 41 per cent of respondents were not aware of any of the three public sector ombudsmen schemes. The figure for socio-economic groups C2, D and E was 51 per cent (Cabinet Office 2000: para. 3.6). As Giddings (2001: 11) observes, widening the availability of an ombudsman's services to include such socio-economic groups is extremely important.

There is also the problem that a single complaint can often involve several delivery agencies, crossing traditional boundaries between delivery agencies – for example, housing benefit claims requiring liaison between Jobcentre Plus and a local authority housing department; a complaint involving a local authority social services department and an NHS body (see Cabinet Office 2000: paras 2.30–2.32). A Cabinet Office review of public sector ombudsmen arrangements, published in 2000, recommended the creation of an integrated public sector ombudsman scheme, incorporating the PCA, the HSC and the local commissioners for administration (Cabinet Office 2000).

The development of ombudsmen at the national and local levels, together with the reforms in the procedures and composition of tribunals dealing with social security appeals, has been part of a series of important developments since the early 1960s, intended to strengthen the users of services in their dealings with the delivery agencies of the welfare state. For many, however, the arrangements for making complaints to, and securing redress against, welfare delivery agencies are still inadequate. As we have seen, the tribunals of the welfare state have been criticized for their excessive judicialization, one important area of the social security system is not covered by tribunals, and the various ombudsmen have yet to achieve their potential.

There is no shortage of suggestions for improving the way that such redress machinery works: they include the provision of legal aid and advice for those appearing before tribunals dealing with social security appeals, direct access to the PCA, and the creation of an integrated public service ombudsmen scheme. As Deakin and Wright (1990: 213) point out, however, redress against the deliverers of public services has meaning only in relation to 'a framework of rights, standards of performance, and legitimate expectations'. According to this view, such a framework should be seen as 'an integral part' of a service users' charter. As we shall see in Chapter 9, some of these ideas were embodied in the Citizen's Charter introduced by the Major government in 1991, and relaunched by the Blair government in 1998.

User participation in welfare delivery

Closely linked to the whole question of 'accountability downwards' to the users of social services is the issue of user participation. In the early years of the post-war welfare state, there was little provision for user participation in the delivery of welfare. The public administration model that underpinned the organization of the delivery of the major social services was dominated by the providers of welfare – the bureaucrats and professionals. According to one commentator, the founders of the welfare state 'never felt called upon' to address the issue of user involvement. Not only was it assumed that the users of social services had little interest in the making of welfare policy, but also it was felt that they had little to contribute to the process (Richardson 1983: 2–3). In the words of Hadley and Hatch (1981: 15–16): 'The public was cast in the role of spectator and consumer, not co-partner': there was no place for 'shared management' with the users of social services. Welfare professionals, bureaucrats and politicians were seen as having the responsibility for ensuring that services met the needs of users.

   One group of writers was later to remark that the 1950s and 1960s had been an era when it was considered 'inappropriate to ask local people what they wanted – the job of deciding what they needed was left to politicians and experts' (Lansley et al. 1989: 3). However, this view began to change in the late 1960s and the early 1970s, when user participation in the delivery of the services of the welfare state became fashionable. As Richardson (1983: 102–14) has shown, the interest in participation was partly the result of pressure from the users of services (such as council house tenants and parents of school children), who became not only more demanding, but also better organized, and partly the result of the needs of the providers of services, who began to seek contact with service users as the growth in the size and scale of delivery agencies widened the gap between the two sides. As a consequence of such factors, the 1970s and the 1980s witnessed the development of a number of initiatives involving user participation in the major social services delivered by both local government and the NHS.

   User participation is now a feature of all three major social services provided by local government. Participatory mechanisms exist within the local education service. Following the recommendations of the Taylor Report 1977 on the management and government of schools, the Education Act 1980 laid down that at least two elected parents be appointed to the board of governors of every local education authority school, a requirement which was extended by the Education Act 1986, which gave parent governors equal representation with governors appointed by the local education authority. Under the Blair government, the proportion of parent governors on governing bodies has increased, and the government has proposed that at least one-third of the places on a governing body should be taken by parents of children at a school. Despite these initiatives, there are difficulties in recruiting and retaining governors, with over a quarter of the respondents to a recent survey of schools reporting vacancies on their governing bodies (Education and Employment Committee 1999a: para. 32).

Since the early 1980s, there has also been an increasing interest in the development of participatory initiatives in local authority housing. The Housing Act 1980 – which introduced a 'tenants' charter' for local authority tenants – imposed a duty on local housing authorities in England and Wales to introduce a form of tenant participation in the management of council housing by requiring them to consult those tenants who are likely to be substantially affected by a matter of housing management. The details of implementation were left to the discretion of the local authority, but most local housing authorities introduced arrangements for tenant participation, ranging from tenant representation on advisory committees or local authority housing committees to questionnaire surveys (Cairncross et al. 1994). A number of local authorities have gone much further. Thus some authorities, such as Hackney, have involved tenants in the management of council estates through estate management boards in partnership with the council, while others, such as Islington, have established tenant management organizations (including cooperatives), involving tenants in an area taking on the responsibility for day-to-day management and repairs (see, for example, Power 1988). But, although tenant participation grew substantially during the 1980s and 1990s, the significance of this 'should not be exaggerated'. As one research study concludes, in some local authorities it has been tenant activists, rather than tenants generally, who have been involved in such participation, and the 'forms and purposes' of participation have varied (Cairncross et al. 1997: vii, 179).

Enhancing the participation of council tenants in the management of council housing is an important part of the Blair government's agenda for social housing, with the government committed to 'empowering tenants through enabling them to be involved in virtually every aspect of the housing service' (Kemp 1999b: 181). Greater participation has been encouraged through formal agreements – compacts – between council landlords and council tenants, setting out how tenants are involved in decisions affecting their homes (Department of the Environment, Transport and the Regions 2000b). Tenants have been given the opportunity to be involved in all stages of the local decision-making process. Compacts are an integral part of the Blair government's Best Value regime – enabling tenants to give their views on housing services and giving them the opportunity to be involved in the planning and delivery of services.

In the case of the third major local authority social service – the personal social services – user participation has been on the agenda ever since the Seebohm Committee reported in 1968. Seebohm (1968: paras 491, 137) argued that the participation of individuals in the planning and delivery of the personal social services was vital if such services were to be sensitive to local needs. It accordingly recommended the involvement of users in both the provision and planning of the personal social services through, for example, representation on local authority social services committees or subcommittees (Seebohm 1968: para. 628). But, as Gyford (1991: 69) points out in his discussion of participation in local government, unlike local authority education and housing services, which both have clearly defined focal points (local schools and housing estates) around which to organize user participation, the personal social services (with their wider range of activities and client groups) do not possess such a clear focus.

Despite this limitation, there have been important developments in user participation in this particular area of local welfare delivery. Thus some local authorities co-opted representatives of voluntary groups on to social services committees, and a national survey of social services departments, carried out in the late 1980s, concluded that user participation was now more broadly established and beginning to become more routine (Beresford and Croft 1990: 18). As we shall see in Chapter 7, user participation was an objective of the community care reforms introduced in the early 1990s. These reforms required not only that assessments of need by local authority social service departments take account of the wishes of the individuals concerned, and where possible include their active participation, but also that social services departments should consult users and voluntary organizations when drawing up community care plans (Department of Health 1989b). Despite this requirement, however, research suggests that local authorities have allowed only limited user involvement in the planning of the delivery of community care. The opinions of user groups are often accepted only when it suits officials (Barnes et al. 1999a: 107; see also Barnes et al. 1999b).

User participation in the NHS

What about user participation in the other major delivery agency of the welfare state, the NHS? For just over the first 25 years of the NHS, the users of its services were what Klein (1989: 77) has graphically referred to as 'the ghosts in the NHS machinery'. Although early plans for the NHS had included a strong emphasis on the desirability of public participation, there was not much evidence of this in the structure that finally emerged in 1948 (Pater 1981: 168).

The tripartite structure set up in 1948 did include members chosen after consultation with voluntary organizations and local authorities. Local authority representation was also built into the unified NHS structure established in 1974 and, although the numbers were reduced, was also included in the streamlined structure introduced in 1982. But this was not user participation in the sense of the users of services influencing the nature of the services being delivered: it was what has been described as community involvement – the representation of the local community through the members of elected local authorities and other concerned bodies (Brown 1975: 262–3). As Brown (1975: 261–2) has pointed out, the most important type of participation in the NHS has been the syndicalist type, in which those working in the NHS (especially the medical profession) have had an important say in the running of the service through representation on health authorities. As another observer has put it, the views of users 'have always come a poor second' to the views of the professionals in the making of decisions about the delivery of health care (Hogg 1990: 174).

Important changes in the arrangements for the representation of user views within the NHS did take place with the reorganization of 1974, when a deliberate decision was taken to separate responsibility for the management of the service and the representation of the community. Thus the RHAs and AHAs established as part of the reorganized service were given managerial responsibilities, while responsibility for representation was given to community health councils (CHCs), set up to represent the interests in the health service of the local community to the management of the local health authority. CHCs were introduced partly to compensate for the absence of any 'direct democracy' in the management of the NHS (Boaden et al. 1982: 120), with their members being nominated by local authorities, voluntary organizations and the RHA. Although advisory bodies, with no executive powers, CHCs were given certain statutory rights, including the right to be consulted about plans, the right to information from health authorities and the right to inspect NHS premises.

However, the impact of CHCs has been limited. Even before they were officially established they were described by an Opposition spokesperson as 'the strangest bunch of administrative eunuchs that any department had yet foisted upon the House – a kind of seraglio of the Secretary of State of utterly useless and emasculated bodies which have no powers' (*Hansard* 1971). Studies of CHCs have emphasized the limitations of these so-called watchdogs. Thus Hogg (1990: 170–1) points to the variations in the standard of the services provided by CHCs, some of which have encouraged the public to participate in their activities, while others have not. The effectiveness of CHCs has also been undermined by their lack of resources (a budget of £120,000 and two full-time staff) and the difficulty of deciding what role they should adopt – that of 'snivelling lapdogs' or that of 'rabid curs' (see Ham 1977: 103).

As a result of the NHS reforms of the early 1990s, the role of CHCs was weakened: they lost their right to be consulted whenever the DHA intended to introduce a substantial change to local services. Using the 'ladder of citizen participation' constructed by the American academic, Sherry Arnstein (1971) – which ranges from manipulation and therapy, through information, consultation and placation, to partnership, delegated power and citizen control – one commentator concluded that the powers of CHCs are restricted to the lower rungs of the ladder (Allsop 1984: 196–7). The Blair government is replacing CHCs with statutory patients' forums for each NHS trust and PCT in England, with the role of ensuring that patients' views are taken into account in the delivery and development of services. Patient involvement is also to be strengthened by the establishment of patient advocacy and liaison services to resolve problems before they become more serious, together with a national Commission for Patient and Public Involvement in Health to oversee the new arrangements (Department of Health 2001a).

As we saw earlier, the mechanisms which attempt to provide service users with the opportunity to participate in the delivery of the three core social services provided by local authorities also appear to be located on the lower rungs of the ladder of participation. Clearly, some benefits have been achieved as a result of these kinds of initiatives, but as Wilson (2001: 301) has observed, participatory schemes 'do not necessarily result in policy impact' and might raise expectations among those participating that are not then met.

Since the mid-1990s there has been the use of more innovative methods of participation in social and other public services, such as citizens' juries and citizens' panels. As we shall discuss further in Chapter 9, such developments have been encouraged by the Blair government, and public participation is central to its Best Value approach to improving service delivery. Both local authorities and the NHS have used focus groups and citizens' juries – groups of 12 to 16 ordinary members of the public, selected to match the profile of the local community – which consider a particular issue or issues, having heard and discussed evidence from experts and other witnesses. Local authorities such as Lewisham have used citizens' juries. Several NHS bodies – including Cambridge and Huntingdon Health Commission and Kensington, Chelsea and Westminster Health Authority – have also used such forums on such issues as health care rationing, priorities in palliative care, and mental health care provision (Coote and Mattinson 1997; Hall and Stewart 1997). As we shall see in Chapter 9, these initiatives are part of the increased emphasis since the late 1980s on improving the position of the user – or 'customer' – of social services.

Further reading

Day and Klein (1987) consider the theories and practice of accountability. The practices of grievance redress are described by Lewis and Birkinshaw (1993). Information on, and reports from, the various public sector ombudsmen can be found via their web sites – www.ombudsman.org.uk for the Parliamentary Commissioner for Administration and the Health Service Commissioner, and www.lgo.org.uk for the local government ombudsman. The claims for, and genesis of, participation in the social services are considered in Richardson (1983), while Lowndes et al. (1998) contains a wealth of material on various methods of public participation.

Part II

New directions in the delivery of welfare

6

The rolling back of the local welfare state

As we saw in our discussion of the government of welfare beyond Whitehall in Chapter 3, local authorities have traditionally been the major delivery agencies of the welfare state, with responsibility for the direct provision of the key collective consumption services of education, housing and personal social services. In providing these 'from the cradle to the grave' services, local authorities (although enjoying a great deal of autonomy and answerable to local electorates) have operated within a framework of central government controls and influences.

Under the Conservative governments 1979–97, developments took place which represented a major shift in the nature of the central–local relationship and which had major consequences for the traditional role of local authorities in the welfare state. Radical changes were introduced in the system of local government finance in an attempt to control the expenditure and income of local authorities. In addition, legislation challenged the role of local authorities as front-line delivery agencies of social services, resulting in a 'rolling back' of the local welfare state. The transformation of the traditional role of local authorities has continued under the Blair government elected in 1997.

An examination of the changing relationship between central government and local authorities under the Thatcher, Major and Blair governments is crucial to an understanding of the role of local government in the delivery of welfare. Before examining these developments, however, we need to discuss the nature of the central–local relationship before 1979.

Central–local relations before 1979: partnership and consultation

In their discussion of the evolving relationship between central and local government in the post-war period, Hartas and Harrop (1991) analyse the relationship between the two sides in the years up to 1979 in terms of two periods: the period from 1945 to 1976, which was characterized by the expansion and consolidation of local authorities as delivery agencies of the welfare state, and the much shorter period from 1976 to the election of the Thatcher government in 1979, which was marked by an increasing concern with the level of local authority spending.

During the first period, covering the 30 or so years following the end of the Second World War, local government played a central role in the launching and consolidation of the modern welfare state, developing the key services of education, housing and what were to be later labelled the personal social services. The development of the local government welfare state was reflected in the increase in local authority spending, which rose steadily in the post-war years. Whereas local authority expenditure as a proportion of total public spending was only about one-quarter at the end of the 1940s, it had risen to nearly one-third by 1976, largely as a result of the growth in spending on the three key services of education, housing and the personal social services (Else and Marshall 1979: 15). Public spending on the education service, in particular, expanded markedly, tripling in constant prices between 1945 and 1965 (Kogan 1978: 26). By 1976, education consumed well over one-third of total local government current spending. Spending on education, housing and the personal social services accounted for nearly 62 per cent of local government current spending in 1976, compared with just over 24 per cent in 1945 (see Table 6.1). There was also a marked increase in the share of capital spending by the three services, particularly on housing.

Table 6.1 Local government current and capital spending on social services in England and Wales 1945 and 1976 (as a percentage of total local government spending)

Sector	Current spending		Capital spending	
	1945	1976	1945	1976
Education	17.6%	37.6%	1.7%	9.9%
Housing	6.6%	17.7%	32.9%	64.9%
Personal Social Services	—	6.6%	—	1.6%

Sources: 1945 figures adapted from figures in Jackman (1985: 151–2); 1976 figures from Central Statistical Office (1979)

The dramatic increase in local government spending during this period was fuelled by increases in the level of central government financial support, notably through the Rate Support Grant after the mid-1960s, underpinned by the steady economic growth of the post-war years. By 1976, central government grants made up nearly 47 per cent of total local government revenue income in England and Wales compared with just over 30 per cent at the end of the war. In the words of one observer, not only did central government extend the territory of local authorities, but also it provided a 'large financial incentive for [them] to cultivate the new territory' (Glennerster 1992a: 74). As Glennerster (1992a: 75) has pointed out, national politicians during this period actually took much of the credit for the schools and council houses built by local authorities under their particular government.

The 1945–76 period was also characterized by a basic consensus between central and local government on the way in which local services were provided. The relationship between the two sides was one of 'partnership' and 'interdependence' (Loughlin 1985: 139). This was a period when both major political parties were 'content to give (when they occupied Westminster) and to receive (when they controlled town halls) local discretion over service provision' (Goodwin and Duncan 1989: 69). The degree of 'local discretion' over service provision during this period has been highlighted by academic studies of local government spending, which have revealed substantial variations in the patterns of spending between different local authorities on the three major social services (see, for example, Boaden 1971; Davies 1972).

'Partnership' has been used to describe the relationship between central government and local authorities in the field of education during this period. The two sides in this 'partnership' were clearly not equal, but as one commentator has argued, 'no other term would do as well'. The contribution of both the central government department responsible for education and the local education authorities was essential, with the two sides working together 'for the good of the service' (Regan 1977: 35). The government of education was dominated by what another writer has described as a 'consensual model', which took account of the two 'potentially conflicting legitimacies' of a central government with a national mandate and local authorities who were legitimized by local government elections (Kogan 1987: 47). In the case of the other major local authority social service (housing) the responsible central government department was described by the standard work on central–local relations, written in the mid-1960s, as having a laissez-faire attitude towards local housing authorities, leaving them to decide local needs and how far they should be met (Griffith 1966: 519). It went on to describe the then Ministry of Housing and Local Government as being 'historically associated with encouraging local authorities to be autonomous' (Griffith 1966: 519), a philosophy confirmed by a former permanent secretary of the ministry who, writing in the late 1960s, asserted that local authorities probably enjoyed greater independence from central government in the field of housing than any other major service (Sharp 1969: 74).

National political leaders during this period were not interested in the detailed supervision of the activities of local authorities: what was regarded as 'real politics' took place at Westminster, with 'proper government' being seen as the concern of Whitehall. As a result, there was what has been termed a 'dual polity': a structure of central–local relations in which central government and local authorities 'operated, by and large, in two separate compartments'. As long as central government was able to control 'high' politics (such as the economy, defence and foreign policy), it was content to leave matters of 'low' politics to local authorities (Bulpitt 1989: 66–7; see also Bulpitt 1983).

There were, of course, occasions when there were clear, and publicly expressed, differences between the two sides concerning the local implementation of particular national social policies. One such dispute concerned the implementation of the Conservative government's controversial Housing Finance Act 1972, with the Labour-controlled Clay Cross Urban District Council in north-east Derbyshire refusing to implement the provisions of the Act which required it to raise council house rents to the level of a 'fair rent'. The council's inaction ultimately resulted in the government using the default powers given to it in the legislation to appoint a housing commissioner to take over responsibility for housing in Clay Cross, culminating in the surcharge and disqualification from holding public office of the councillors involved.

Another well-documented example of local authority recalcitrance during this period, this time involving a Conservative-controlled local authority, was the case of Tameside Metropolitan Borough in Greater Manchester, which decided in 1975 not to proceed with the outgoing Labour council's plans for the reorganization of its secondary schools on comprehensive lines. The Secretary of State for Education argued that the local education authority was acting unreasonably and, exercising his powers under the Education Act 1944, issued a directive requiring Tameside to go ahead with the reorganization plans. After a protracted court case, the House of Lords rejected the government's case, declaring that there was no evidence that the Tameside council was acting in a way that no reasonable council would do.

But, despite these and other conflicts, the normal style of central–local relations between 1945 and the mid-1970s was one of partnership. Dunleavy and Rhodes (1986: 125) have argued that central government's dependence upon local authorities for the delivery of such key services as education and housing meant that 'they trod carefully' around the issue of local government autonomy, relying more on partnership and consultation than on the full exercise of the instruments of control available to them. The partnership between central government and local education authorities was part of the post-war settlement. Thus when the Labour government of the mid-1960s decided to press ahead with its controversial policy of introducing comprehensive education in secondary schools, it deliberately decided to rely on a policy instrument which emphasized local authority cooperation. It issued a departmental circular 'requesting' local education authorities to submit reorganization plans for their areas on comprehensive lines, rather than choosing the 'big stick' of legislation, which would have compelled those authorities to go comprehensive (Kogan 1971: 191; Dunleavy and Rhodes 1983: 123).

The local government spending which helped to fuel the post-war expansion of the welfare state reached its peak in 1976, when it accounted for nearly one-third of public expenditure. The period of expansion came to an end with the economic recession of the mid-1970s, brought about by the quadrupling of oil prices and double figure inflation. In 1976, the Labour government was obliged to negotiate a loan from the International Monetary Fund, a condition of which was sharp cuts in public expenditure. An era of public expenditure growth was replaced by one of public expenditure restraint. In the oft-quoted words of Anthony Crosland, the then Cabinet minister responsible for local government, 'the party' was over (see, for example, Crosland 1982: 295; Whitehead 1985: 150). A new phase of central–local relations had begun.

The central–local relationship during the period 1976–79 was dominated by Labour government attempts to achieve reductions in local authority spending as part of its wider attempt to reduce public expenditure, through cuts in central government grant and the setting of annual targets for local authority spending. Apart from the controls on borrowing, however, the financial instruments used by central government were 'ones of influence rather than control' (Elcock et al. 1989: 28): the mechanisms of central government intervention were based on 'consultation and persuasion rather than coercion' (Alexander 1982b: 104). Furthermore, the Labour government of the late 1970s was concerned only with the total of local government expenditure and not with the spending of individual local authorities. Labour's approach involved the 'incorporation' of the local authority associations (who represented the individual local authorities in negotiations with central government) into the policymaking process, with the government trying to persuade them of the harsh realities of the economic situation (Rhodes 1992a: 53). The key forum for this particular approach was the Consultative Council on Local Government Finance, which brought together the Treasury and representatives of the local authority associations to discuss local government expenditure, and was what one observer has described as an institutionalized means of reaching 'gentlemen's agreements' on local government spending (Glennerster 1992a: 76). Such agreements were generally successful, with the eventual out-turn of local government spending in each of the years 1976–79 being within 2 per cent of the targets set by central government.

Reviewing the nature of the central–local relationship in the post-war years up to 1979, John (1990: 59) concludes that it was a model of central–local relations where (although the centre had a wide range of controls available to it) central government 'tended to be concerned with setting the broad lines of policy, its implementation being left in local hands'. Although responsible for the implementation of centrally determined policies, local authorities had a certain amount of discretion in the way they did this. This relationship was to undergo a dramatic change with the election of the Conservative Thatcher government in 1979.

Central–local relations 1979–97: trying to put the cap on spending by local authorities

The partnership between central government and local authorities from 1945 to 1979 was part of a wider consensus that underpinned British politics during the post-war period. As long as the assumptions underpinning the post-war welfare state remained unquestioned, issues about the central–local relationship were of 'peripheral importance' (Loughlin 1986: 3). But 1979 saw the election of a Conservative government opposed to the traditional consensus of the post-war years. It was committed to the reduction of public expenditure, a policy that was seen as central to its goal of cutting public borrowing. As Travers (1986: 80) has pointed out, given that the new government had promised in its election campaign to increase defence spending and protect spending on social security and the NHS, its commitment to reducing public spending was, in effect, a commitment to cut spending on those services which were mainly delivered by local government. The Thatcher government's commitment to rolling back the state and encouraging the values of independence and self-reliance also clearly had implications for the welfare state role of local authorities. As a result, local government was elevated from the level of 'low' politics to become a subject of relatively 'high' politics.

A major theme which ran through the developments of the 1980s was the search by successive Conservative governments for more effective control over local government spending, as opposed to the attempts to influence local government spending associated with the more consensus-based approach before 1979 (see, for example, Rhodes 1992a: 51). In addition to its commitment to reduce local authority spending as part of its wider goal of reducing public expenditure, the government's concern with local government spending reflected more specific right-wing criticisms of local authorities, ministers claiming that local government was 'wasteful, profligate, irresponsible, unaccountable, luxurious and out of control' (Newton and Karran 1985: 116).

Since central government had no direct means of controlling local government spending (having to rely upon the influences of exhortation and cuts in central government grant: Travers 1986: 81), successive Conservative governments since 1979 attempted to remedy this omission by introducing a series of measures designed to strengthen central government controls over local government spending. As we shall see, the Conservative government came to see central government grants (which had been such an important factor in the expansion of local government services in the late 1960s and early 1970s) as a form of control.

Attempts to control the level of local government spending began with the reform of the complicated system of Rate Support Grant – once described by one local government minister as 'byzantine in its complexity' and 'probably fully comprehended by those who have a taste for scholastic theology' (*Hansard* 1985). The old system of RSG (in which the distribution of central government grant was determined by the past spending patterns of local authorities) was replaced by a system of block grant. Under the new system, the distribution of grant was determined by the government, a local authority's grant being reduced if its spending rose above the level that the government considered was required to meet a standard level service.

Despite the introduction of this new system, local government spending continued to rise in real terms, many local authorities circumventing cuts in grant by raising extra revenue through the local property tax, the rates. When further measures (the introduction of a complicated system of targets, with penalties in the form of loss of grant if they were exceeded, and the abolition of the power to levy supplementary rates) failed to curtail local spending, the Conservative government turned its attention to restricting the sources of local government revenue. The year 1985 saw the introduction of 'rate capping', with the government being given the power to fix an upper limit to the rates levied by 'high-spending' local authorities, thereby removing the means to maintain service levels through increases in local taxation. But despite this plethora of legislation, the government still found itself, in the words of Stoker (1988: 170), 'constrained by [its] lack of direct control over local government'. Many local authorities evaded the new controls by the use of such devices as creative accounting to offset their loss of income.

The next stage in what has been described as the 'knee-capping' of local government (Newton and Karran 1985: 114) was the abolition of the rating system and its replacement in 1990 by the community charge (popularly known as the 'poll tax'), a flat rate charge payable by all adults over the age of 18 years. Like the rates it replaced, the community charge could be 'capped' by central government. In addition, RSG was simplified and renamed Revenue Support Grant, which was to be allocated on the basis of central government's assessment of the necessary level of spending, while non-domestic rates were set and collected centrally and then redistributed to local authorities.

A major strand in this new reform package was the perceived need to strengthen local accountability, which was (as we shall see later) to become a central theme in the developments which followed the Conservatives' 1987 general election victory. The government argued that if local electors were aware of the costs of local authority services, they would then penalize high-spending councils at local elections. But for its critics, the real task of the community charge was to contain local government spending, the view of one of the local authority associations being that the measures revealed 'only too clearly that the Government's long-term aim is to use the poll tax to force councils into providing the barest minimal services for use only by those who can't afford to buy them in the market place' (Association of Metropolitan Authorities 1987).

Observers have described the legislation which introduced the controversial community charge as one of a succession of Acts of Parliament in the late 1980s which marked 'the most decisive break in British social policy' since the Labour government of the early post-war years (Glennerster et al. 1991: 389). (We shall discuss the other legislation later.) For those on the New Right, this new form of local government taxation was seen as an important element in what has been described as a system of local government conforming to 'the Neo-Conservative dream', in which there was no reason why local government services should be provided by the public sector at all. According to this vision of local government, most of the major social services provided by local authorities could be hived off to the private sector or voluntary organizations. The community charge was seen as an important element in such a system, as it was viewed as a way of discouraging local government spending and thus encouraging local authorities to privatize services and to surrender functions (Glennerster et al. 1991: 390–1, 408).

The Conservative government, now headed by John Major, decided to abandon the controversial community charge soon after Margaret Thatcher's resignation as prime minister in 1990. The charge was replaced by a council tax in 1993. Labelled 'son of poll tax' by Glennerster (1992a: 86), the new tax is based on property values, but, like its predecessor, takes into account the number of adults in each household. One result of the new system was that local government had an even narrower tax base than before (central government now controlled some 85 per cent of local authority income, including non-domestic rates), and the capping powers of central government had been strengthened. This combination of controls was seen as giving central government 'almost unlimited powers' to dictate both the level of spending of local authorities and the level of local taxation (see Midwinter and Monaghan 1993: 132).

The changing role of local education authorities

The first two terms of the Thatcher government, 1979–87, focused on attempts to control the spending of the local government welfare state.

But, following the Conservatives' third successive victory in the 1987 general election, the government's programme for local government entered a much more radical phase. As Rhodes (1992b: 213) has observed, the Conservatives' 'narrow fixation' on local government spending was replaced by a market-orientated strategy intended to return control of local authority services to their users. Described by some observers as 'revolutionary' (see, for example, Audit Commission 1988a: 1) and by others as inaugurating a 'new era for social policy' (Glennerster et al. 1991), the post-1987 programme involved fundamental changes in the arrangements for the delivery of all three social services traditionally provided by local authorities.

A significant part of this new approach to the delivery of welfare was a piece of legislation intended to transform the local government education system. Described as creating 'the most radical recasting of the government of education' since the Education Act 1944 (Ranson 1992a: 10), the Education Reform Act 1988 introduced a series of changes that substantially diminished the traditional role of local education authorities (LEAs). As a result of the Act, local education authorities were obliged to share their powers with three other groups – upwards with the Secretary of State for Education, downwards with individual schools, colleges and their governors, and outwards with parents and other groups in the community (Audit Commission 1989: 2–3).

The 1988 Act was the culmination of a long period of debate about local authority education. As we saw in Chapter 1, the local education service had been seen by critics on the New Right as having been 'captured' by the 'producers'. Typical were the views of the Hillgate Group, who argued that: 'Like every monopolized industry, the educational system has begun to ignore the demands of the consumers – parents and children – and to respond instead to the requirements of the producers – LEAs and teachers' (Hillgate Group 1986: 3). This view of the delivery of local education was echoed in 1987 by the Secretary of State for Education, Kenneth Baker, who believed that 'education was too serious a business to leave to the professional educationalists' (see Jenkins 1987: 268). The panacea for the perceived ills of the local education system was seen as increased consumer accountability. As Ranson (1990: 189, 195) put it, parents were to be 'brought centre stage in the establishment of an education market place'.

The notion of market accountability was at the heart of the 1988 Act, described by one observer as a piece of legislation intended to produce a consumer-orientated education system 'driven by the twin engines of choice and competition' (Wilcox 1989: 31). Thus the Act permitted schools to opt out of local authority control, following a ballot of parents, and be financed directly by the DfE as grant-maintained schools. It also permitted the establishment of city technology colleges, specializing in science and technology and funded directly by central government and private industry. Parental choice and the promotion of competition for pupils were also to be increased by the introduction of open enrolment, which removed the right of local education authorities to set limits on the number of pupils enrolling at particular schools.

In addition to increasing parental choice, the 1988 Act also pushed power downwards to schools, giving them the freedom to manage their own budgets, which were delegated to boards of governors through the new system of local management of schools (LMS). The powers of the secretary of state were also strengthened, notably over the establishment of the national curriculum. The Act also removed local education authority responsibility for higher education, giving the then polytechnics and colleges of education self-governing corporate status with direct funding from the Polytechnics and Colleges Funding Council (later replaced by the Higher Education Funding Council).

Although the 1988 Act was seen as consigning the local education authority to 'a distinctly subordinate role' in the implementation of educational policy (Whitty 1990: 315), it still left it with potentially an important role to play in strategic planning and quality assurance (Ranson 1992a: 32). In the event, the functions of local education authorities were further diminished. Following the Further and Higher Education Act 1992, local education authorities lost their responsibility for further education colleges, tertiary colleges and sixth form colleges, which were given independent status as corporations financed directly by the Further Education Funding Council. What was seen by some as the 'final nail in the local education authority's coffin as a provider of local education services' (Wilson et al. 1994: 90), however, was the Education Act 1993. In an attempt to increase the number of grant-maintained schools – fewer than 300 of the 25,000 local authority schools had opted out by the end of 1992 – the 1993 Act streamlined the procedures for grant-maintained status. Opting-out was also encouraged by the introduction of the technology colleges scheme (restricted to grant-maintained and voluntary aided schools), involving additional government funding for schools which emphasized science, technology and mathematics and which developed a close relationship with business sponsors. The 1993 Act also provided that schools identified as failing to deliver a reasonable standard of education to their pupils would become grant maintained once they had been taken over and improved by newly created education associations.

Local government control of the education service was also reduced by the creation of a new quasi-governmental body, the Funding Agency for Schools (FAS), which took over responsibility for the funding of grant-maintained schools, as well as the monitoring of their expenditure and wider planning responsibilities. Once 10 per cent of school pupils in a local education authority area were in grant-maintained schools, the authority had to share its duty for providing sufficient school places with the FAS. The local education authority ceased to have responsibility for securing sufficient places once this figure reached 75 per cent, when the duty passed to the FAS. A similar funding authority was introduced for Wales.

The 1993 Act's abolition of the requirement for local education authorities to establish education committees was a further indication of the government's intention to dismantle local government control of education. Symbolically, the 1993 Act removed the reference in the Education Act 1944 to national policy for providing an educational service being secured by local authorities under the control and direction of the minister, thereby removing the local education authority from its central position in the delivery of local education (Ranson and Travers 1994: 227). To quote one observer, under the Conservatives the predominant place that education had played in local government was 'fast disappearing' (Ranson 1992b: 140).

The decline of local authority housing

The themes of choice and competition which were such an important feature of the development of the Conservative government's education reforms during the late 1980s could also be found in its approach to local authority housing. A number of radical changes took place that affected the traditional role of local housing authorities as providers of social housing.

As we shall discuss in greater detail in Chapter 7, the centrepiece of the government's housing policy in the early 1980s was the 'right to buy', with the Housing Act 1980 providing certain council house tenants with the statutory right to purchase their properties at substantial discounts of the market value. As with the education reforms of the late 1980s, for the New Right the 1980 Act represented an escape from the bureaucracy and paternalism of local government, council house sales being compared by the Conservative Party to the 'freeing' of 'feudal tenants' who were 'subjugated to the patronage and paternalism of local political barons' (Bassett 1980: 291). The introduction of the 'right to buy' signalled an important change in the relationship between central government and local authorities. As Forrest and Murie (1991: 200) have put it, the policy eroded what had been 'one of the most significant and visible' of local government activities, and was seen as not only a threat to locally determined housing policies, but also an undermining of local democracy. Nearly 1.7 million local authority houses were sold under the 'right to buy' between 1980 and 1997, equivalent to about one-third of the 1979 local authority housing stock.

The Conservative government's attempts to break up the near monopoly position of local authorities in the field of social housing were continued with the Housing Act 1988. As the Minister for Housing put it in 1987: 'The next great push after the right to buy should be to get rid of the State as a big landlord and bring housing back to the community' (Waldegrave 1987). This 'great push' involved the run down of local authorities as major providers of housing and the development of housing associations, who would become what one commentator has called 'the new main engine' of social housing (Spencer 1989: 95). This approach reflected increasing criticism of the role of local housing authorities. There was a growing feeling (not restricted to those on the right of the political spectrum) that there were problems with both the scale and management of council housing. In 1986 the Audit Commission referred to a 'crisis' in local authority housing (Audit Commission 1986). One academic study depicted local housing departments as 'unwieldy, bureaucratic structures remote from tenants' (Power 1987: 1), a description echoed in 1987 by the Secretary of State for the Environment, who referred to insensitive allocation procedures and management arrangements which were often cumbersome, remote and inflexible (*Hansard* 1987). Another housing minister later argued that the 'basic conditions for customer satisfaction' simply did not exist in the local authority housing service: 'People became council tenants not on the whole by choice but because there is practically nowhere else to go. Escape is only possible if their financial circumstances change' (Trippier 1989). As one observer later concluded, all this criticism amounted to 'an assault on the confidence and credibility of local authorities as housing providers' (Malpass 1992: 15).

It was the intention of the Conservative government to encourage local housing authorities to move away from their traditional role as direct providers of housing and to see their role as being essentially a strategic one, identifying housing needs and demands (Department of the Environment 1987: para. 5.1). Local authorities were expected to see themselves as enablers who would ensure that people in their area were adequately housed. As part of this process, the 1988 Act introduced the so-called 'tenants' choice', under which council tenants could ballot on whether they wished to be transferred from local authority control to an alternative landlord (who had to be approved by the Housing Corporation) in the housing association or private sector. Although this measure was not very successful, over 50 local authorities voluntarily sold their complete stock of rented homes, under the large-scale voluntary transfer mechanism, to newly created housing associations in the period 1988 to 1997 (see Chapter 7). Tenants were also given the right to own and run their own estates as tenant cooperatives. The Conservative government clearly saw housing associations as the main vehicle for social housing in the 1990s, either as builders of new rented housing or as alternative landlords for dissatisfied council tenants through 'tenants' choice'.

Another mechanism introduced by the 1988 legislation to 'rescue' council tenants from incompetent local housing authorities was that of housing action trusts (Karn 1993: 75). Central government gave itself powers to set up HATs, modelled on the UDCs set up to regenerate certain inner-city areas, to take over selected local authority estates and to renovate the housing stock before handing it over to private landlords.

Although (as we shall see in Chapter 7) 'tenants' choice' and HATs did not have the impact hoped for by the Thatcher government, developments in local authority housing under the Conservatives cannot be ignored. As Malpass and Murie (1990: 131–2) put it, the government's preference for housing associations as providers of social housing and the promotion of an 'enabling' role for local authorities marked 'a final phase in the breakdown of central government's use of local authorities as the major instruments of housing policy'. The building of new social housing was also shifted away from local authorities and towards housing associations. By the election of the Labour government in 1997, local authorities 'had all but ceased to be a major supplier of new rented homes' (Kemp 1999b: 171).

Community care: the contract culture

The theme that local authorities should no longer perform the role of direct providers of services was also applied by the Conservative government to the third major local authority social service, the personal social services. The personal social services had long been characterized by a 'mixed economy of welfare' (in which substantial contributions to the delivery of welfare have been made by the voluntary and private sectors) and Conservative governments emphasized the desirability of local authority social services departments making the fullest possible use of the non-statutory sectors in the delivery of social care.

Following increasing criticisms about the delivery of community care policies, including concern about the fragmentation of responsibilities between local authorities and health authorities (see Chapter 4), the Griffiths Report of 1988 made a number of proposals for radical change. Griffiths (1988a) recommended that local authorities should no longer be monopolistic providers of community care services, but should ensure that services are provided within the appropriate budgets by the public or private sector, according to where they can be most economically and efficiently provided (Griffiths 1988a: vii). As one group of commentators was to put it some years later, Griffiths was 'looking back to the traditional emphasis on stimulating community resources' and looking 'forward to the new world of purchasing and provision in which the private sector would be encouraged to compete alongside statutory and not-for-profit agencies' (Wistow et al. 1992: 27). This latter emphasis upon the purchasing role of local authorities was central to the government's response to Griffiths (Department of Health 1989b: para. 3.1.3), which said that local authority social services departments would be responsible for securing the delivery of services 'not simply by acting as direct providers but by developing their purchasing and contracting role to become "enabling authorities"'.

Accordingly, as a result of the National Health Service and Community Care Act 1990, with effect from April 1993 local authorities were expected to see themselves as purchasers rather than providers of community care services. Local authority social services departments were given the duty to assess the community care needs of any individual they believe requires such care and to decide what services that individual needs. Local authorities could then either provide the services themselves through 'self-managed' units, invite tenders from private and voluntary bodies, stimulate the establishment of not-for-profit agencies or encourage new voluntary sector activity (Department of Health 1991a: para. 2.1.4).

The community care reforms, together with those that had been introduced in housing and education, questioned the traditional assumption that local authorities should both finance and provide services. The result was the separation of the purchaser and provider roles and the development of what were labelled 'quasi-markets' (see Chapter 7).

Losing a welfare empire, finding a role: from providing to enabling

It has been argued that the Conservative government's post-1987 programme for local government went beyond the changes of the 1979–87 period because of 'the breadth and common themes of the restructuring' that it proposed, including a commitment to competition, an increased emphasis on consumer choice, the separation of the responsibility for a service from its actual provision, and an emphasis on new forms of accountability (Stewart and Stoker 1989: 2–4). All of these themes underpinned changes in the delivery of welfare under the Conservatives in the late 1980s and 1990s.

One concept that helped to draw together all these developments was that of 'enabling'. Indeed, it was suggested that if the Conservative government had a vision for local government in the 1990s, then it was that of the 'enabling authority' (Leach 1992: 5), while other observers described the enabling role as 'the new orthodoxy' (Hollis et al. 1992: 28). The concept of enabling was first made fashionable in the late 1980s by the then Secretary of State for the Environment, Nicholas Ridley, who argued that local authorities should be concerned with 'enabling not providing'. In Ridley's opinion, the role of local authorities should be reduced from that of universal, front-line providers of such major services as housing and personal social services to that of minimalist, enabling authorities. According to this view of local government, there should be a much more pluralistic system of local service provision, with a variety of public, private and voluntary agencies working alongside local authorities. Although local authorities would no longer be the universal providers of services, they should continue to have a key role in ensuring that there was adequate provision to meet needs (Ridley 1988a: 16–17, 25). The Conservative government's dissatisfaction with the historical role of local authorities as the direct providers of services was also emphasized in its Citizen's Charter (Prime Minister 1991: 34), which argued that it was time for a new approach to the delivery of local services. What it described as 'the real task' for local authorities lay in concentrating on 'strategic responsibilities', setting priorities, determining the standards of service and finding the best ways of meeting them.

This was the role envisaged for local authorities in the government's housing reforms of the late 1980s, with the 1987 White Paper on housing (which preceded the Housing Act 1988) maintaining that rather than acting as local landlords, local authorities should 'increasingly see themselves as enablers who ensure that everyone in their area is adequately housed; but not necessarily by them' (Department of the Environment 1987: para. 1.16). The approach was later elaborated in a departmental circular in 1989:

> Local authorities are ceasing to be the main providers of subsidized housing for rent; but they will remain responsible for ensuring, as far as resources permit, the needs for new housing in their areas are met, by the private sector alone where possible, with public sector subsidy where necessary. This will require some of them to take a broader view of their responsibilities than they have in the past, and to develop their information sources and monitoring arrangements accordingly.
> (Department of the Environment 1989: 1–2)

According to this approach, local authorities should facilitate the efforts of housebuilders, housing associations and private landlords to deal with local housing needs. Various ways in which local authorities could undertake this new enabling role were identified by the Cabinet minister responsible for the 1988 legislation and included the use of planning powers; assessing housing needs and conditions; offering improvement grants; the provision of assistance to schemes for private renting; sponsoring housing association schemes; cooperating with housing associations over their allocation of tenancies; and working with housing associations to make sure that housing is available for vulnerable groups (Ridley 1988b).

The Conservative government also envisaged an enabling role for local education authorities following the Education Reform Act 1988, with local authorities becoming promoters of education policies rather than pro-viders of education services (John 1990: 34, 37). In its discussion of the 1988 Act, the Audit Commission (1989: 2) argued that although local education authorities might have lost their 'empires', they still had an important role to play. Despite their loss of powers to grant-maintained schools in some areas of England, they still retained important responsibilities in the areas of finance and resources, the curriculum, planning and provision, quality assurance, information and training. Other observers argued that the development of new relationships with individual grant-maintained schools, further education colleges and TECs could be seen as a shift to an enabling role in which local education authorities took on the kind of functions highlighted by the Audit Commission (Hollis et al. 1992: 85–8).

As we saw in the previous section, the post-Griffiths developments in community care were also intended to give local authorities more of an enabling, and less of a providing, role. Local authority social services departments were to become responsible for assessing local care needs, purchasing that care from either the social services department itself or the private or voluntary sectors, and monitoring performance.

Thus the enabling concept was a feature of developments in all three local authority social services under the Conservative governments between 1979 and 1997. To paraphrase the Audit Commission (1989), local authorities might have lost a welfare empire, but they appeared to have found a new role to perform – that of enabling – in the aftermath of these changes.

The Blair government and the local welfare state

The movement of local authorities away from their traditional role as direct service providers continued under the Blair government elected in 1997. The Labour Party's election manifesto declared that it saw 'no reason why a service should be delivered directly [by local councils] if other more efficient means are available' (Labour Party 1997: 34). This approach was reiterated by the new administration, which stated that there was 'no future in the old model of councils trying to plan and run most services' (Department of the Environment, Transport and the Regions 1998: 5). According to Blair himself (1998a):

> It is in partnership with others – public agencies, private companies, community groups and voluntary organisations – that local government's future lies. Local authorities will still deliver some services but their distinctive leadership role will be to weave and knit together the contributions of the various local stakeholders.
>
> (Blair 1998a: 13)

Thus the enabling role has continued under the Blair government, but the concept has been given a broader interpretation than the one associated with the Thatcher and Major governments. As Wilson (2000b: 258) has observed, the Blair government has adopted a view of enabling that largely reflects that of Clarke and Stewart (1988: 1), who see the role of an enabling local authority as being 'to use all the means at its disposal to meet the needs of those who live within the area'. The Labour government has moved towards an approach in which partnership and collaboration have become key features of local service delivery – there is a 'mixed economy' of service provision (Wilson 2000a: 46).

Thus, in the field of education, the White Paper on schools of 2001 (Department for Education and Skills 2001: paras 5.22, 5.27) expressed the view that educational standards would be raised by the development of new partnerships and allowing new providers to work with schools. As we have seen, under the Thatcher and Major administration, the role of local education authorities had been dramatically diminished. Although the Blair government reabsorbed grant-maintained schools into local education authorities, Labour's 1997 election manifesto spoke of 'a new job description' for local education authorities, who would be required to devolve powers and more of their budgets to schools (Labour Party 1997: 8). Once in office, the new administration warned local education authorities that they did not have a 'God-given right to run and lead everything' (Lightfoot 1998a). Under the *Fair Funding* system – which has superseded LMS – local education authorities have to delegate far greater funding to schools, and they are now subject to Ofsted inspections. The Blair government has also created education action zones in areas of educational under-performance, with the aim of raising educational standards and to foster innovation. Each zone is based on a cluster of secondary, primary and special schools in a local area, and is run by a forum made up of school governors, teachers, parents, local councillors and business representatives. By the end of 2001, there were 73 zones, each set up for a five-year period. The zones were viewed by the government as emblems of the 'third way' in public services (Gewirtz 1999). The Local Government Association saw them as the beginning of the break-up of local education authorities (Lightfoot 1998b; see also Chapter 7).

As a result of such developments, local education authorities have moved even further from being 'barons' to 'postmen' (*The Economist* 27 May 2000: 36). Their position was further threatened by the establishment in 2001 of learning and skills councils with responsibility for all post-16 education and training, excluding higher education (see Chapter 3). It has been suggested that the transfer of local education authority responsibilities to these new bodies could restore the 'seamless robe' of education (Leach and Percy-Smith 2001: 237).

In the field of housing, the Blair government has shared the view of the Thatcher and Major administrations that local authorities should move away from their traditional role as large-scale monopoly landlords. It has continued the policy of large-scale stock transfer to housing associations begun under the Thatcher government in 1988, supporting the transfer of up to 200,000 dwellings each year from 2001. Stock transfers are seen as enabling local authorities to concentrate on their strategic responsibilities for housing. According to the Blair government, local authorities 'should be concerned with the full range of strategic issues surrounding the housing needs of their communities, rather than focusing more narrowly on the day-to-day management of social housing' (Department of the Environment, Transport and the Regions 2000a: para. 7.15).

In the third major local authority social service, the personal social services, the Blair government has criticized 'the near-monopoly local authority provision' that used to be a feature of the delivery of social care. What it described as a 'one size fits all' approach, where the users of services were expected to accommodate themselves to the services that existed, was to be replaced by a 'third way' for social care. This approach moved the focus away from who provides the care, and placed it firmly on 'the quality of services' (Department of Health 1998: para. 1.7). There was an emphasis on partnership, including partnerships involving the voluntary sector and independent social care providers.

Thus, under the Blair government, arrangements for the delivery of all three local authority social services have been characterized by an emphasis on partnership and collaboration between public, private and voluntary bodies at the local level in order to promote the well-being of their local communities. In the words of the prime minister: 'There are all sorts of players on the local pitch jostling for position where previously the council was the main game in town' (Blair 1998a: 10).

Within this new local governance, the Blair government promised to give local authorities greater freedom, including financial freedoms. It has made it clear, however, that where it thinks that a local service is falling below an acceptable standard, it will work with the authority concerned to secure improvements, but will intervene in cases of serious or persistent failure in the delivery of a service. It has set up special improvement teams – inevitably labelled 'hit squads' – to address serious failings in local authority service delivery of education and the personal social services. Within days of the 1997 election victory, 18 schools were 'named and shamed' by the government. The Schools Standards and Framework Act 1998 gave the Secretary of State for Education powers to intervene in 'failing' schools. Up to November 2001, the secretary of state had intervened in 21 local education authorities following a critical Ofsted report. Ten of these interventions involved private sector companies delivering services or functions under contract, notably the award of a seven-year contract to a private sector firm to run education services in the London Borough of Islington from April 2000. A year later, the DfES transferred education services in the London Borough of Hackney to an independent, non-profit-making trust. The Blair government has also served notice on local authorities which deliver sub-standard personal social services, stating that it would be ready to use its powers to intervene in the running of such services, if necessary (see, for example, Department of Health 1997b). Inspectorates are seen as an important means for ensuring improvements in the quality of all three major local authority social services. In 1996, the Major government had extended the activities of the Social Services Inspectorate to enable it – jointly with the Audit Commission – to review the overall performance of each social services department. The Blair government has strengthened the role of the other inspectorate that it inherited from the Conservatives, giving Ofsted additional powers to inspect local education authorities. It has also established a Housing Inspectorate.

The Blair government's emphasis is on improving the quality of services. As we shall discuss in Chapter 7, the government's Best Value regime requires local authorities to make arrangements to continuously improve services. As part of its attempts to improve local authority performance, Labour has also designated 'beacon' councils – the best performing local authorities – which are expected to help improve the standards of service delivery by sharing best practice with other local authorities. Local authorities are able to apply for beacon status in relation to particular service areas – there will be beacon housing councils, beacon education councils and beacon councils for the personal social services. In awarding 'beacon' status, the government takes account of performance in service delivery against national and local performance targets and indicators, inspectorate reports, and auditors' reports on financial management.

The Blair government has made it clear that local authorities that embrace its performance agenda, and demonstrate that they can provide value for money and quality in the delivery of education, housing, the personal social services and other local services, will be rewarded with new powers and extra finances. However, those local authorities considered to be 'failing' will be subject to direct central intervention and the possible transfer of services to other delivery agencies (see, for example, Department of Transport, Local Government and the Regions 2001). As one leading writer on local government has observed, the Blair government's policies on local government are characterized by a tension between 'a commitment to decentralisation and an emphasis on inspection, centrally developed procedures and powers of intervention' (Stewart 2000: 289–90).

Further reading

See Hartas and Harrop (1991) for a discussion of the relationship between local authorities and central government in the post-war local welfare state. Wilson and Game (1998) and Byrne (2000) provide detailed discussions of developments in local government since 1979. On developments in specific services, see Kendall and Holloway (2001) on education, Kemp (1999a) on housing, and Johnson (1999) on the personal social services and community care. Those interested in the Blair government's modernization agenda for local government should consult Department of the Environment, Transport and the Regions (1998). Readers can keep up to date with developments by looking at the two weekly publications, *Local Government Chronicle* and *Municipal Journal*.

7

The privatization of welfare delivery

One major, and controversial, policy response to the problems perceived to be associated with traditional approaches to the provision of services by the delivery agencies of the welfare state, has been privatization. The privatization of welfare delivery was one of the major strategies employed by Conservative governments between 1979 and 1997 in their attempts to restructure the arrangements for the delivery of social services. Private sector involvement has been a major feature of the arrangements for the delivery of social services under the Labour government elected in 1997.

Associated with the views of the New Right, privatization is a policy which, in the words of Hambleton and Hoggett (1988: 14), sets out to challenge the very idea of collective and non-market provision for social need. As we shall see, the privatization of welfare delivery is a strategy which covers a number of different approaches, ranging from the selling of the assets of welfare delivery agencies to the application of market principles and practices to their operations.

Privatization is a concept beset with definitional uncertainties. As Donnison (1984: 45) has observed, it is a word which should be 'heavily escorted by inverted commas as a reminder that its meaning is at best uncertain and often tendentious'. For Donnison, 'privatization'

> is a word invented by politicians and disseminated by political journalists. It is designed not to clarify analysis but as a symbol, intended by

advocates and opponents of the processes it describes to dramatise a conflict and mobilise support for their own side.

(Donnison 1984: 45)

The confusion about the meaning, and the use, of the concept of privatization is well illustrated by the debate over the use of public–private partnerships following the re-election of the Labour government in 2001. Critics of the government's public–private partnership initiative, particularly public sector trade unions, protested at what they saw as a 'privatization' policy, with one union leader describing such measures as a 'Trojan horse' that heralded a full-scale 'privatization agenda' (McHugh 2001). Government ministers maintained that, although there was a partnership role for the private sector, there would be no private sector take-over of public services (see, for example, Adams et al. 2001).

We consider these problems of definition in the first section of this chapter. Having provided a brief overview of the subject, we then examine in more detail some of the main forms that the privatization of welfare delivery has taken since 1979.

Approaches to the privatization of welfare delivery

One definition of privatization is that suggested by Young (1986: 236), who defines it as 'a set of policies which aim to limit the role of the public sector, and increase the role of the private sector, while improving the performance of the remaining public sector'. A similar approach is taken by Ascher (1987: 4), who views privatization as an umbrella term used to describe 'a multitude of government initiatives designed to increase the role of the private sector'.

Privatization takes a number of forms. Young (1986) identifies seven distinct forms of the process, including the selling of public sector assets and the contracting out of services to the private sector. The privatization of welfare delivery has included both these forms, as well as the encouragement of welfare provision by the private sector as an alternative to public sector provision, and the application of market principles to the operations of delivery agencies. Also, as we shall see later in the chapter, a major strand of government policy on the privatization of welfare delivery has involved developing the role of the voluntary sector. Thus privatization 'involves much wider and deeper changes than is usually appreciated' (Young 1986: 238).

The privatization of welfare delivery is not new. Local authorities and the NHS have long contracted out services to the private sector, while local authority social services departments have also made use of voluntary organizations in the delivery of certain services. But, although the idea may not be new, the context of the concept of privatization in welfare delivery has changed dramatically since the election of the first Thatcher government in 1979.

Selling the welfare state: the case of council house sales

One form of privatization has involved the sale of the assets of welfare delivery agencies to the private sector. The major example of this particular kind of privatization has been the sale of council houses under the Conservative administrations, a policy described by Forrest and Murie (1991: 1) as 'the most important element in the privatisation programme of the Thatcher Governments' in social, political and economic terms.

Privatization was a dominant theme in the Thatcher government's approach to council housing during the 1980s. Indeed, as Malpass and Murie (1990: 22) observe, the government's whole housing strategy during this particular decade was based on the assumption that council housing was 'both unnecessary and unsuccessful', and that it was possible to develop a housing system which is almost entirely located in the private sector. Central to this strategy was the sale of council housing to sitting tenants through the 'right to buy' policy.

In 1979, council housing made up just over 31 per cent of the total housing stock in Britain, far in excess of the 14 per cent accounted for by the privately rented and housing association sectors. It is possible to identify two waves of policymaking on council housing since the election of the first Thatcher government in 1979 (Hills and Mullings 1991: 140–2). The first wave was represented by the Housing Act 1980, which gave local authority tenants the statutory right to buy their homes at attractive discounts of the market value – up to a maximum of 50 per cent (later increased to a maximum of 60 per cent on houses and a maximum of 70 per cent on flats) – together with a guaranteed mortgage from the local authority. The scheme was extended even further in 1993 with the introduction of a 'rent to mortgage' scheme, allowing tenants to purchase their homes for the same cost as their council rent. The 'right to buy' policy was extremely popular – the programme was described by one writer as 'the sale of the century' (Stoker 1988: 176) – with 1.7 million local authority properties being sold between 1980 and 1997.

But by the late 1980s it had become clear that this particular approach to the privatization of local authority housing was in decline, with council house sales in England and Wales having peaked at just over 200,000 properties in 1982. The residualization of council housing once better-off tenants had purchased their homes reduced the number of potential purchasers, and the Conservative government had to develop other initiatives in its attempt to demunicipalize local authority housing. Its solution was contained in a second wave of policymaking – the major component of which was the Housing Act 1988 – which extended the privatization policy to involve the sale of local authority houses not only to sitting tenants through the 'right to buy', but also to alternative landlords. The 1988 Act gave approved private landlords and housing associations the right to purchase blocks of council housing or even whole council estates, provided that such sales were preceded by successful ballots of the tenants concerned, a policy described by the government as 'tenants' choice'. The initiative for the transfer of ownership through 'tenants' choice' could come from either the tenants themselves or prospective alternative landlords, irrespective of whether or not the local authority wished to participate in such transfers. In the event, very few transfers of housing stock took place as a result of 'tenants' choice'. Neither alternative landlords nor local authority tenants demonstrated much interest in this particular type of transfer of ownership.

The Housing Act 1988 also gave the government powers to introduce housing action trusts which, following a ballot of the tenants involved, would take over large, run-down council estates and transfer them to private or voluntary sector landlords after necessary repairs and improvements had been carried out. Eighteen local authority estates were originally designated by the DoE for HAT status, but, following a marked lack of support from tenants, none of the schemes were actually established. According to one observer of this initiative, a combination of the confrontational way in which the new policy was presented by the government, the fear of privatization and the loss of democratic accountability made HATs unacceptable to both local authorities and tenants' associations (Karn 1993: 76). Subsequently, the original concept of HATs was 'redesigned' and six local authorities – Hull, Liverpool, Birmingham, and the London boroughs of Waltham Forest, Tower Hamlets and Brent – set up 'voluntary' HATs on estates in their areas. The terms of these new model HATs were very different from those originally laid down, the tenants involved having the right to choose to return to local authority control after their estates had been improved (Baker 1993: 41). The HAT in Hull completed its work and ceased operation in 1999.

Despite the limited impact of 'tenants' choice' and the HAT initiative, they had important consequences for the organization of housing delivery by local authorities. According to one observer, the threat of potential competition 'galvanized' many local housing authorities into developing more efficient and responsive services (Bramley 1993: 159). As a result, housing management in many local authorities was 'reformed from within' (Cole and Furbey 1994: 217), key features of such reforms being the decentralization of the housing service and the development of more customer-orientated approaches (see Chapter 9).

A far greater contribution to the privatization of local authority housing than either of the two policy instruments introduced by the Housing Act 1988 has been the large-scale voluntary transfer of housing by many local authorities. Large-scale voluntary transfers were originally undertaken as a means of countering the perceived threat of 'tenants' choice', and were subsequently stimulated by government restrictions on local housing authorities (Mullins et al. 1993: 171). Under the Conservative government, large number of local authorities transferred – after a successful ballot of tenants – all, or nearly all, their housing stock to housing associations, most of which were specifically formed by the local authorities concerned. One of the local authorities that led the early pace was the London Borough of Bromley, which transferred 12,000 homes to the newly formed Broomleigh Housing Association in 1992. By 1997, nearly 250,000 homes had been transferred from local authorities to housing associations as a result of large-scale voluntary transfer, with over 50 local housing authorities having transferred all their housing stock. The transfer of local authority housing stock has continued under the Blair government, which sees stock transfer as a way of improving the quality of social housing by bringing in private investment (Department of the Environment, Transport and the Regions 2000a: para. 7.11). The Blair government has provided resources to fund the transfer of up to 200,000 homes per year to housing associations and local housing companies – non-profit-making bodies set up by local authorities to expedite stock transfers – in the period 2001–04 (Department of the Environment, Transport and the Regions 2001a: para. 4.13). Large-scale voluntary transfers represent a significant contribution to the privatization of local authority housing, and it has been predicted by leading figures in the housing movement that council housing could effectively cease to exist by 2014 (Weaver 2000).

Contracting out welfare provision

Another important manifestation of the privatization of welfare delivery is contracting out, the purchase of services, which would otherwise have been provided by in-house staff, from private contractors (Ascher 1987: 7–8). This form of privatization has operated for many years in the delivery of social services. Thus some NHS hospitals have long contracted out their cleaning and catering services, while many local authority personal social services (such as meals on wheels) have long been supplied by voluntary organizations. In 1978–79, over 11 per cent of local government's spending on the personal social services was contracted out, the bulk of it on residential care (Judge 1982: 399). Contracting grew in importance in the 1980s, when it was closely linked not only with the Conservative government's search for efficiency in the public sector (see Chapter 8), but also with another central principle of Conservative policy: that is, encouraging the expansion of the private sector (Key 1988: 65).

Contracting out was an important feature of attempts to improve the efficiency and cost-effectiveness of the NHS. Early attempts by the first Thatcher government to persuade health authorities to introduce this form of privatization in the hospital ancillary services were unsuccessful, and the government resorted to compulsory competitive tendering (CCT). In 1983 a DHSS circular instructed health authorities to put the three hospital ancillary services of cleaning, laundry and catering (the so-called 'hotel services') out to competitive tender. In the event, however, CCT had only limited success in transferring these services to the private sector, as the majority of contracts were won by in-house tenders. By the mid-1990s, only 40 per cent of contracts by value had been awarded to private companies (Baggott 1998: 163).

The financial savings produced by competitive tendering in the NHS under the Conservative governments are difficult to quantify. Writing in the late 1980s, Key (1988: 79) concluded that there were indications that the ultimate savings varied not only between different health authorities, but also between different services, estimating that the total savings might amount to no more than 10 per cent of NHS domestic spending. Official figures in the early 1990s, however, stated that savings were substantial: the cost of cleaning and other domestic services fell by 29 per cent in real terms between 1984–85 and 1989–90 (HM Treasury 1991: 14).

Contracting out did not progress nearly as fast under the Conservatives in the social services delivered by local authorities. While the Local Government Act 1988 introduced CCT for certain 'defined areas' of local government, the areas included were mainly technical and ancillary services outside the mainstream social services. The list did, however, include catering for schools and the personal social services, as well as the cleaning of buildings, and local authority education departments were usually the main clients for both these types of services (Council of Europe 1993: 68). Despite the limitations of the 1988 Act, some local authorities took much more radical initiatives in the contracting out of social services. Thus the London Borough of Wandsworth, for example, contracted out residential care for its old people.

In the early 1990s, the Conservative government stated that local authorities 'should be looking to contract out work to whoever can deliver services most efficiently and effectively' (Department of the Environment 1991b: para. 4), an approach clearly linked with the enabling concept discussed in Chapter 6. The Local Government Act 1988 gave central government the power to add to the list of services subject to CCT, and the process of implementing CCT in the important area of council housing management was phased in by local housing authorities from 1996. As part of the government's market-testing plans (see Chapter 8), the NHS was asked to further exploit the opportunities for tendering support services (HM Treasury 1991: 17). Having seen the benefits of applying competitive tendering to the hospital 'hotel services', managers in many health authorities had already put other support services, including transport, out to tender (HM Treasury 1991: 15).

While competitive tendering undoubtedly led to efficiency savings within both the NHS and local government, it was argued that its main significance was to facilitate a new style of management in these key delivery agencies of the welfare state, encouraging the introduction of market mechanisms and disciplines (see, for example, Walsh 1989: 48–9; Flynn 1992:

162). As we saw earlier in the chapter, similar conclusions were made about the impact of attempts to privatize council housing on the management of local authority housing departments.

Efficiency savings and management improvements are, of course, only one side of the coin when attempting to evaluate the impact of this form of privatization under the Conservative governments. Critics of contracting out argued that it had major implications for the quality of services, and there were many alleged cases of poor service delivery by outside contractors. It was claimed, for example, that standards of ancillary services in hospitals fell as a result of contracting out, with private contractors failing to perform to the standards specified in contracts (see, for example, McGregor 1990). Some contractors had their contracts terminated, one example involving Bromley DHA, which cancelled a contract with a private cleaning company following allegations of falling standards of hygiene (Baggott 1994: 150, 152). At the local government level, the London Borough of Wandsworth discharged the private contractor responsible for running old people's homes in its borough after discovering that the meal portions provided had been severely reduced in order to protect profit margins (Elcock 1996: 193). But, despite such cases, research showed that few local authorities felt that overall standards had worsened (Walsh and Davies 1993: para. 15.3).

Observers also pointed to the fact that contracting out had consequences for accountability, as it changed the pattern of control over welfare delivery. Under contracting out, the direct control that had traditionally been exercised over staff and levels of service within delivery agencies was replaced by a form of indirect control (Wood 1988: 127). Such a change had important implications for the redress of grievances in the services concerned, with complaints about service quality no longer being handled directly, but having to be referred to the contractors for their comments.

Despite these kinds of misgivings, however, advocates of privatization argued that the process of contracting out in both the NHS and local government did not go far enough. Thus the Adam Smith Institute argued that the number of local authority services open to CCT should be increased to include such services as the provision of residential homes and day centres (see Mather 1989: 222), while the then general director of another right-wing pressure group, the Institute of Economic Affairs, argued that contracting out need not be confined to support services, pointing out that many personal social services were already delivered by voluntary organizations acting on behalf of local authorities (Mather 1989: 223). As we saw in Chapter 6, as a result of the Conservative government's community care reforms, local authority social services departments were expected to invite tenders from private and voluntary bodies.

Compulsory competitive tendering was criticized for its inflexibility and bias towards the private sector, and the Blair government replaced it with the Best Value initiative. Best Value involves a duty to deliver services to clear standards by the most economical, efficient and effective means possible (Department of the Environment, Transport and the Regions 1998: para. 7.2). While there is no compulsion to put services out to tender, the Blair government has made it clear that competition remains an important feature of the new regime. Competition is seen as an essential part of the performance reviews that form part of the management of Best Value (Department of the Environment, Transport and the Regions 1998: para. 7.18). The government emphasized that 'Services should not be delivered directly if other more efficient and effective means are available' – there is still an important role for the private sector in the delivery of local services (Department of the Environment, Transport and the Regions 1998: para. 7.27). Thus, as Harries and Vincent-Jones (2001: 89) observe, 'the spirit of CCT lives on in the continuing pressure on local authorities to reform traditional modes of provision'. Although it will be some years before it is possible to evaluate the impact of the Best Value regime, evidence from the pilot programme that preceded its introduction in 2000 – including the major social services – suggests that Best Value has had a positive impact on service quality (Boyne et al. 2001). Initiatives have included the market-testing of in-house provision of residential homes for elderly people, externalizing the administration of housing benefit, Private Finance Initiative (PFI: see p. 134) deals covering some personal social services, and private investment in elderly people's homes and school buildings (Martin 2000: 218–19). In 2001 the Audit Commission concluded that both Best Value performance indicators and findings by Ofsted and the Social Services Inspectorate showed a picture of improvement in the areas of education and the personal social services in many local councils (Audit Commission 2001: para. 23). We shall have more to say about Best Value in Chapter 8.

Under the Blair government, CCT for NHS support services has also been dropped. It has been replaced by a system in which NHS trusts and PCTs measure themselves against the best that the NHS can offer, with patient satisfaction as well as efficiency being central to the process. If services are not meeting value for money and high standards, they should be market tested (Department of Health 2000b).

Encouraging the private provision of welfare

Another form of privatization is government encouragement of the provision of welfare by the private sector. One part of the private sector that was particularly encouraged when the Conservative government came into office in 1979 was the private health sector. Part of the compromise between the Labour government and the medical profession which underpinned the creation of the NHS in 1948 was that private practice and pay beds in NHS hospitals were allowed to exist alongside the public sector. The potential for private medicine was increased by a number of initiatives following the election of the Thatcher government in 1979. Higgins (1988) identified four such developments:

- the introduction of legislation in 1980 designed to reduce the restrictions on private medicine imposed by the previous Labour government
- the use of tax concessions to encourage the growth of private health insurance
- changes in contracts enabling all NHS consultants to engage in private practice
- government encouragement of greater collaboration between the NHS and the private health sector.

(Higgins 1988: 84–9)

The effect of these developments was to 'set in train a cumulative process which altered the traditional balance between public and private medicine' (Higgins 1988: 84). The private health care sector underwent huge changes under the Conservatives: the percentage of the UK population covered by private health insurance increased from 4 per cent to 11 per cent between 1979 and 1995. There was also a rapid growth in the number of private hospitals, the private sector's share of hospital-based health care in the UK increasing from 7.5 per cent to 20 per cent between 1984 and 1995 (Baggott 1998: 165, 167). Tax relief on private health insurance for those aged 60 years and above was abolished by the Blair government in 1997.

The Conservative government's encouragement of the role of the private sector in the delivery of welfare also included the arrangements for pensions and residential care for elderly people. Thus the social security reforms of 1986 provided generous incentives for those individuals taking out occupational pensions with private companies. This particular aspect of privatization was described by Bradshaw (1992: 96) as 'a roaring success', with nearly 5 million people opting out of the state scheme by 1993, although sales then 'flattened off' following criticisms about hard-selling and misleading advice (Burchardt and Hills 1999: 34; Drakeford 2000: 77). The period of the Thatcher and Major governments also saw the expansion of private residential care. Between 1984 and 1995, the number of private residential care homes more than doubled, while the number of local authority homes fell by one-third (Department of Health 1996). According to one commentator, the rapid development of private residential care in the 1980s was the result of a combination of stick and carrot (Walker 1989: 207–8). The stick had involved reducing the financial resources available for personal social services to local authorities, while the carrot had involved the then DHSS agreeing to pay the full cost of care in private residential and nursing homes for those receiving supplementary benefit (later replaced by income support). In the 1990s, the development of the private sector was strengthened by the Conservatives' community care reforms, which required local authorities to make the maximum possible use of voluntary and private sector provision. By 2001, the independent sector provided 92 per cent of all residential care homes and 85 per cent of places (Department of Health 2001d).

Another example of a policy designed to promote the role of the private sector in the area of welfare delivery under the Conservatives was the increased public funding of private education. The Education Act 1902, which (as we saw in Chapter 3) introduced local authority control of education in England and Wales, launched a scheme whereby independent schools received a direct grant from central government in return for providing a number of places (up to 25 per cent) for children nominated by local education authorities, an arrangement which had been abolished by the Labour government in 1976. Under the Assisted Places Scheme introduced by the first Thatcher government in 1981, selected independent schools were allowed to offer places to children at reduced fees related to the income of parents, the difference in the fee income being reimbursed by central government. By the mid-1990s the scheme offered nearly 34,000 places. The scheme was abolished by the Blair government.

The marketization of welfare delivery: quasi-markets

As Le Grand (1991: 1258) notes, the contracting out of ancillary services by health authorities in the early 1980s, the payment of the cost of care for elderly people in residential homes, and the introduction of the Assisted Places Scheme for independent schools were all early examples of attempts to move the state away from its traditional role as both funder and provider of social services. The introduction of what became known as 'quasi-markets' into the delivery of social services continued with even more radical developments in the late 1980s and early 1990s in the core social services of housing, education, personal social services and the NHS. As Le Grand (1991) put it, in each case, the intention was

> for the state to stop being both the funder *and* the provider of services. Instead it is to become primarily a funder, purchasing services from a variety of private, voluntary and public providers, all operating in competition with one another.
>
> (Le Grand 1991: 1257, original emphasis)

What was described as the 'big bang' occurred in the late 1980s (Le Grand 1991: 1258). The 'tenants' choice' provisions of the Housing Act 1988 introduced a degree of competition within social housing by giving council tenants the opportunity to opt out of local authority control and choose alternative landlords, either from the private sector or from the housing association sector. The Education Reform Act of the same year allowed schools to opt out of local education authority control and become grant-maintained schools. As well as being in competition with each other for pupils, grant-maintained schools were also in competition with the schools that remained under the control of local education authorities. Market mechanisms were also introduced within the local education authority sector with the introduction of 'open enrolment', under which local education authority schools were obliged to admit pupils up to their standard numbers. The introduction of this provision meant that local education authorities could not protect the less popular schools in their authorities by restricting the entry to popular schools.

The introduction of competition was also a feature of the community care reforms of the early 1990s. Thus local authority social services departments were required to appoint care managers, with budgets, who were responsible for constructing packages of care for individual clients, after considering bids from competing service providers in the public, private and voluntary sectors. Conservative government reforms in the organization of health care delivery also involved the introduction of quasi-markets. From 1991, district health authorities, fund-holding GPs (those with more than 7000 patients) and private insurers were able to purchase health care on behalf of their patients from DHA-managed hospitals, self-governing hospitals and hospitals in the private sector, who would be in competition for patients. We shall discuss this particular package of reforms in more detail in Chapter 8.

All these developments were examples of what Le Grand (1991: 1259–60) termed 'quasi-markets'. They were 'markets' because they replaced the traditional monopolistic providers of the welfare state with competitive independent providers. They were 'quasi' because they were different from conventional markets: the competing suppliers of services (for example, housing associations and grant-maintained schools) were not necessarily privately owned nor concerned with the maximization of profits; and in areas such as community care and health care the consumers were represented in the market, not by themselves, but by agents (for example, a care manager in a local authority social services department or a fund-holding GP). Such developments were also 'quasi' markets because the purchasing power of consumers under these new arrangements was not expressed in money terms, but in the form of an ear-marked budget which could be used only for the purchase of a specific service (for example, the budgets of fund-holding GPs).

The introduction of quasi-markets into the delivery of welfare was defended on the grounds that such arrangements would promote not only a more economical use of resources, but also an expansion of consumer choice, as the users of social services would have alternative sources of supply. Despite such claims, however, many observers expressed scepticism. Thus, Le Grand (1991: 1263–5) concluded that, far from reducing the cost of services, quasi-markets might actually lead to overall cost increases. Thus, it was estimated that the costs of monitoring the new internal market system in the NHS could be as high as £500 million per year. There would also need to be a very large investment in the development of the infra-structure needed to operate the new system for delivering community care. It was also pointed out that improvements in efficiency resulting from quasi-markets would need to be balanced against the costs of setting up these new systems (Hudson 1992: 133, 137).

Doubts were also raised about the impact of quasi-markets on con-sumer choice. Critics argued that the consumers of health care were not really empowered. Thus, in reality, consumers had little say over the kind of care they received in the NHS: the purchasing agencies acted as the patient's agent (see Harrison and Pollitt 1994: 127; Ranade 1994: 71). It was also suggested that a quasi-market in the field of health care would result in worse access to services for certain groups (for example, the poor and less educated people) and that individuals most in need of a service (such as chronically sick people) might be excluded from access to that service on the grounds of their high cost (Le Grand 1990: 358). The securing of choice and equity was also seen as 'problematic' in the new arrangements for the delivery of community care, as the users of such services had no 'market power' to reveal their preferences. As with the case of health care reforms, there was also the danger of 'adverse selection' of the users of community care, with private residential homes possibly being reluctant to provide accommodation for difficult cases (Hudson 1992: 137).

In the light of such misgivings, one commentator observed that it was 'difficult to avoid the conclusion that the benefits of a quasi-market in both health and social care . . . tended to be *asserted* rather than *demonstrated*' (Hudson 1992: 141, original emphasis). Certainly, there was a lot of debate about the benefits of the introduction of a quasi-market in health care when the new system was set up in 1991. The NHS Management Executive's review of the early stages of the NHS reforms indicated that more patients were being treated and waiting lists were falling as a result of the new system (NHS Management Executive 1991). Critics of the new arrange-ments, however, argued that the NHS was disintegrating, pointing to the hospital trusts that were facing severe financial difficulties, the cancellation by some hospitals of non-urgent operations half-way through the financial year, and the allegations that a two-tier NHS was emerging as hospitals gave preference to patients referred by fund-holding GPs (see, for example, Mason 1993). In the event, the Major government laid down ground-rules for DoH intervention in certain circumstances (such as closure of services), thus accepting 'that the market, left to its own devices, threatened wider policy objectives' (Baggott 1998: 204). As we shall discuss in Chapter 8, the internal market was abolished by the Blair government, although the provider–purchaser distinction remains in the new arrangements for com-missioning health care.

Privatization and the voluntary sector

The privatization of welfare delivery does not simply mean the selling of public assets, the contracting out of social services to the private sector, the encouragement of private sector provision or the introduction of quasi-markets. The concept is also used to include the development of the role of the voluntary sector as a vehicle for the provision of welfare. As Sugden (1984: 70) has pointed out, voluntary organizations are 'private' in the sense that they are outside the public sector. Indeed, he suggests that the voluntary sector can be seen as 'the counterpart of the private market in the realm of public goods. Like the market system, the voluntary sector is adapted to supply diverse goods in response to individuals' wants' (Sugden 1984: 88).

The voluntary sector has played an important role in the delivery of welfare in Britain for many years: indeed, it was a major provider of welfare for much of the nineteenth and early twentieth centuries. With the establishment of the post-war welfare state, however, the voluntary sector came to be seen as marginal to state provision. As we saw in Chapter 1, the welfare state that was developed and consolidated in the post-war years was deliberately based upon large-scale state social services, organized on the basis of bureaucratic structures and staffed by professionally qualified personnel. The voluntary sector was seen as either unnecessary or a threat to the adequacy of public provision (Webb and Wistow 1982: 59). But, despite the downgrading of the voluntary sector in the post-war period, there continued to be a 'mixed economy of welfare' consisting of the public, private and voluntary sectors (together with the informal sector of care provided by families and friends). Voluntary organizations continued to play an important role in the provision of welfare, and in some fields (such as care for elderly and handicapped people) it made a substantial contribution (see, for example, Hatch 1980).

Voluntary organizations do not match a single stereotype. How could they, given that there are thousands of them, of all shapes and sizes, ranging from large national bodies such as Barnados and Help the Aged to locally based organizations like local community housing associations and small local self-help groups, all with different organizational structures, funding arrangements and types of activities? The world of the voluntary sector is bewildering, as is the variety of bodies and activities within it. As one writer in this area has commented, the voluntary sector has a 'chameleon-like character': 'the many different bits of the sector between them, can sing almost any tune provided the score is clearly written and the fee is adequate' (Hatch 1986: 390).

But what score should the voluntary sector play with regard to the delivery of welfare? In the late 1970s, the Wolfenden Committee (1978: 26), reporting on the future of voluntary organizations, argued that the voluntary sector complemented, supplemented, extended and influenced the informal and statutory sectors of welfare provision. Wolfenden stressed the importance of a pluralistic system of welfare delivery, in which the voluntary sector would play a greater role in delivering welfare alongside the delivery agencies of the welfare state. This was a theme that was taken up by writers in what has become known as the welfare pluralist tradition. Thus, Hadley and Hatch (1981) referred to the 'failure' of the state in social welfare and emphasized the importance of voluntary organizations in contributing to greater diversity and participation in welfare provision. Another writer in this tradition argued for a 'de-monopolising strategy', involving a greater role for voluntary action (Gladstone 1979: 100).

Other observers, notably on the New Right, have argued a very different case for extending the role of the voluntary sector. For these critics of the public face of welfare, the voluntary sector is not so much an opportunity for increasing diversity and participation in welfare provision, as a means of providing a substitute for public provision (Harris 1986: 11). In 1980, one Conservative minister actually spoke of the statutory sector as a 'long stop' for the special needs going beyond the scope of the voluntary sector (Patrick Jenkin, quoted in Webb and Wistow 1982: 73).

The early 1980s witnessed what has been described as 'a crescendo of political rhetoric' in support of the voluntary sector, particularly in relation to the personal social services (Brenton 1985b: 177). The Conservative government elected in 1979 had campaigned on a manifesto which argued that central government should encourage the voluntary sector, the reasons for this being spelt out by the newly appointed Secretary of State for Social Services, Patrick Jenkin, later that year:

> As the Government sets about the tasks for which it was elected – cutting income tax, cutting public spending and curbing the burgeoning bureaucracies of the public sector – we shall be looking to the voluntary movement to take up more of the running.
>
> (quoted in Brenton 1985a: 147)

During the 1980s, Conservative government ministers praised the value of the voluntary sector's contribution to welfare provision. Thus in 1984, Jenkin's successor as secretary of state, Norman Fowler, referred to a 'wider conception' of social services, declaring that society must look away from the state and tap 'a great reservoir of voluntary and private effort'. As one commentator later observed, the advantages of such an approach were clearly seen to lay in the opportunity to cut public expenditure and diminish the role of the state, as well as according with the Conservative government's values of self-help and individual responsibility (McCarthy 1989: 43).

Similar sentiments were expressed in the 1983 Conservative Party manifesto, which welcomed what it described as the 'vital contribution' made by voluntary organizations to the social services, and pledged to continue to give such organizations strong support (Conservative Party 1983). Government funding of the voluntary sector increased considerably during the 1980s, amounting to over £4 billion by 1987, an increase in real terms of over 90 per cent since 1979 (Taylor 1992: 163). The Thatcher government also introduced additional tax concessions to encourage financial donations to charities. Writing in 1985, Brenton (1985a: 213) commented that the Conservative government's enthusiasm for the voluntary sector was 'a refraction of the market ideology'. The personal social services were particularly important, as the use of the voluntary sector in this area offered 'the possibility of privatising this part of the welfare state in a non-market form' (Brenton 1985a: 143).

Further significant developments followed the Conservative Party's victory in the 1987 general election, with the voluntary sector moving from a position where it complemented state provision towards one where it was expected to provide a substitute for such provision (Taylor 1992: 156). As we saw in Chapter 6, one manifestation of this movement was the housing legislation introduced in 1988, which gave local authority tenants the right to choose their own landlords, a policy designed to encourage the expansion of a particular part of the voluntary sector – housing associations – as alternatives to local authorities as the major providers of social housing. An even more important development introduced by the Conservative government which had implications for the voluntary sector was the introduction of quasi-markets in the personal social services. As we have already seen, the community care reforms of the early 1990s separated the roles of local authorities as purchasers and providers of community care and introduced arrangements in which voluntary organizations and private firms bid for contracts. Under these new arrangements, local authorities were expected not only to make the maximum use possible of the voluntary and private sectors in the provision of community care, but also to stimulate the development of new voluntary sector activity.

Thus, developments under the Conservative governments envisaged a greater role for the voluntary sector in the delivery of welfare, particularly in the field of housing and the personal social services. This emphasis on the service role of voluntary organizations was developed under the Blair government, which expressed its preference for a multi-agency partnership approach to the delivery of local services. It views voluntary organizations as the 'potential partners' of local authorities in securing improvements in both the quality and the cost of local service delivery (Department of the Environment, Transport and the Regions 1998: para. 7.27). In 1998, the Blair government launched a compact on relations between government and the voluntary sector. The compact seeks to develop 'undertakings' for both central government and the voluntary sector that will provide the basis for partnership in the making and implementation of public policy, and there is an expectation that similar compacts will be developed at the local government level (Home Office 1998).

But how desirable is the expansion of the voluntary sector in areas that have traditionally been provided directly by the delivery agencies of the welfare state? As Johnson (1987: 122) has noted, the voluntary sector has several features that give rise to serious misgivings. Not only is it characterized by an uneven coverage of services, but also it has been criticized for its weak accountability and lack of internal democracy. Housing associations, which are controlled by voluntary unpaid management committees, have been the subject of particular criticism, with suggestions that such groups run the danger of not only becoming self-perpetuating oligarchies, but also becoming merely rubber stamps for the decisions of their full-time managers (Hills 1987: 34). In Johnson's view, these kinds of defects are 'major failings' that can be tolerated only so long as the voluntary sector plays a relatively marginal role in the delivery of welfare (Johnson 1987: 122).

Anxieties have also been expressed that the development of contracts – as in community care – for the purchase of services may compromise the independence of voluntary organizations. There is the danger that as such organizations diversify into areas that will attract contract funding they will be diverted from more innovative and consumer responsiveness functions (Taylor 1992: 156–7). Similar concerns have been expressed by voluntary organizations themselves (see, for example, Common and Flynn 1992: 32). There is also the danger that local government's contractual/partnership relationship with the voluntary sector might lead to voluntary organizations becoming increasingly like bureaucratic and professional organizations (Lowndes and Wilson 2001: 635).

Partnerships between the public and private sectors

An extremely important manifestation of private sector involvement in the arrangements for the delivery of welfare under the Blair government has been the development of public–private partnerships. The Blair government has stated that it will adopt a pragmatic approach to the delivery of public services, 'looking hard – but not dogmatically – at what services government can best provide itself, what should be contracted to the private sector, and what should be done in partnership' (Cabinet Office 1999: 35). Public–private partnerships have been described as the Blair government's 'flexible friend' – 'a conveniently malleable term covering a host of diverse arrangements'. What such partnerships have in common is that public sector agencies commission and pay for services to be supplied by the private sector (The Economist 30 June 2001: 37). There have been a number of different partnership initiatives involving private sector organizations in the delivery of the major social services, ranging from the Private Finance Initiative, to partnership through education action zones, to the management of particular services. According to one Cabinet minister, partnerships between the public and private sectors are 'a cornerstone' of the Blair government's programme for modernizing the public services (Commission on Public Private Partnerships 2001: 33).

Central to PPPs has been the PFI. Under PFI, a private sector consortium contracts to design, build, finance and operate an asset-based service, which is leased to the contracting public sector agency, and which reverts to public ownership after a given period of time. The PFI was introduced by the Major government in 1992, with the aim of encouraging private sector investment in large-scale capital projects, but got off to a slow start. Although in opposition the Labour Party had been very critical of the PFI, the Blair government modified and relaunched the Initiative, which it sees as a key factor in its strategy for the delivery of high quality public services.

The PFI is central to the Blair government's strategy for modernizing the NHS, with private sector funding being used to build new hospitals, which are then leased to the NHS. In the first four and a half years of the Blair government, 64 major PFI hospital developments were approved. The NHS Plan published in 2000 included the planned delivery of over 100 new hospital schemes between 2001 and 2010, with an extended role for the PFI. Private sector investment under the PFI will rise to £7 billion over the period 2001–10 (Department of Health 2000a: paras 4.7–4.10). However, the use of the PFI in the NHS has been controversial. Some observers have pointed to the lack of convincing value for money gains for the NHS from the PFI (Commission on Public Private Partnerships 2001: 92). For example, it has been calculated that the cost of the PFI contract involving the design, ownership and service of the new Edinburgh Royal Infirmary, and its renting back to the NHS, will total some £900 million over a 30-year period, as contrasted with a cost of £180 million if the project had been financed from taxation or government borrowing (Cohen 1999). Critics of the PFI also argue that NHS trusts and health authorities have been forced to make savings on other budgets in order to make the high costs of investment affordable (Gaffney and Pollock 1999: 62).

The PFI has also been used by many local authorities as a way of injecting new capital investment into local public services such as education, the personal social services and housing. Schools have seen a particularly large number of PFI deals, including contracts with Waltham Forest London Borough Council, East Sussex County Council and Sheffield City Council to build secondary schools. Other local authority PFI deals have included an arrangement by Dudley Metropolitan Borough Council with NHS partners for the construction of a 'one-stop shop' for health and personal social services, and a contract with Surrey County Council for the replacement of 17 residential homes for elderly people (*Local Government Chronicle* 29 May 1998: 14; 28 April 2000: 20). One of the key measures in the Blair government's approach to improve council housing has been to promote and fund PFI schemes (Department of the Environment, Transport and the Regions 2001a: paras 4.7, 4.12), and a number of local authorities are taking part in pathfinder PFI schemes to improve their housing stock.

The PFI has been complemented by a variety of other public–private partnership approaches. In 2000, the DoH signed a Concordat with the

Independent Healthcare Association, under which the NHS in England is able to make greater use of hospital beds in the private sector. The private sector is also being used to develop 20 new diagnostic and treatment centres. In education (as we saw in Chapter 6) education action zones involve business and other partners to enable zone schools to form partnerships that can develop more effective ways of delivering education. Reports by Ofsted and the National Audit Office, however, criticized the initiative, and private sector sponsorship pledged for the zones was only expected to total £37 million. In late 2001 the government announced that it would not continue with zones beyond their initial five-year terms (Woodward 2001b). Private sector bodies also act as sponsors of the 15 CTCs – established by the Conservative government under the Education Reform Act 1988 (see Chapter 6) – operating in urban areas in England. The Blair government is committed to the establishment of city academies – publicly funded independent secondary schools to be set up in disadvantaged urban areas – which will be owned and run by sponsors from the private and voluntary sectors. This initiative was launched in 2000, and 13 partnerships had been announced by September 2001.

In addition to playing a key role in modernizing the infrastructure of public services such as health care, education, housing and the personal social services, private sector organizations have also developed a partnership role in the management of publicly funded services. A significant example is education, where, under the School Standards and Framework Act 1998, the Secretary of State for Education may direct a local education authority to contract out some or all of its education services if satisfied that the current discharge of its functions is inadequate. Following the passage of the 1998 Act, 17 organizations were approved as service providers, capable of providing the functions of a failing local education authority. As we saw in Chapter 6, the Blair government has intervened in a large number of local education authorities, and private sector organizations have been awarded contracts to run certain education services. Thus, in 1999, the London Borough of Hackney was directed to contract out two services – the School Improvement Service and the Ethnic Minority Achievement Service. Following a critical Ofsted inspection report in 1999, a private company took over the management of the local schools service from Islington. The following year, Leeds lost all its school support services to a new joint venture company, in which both Leeds City Council and a private sector company have a share.

Under the Blair government, there has also been private sector involvement in the running of schools. The first state school to be managed by a private company was King's College in Guildford. This followed the award of a contract by Surrey County Council to a private company in 1998 to establish a new school to replace the King's Manor school and to manage it on behalf of the local education authority. In 2001, another private sector firm signed a seven-year contract to manage another Surrey school (Woodward 2001a). One education minister has stated that 'as far as the Local Education Authorities are concerned, the private sector is here to stay' (Education and Employment Committee 2000: Q.161). Shortly after its re-election in 2001, the Blair government published a schools White Paper, which guaranteed private sector and voluntary organizations the opportunity to bid to run all new maintained schools. Ministers were also to be given reserve powers to require that private sector firms be involved if necessary in helping to turn around failing schools (Department for Education and Skills 2001: para. 6.24).

Public–private partnerships are clearly an important 'new element in the repertoire of public sector managerialism' under the Blair government (Ling 2000: 100). Advocates of this approach maintain that partnerships play an important role in developing a 'pluralist model of public management' (Commission on Public Private Partnerships 2001: 33). Critics, however, including some public sector unions, fiercely argue that such partnerships are a stage on the road to full-scale privatization – 'privatization by stealth' (Commission on Public Private Partnerships 2001: 24). As one writer has observed, however, 'the concept of public–private partnerships is clearly here to stay' (Curwen 2000: 19).

Further reading

For definitions and approaches to the notion of privatization, see Young (1986). Drakeford (2000) discusses the impact of privatization on the five core social services. Bartlett and Le Grand (1993) discuss quasi-markets. The relationship between the voluntary sector and the state, and the impact of New Labour, is examined by Lewis (1999). Essential reading on public–private partnerships is the report of the Commission on Public Private Partnerships (2001).

8

The search for efficiency and value for money

Attempts to introduce greater private sector involvement and market mechanisms into the delivery of welfare are part of a wider series of developments since 1979 designed to improve the management and efficiency of the delivery agencies of the welfare state. Such developments have been part of what has been described as 'a set of beliefs and practices, at the core of which burns the seldom-tested assumption that better management will prove an effective solvent for a wide range of economic and social ills' (Pollitt 1993: 1).

Concern with management and efficiency had, of course, been a theme in the debate about the delivery agencies of the welfare state long before the 1980s. As we saw in Chapter 4, developments in the management of local authority services in the late 1960s and early 1970s centred around the issues of improved coordination and the introduction of corporate management. In the NHS, the restructuring which took place in 1974 emphasized better management as being the key to successful reorganization. However, the turning point in the debate about efficiency came in 1979 with the election of the first Thatcher government, concerned to reduce both the cost and scale of the state. According to a former member of Margaret Thatcher's Efficiency Unit during this period, a major reason for this concern was that the theory of the welfare state had not included any emphasis on efficiency or value for money (Priestley 1986: 115).

As Pollitt (1993: 49) has pointed out, managerialism was a key element in the policies of the New Right towards the public sector, 'better management' providing a banner under which various initiatives could be introduced, including the injection of private sector disciplines, cost cutting, the reduction of professional autonomy, and the setting up of a quasi-competitive framework to 'flush out the "natural" inefficiencies of bureaucracy'. The 1980s were also, of course, a period dominated by the idea that the public sector had a lot to learn from the management systems and techniques employed in the private sector. Typical were the views of Michael Heseltine (1980: 68), the then Secretary of State for the Environment, with responsibility for local government, who argued in 1980 that 'the management ethos' should run throughout central government, local authorities and the NHS, as well as the private sector. This was a theme that was to be central to the Thatcher governments' emphasis upon greater efficiency and better value for money in the delivery of social and other public services.

According to Mather (1989), the Thatcherite commitment to better value for money was

> a straightforward concept, based on the underlying premise that monopoly services provided free at the point of consumption and untested by competitive forces are unlikely to be efficient in the medium and long-term; that they are likely to perpetuate restrictive practices and producer-led service delivery; and that they entangle the interests of those specifying the services . . . with those providing them.
>
> (Mather 1989: 213)

The result was that the gospel of public sector reform in the 1980s became what was described as 'managerialism couched in the language of the health farm'. Public sector organizations such as local authorities and the NHS were seen as being fat and needed to be slimmer (Gray and Jenkins 1982: 47). The principles behind this new approach were the search for efficiency, effectiveness and value for money (Gray and Jenkins 1986: 171). This commitment led to a series of important initiatives in all of the organizations responsible for the delivery of welfare: central government's social service departments – particularly the DSS (formerly the DHSS, and now revamped as the DWP) – and the other delivery agencies of local government and the NHS. This concern with the pursuit of efficiency and value for money has also been a central element in the Blair government's approach to the public services.

At the heart of the debate about the management of the delivery agencies of the welfare state since 1979 has been the emphasis on the achievement of the so-called 'three Es' – the values of economy, efficiency and effectiveness. The three concepts have been defined by the Audit Commission (1983):

> *Economy* may be defined as the terms under which the authority acquires human and material resources. An economical operation acquires those resources in the appropriate quality and quantity at the lowest cost.

Efficiency may be defined as the relationship between goods and services produced and the resources used to produce them. An efficient operation produces the maximum output for a given set of resource outputs; or, it has minimum inputs for any given quantity and quality of service provided.

Effectiveness may be defined as how well a programme or activity is achieving its established goals or other intended benefits.

(Audit Commission 1983: para. 36)

Effectiveness is the most difficult of the three concepts to measure, not only because of the problems involved in assessing the achievement of the goals of welfare delivery agencies, but also because the measurement of effectiveness invariably involves political issues (Radford 1991: 929). There have also been criticisms that too many Conservative government inspired managerial initiatives since 1979 used effectiveness and efficiency as substitutes for economy, the three concepts in practice often being reduced to economy or cost cutting (Greenwood and Wilson 1989: 12–13).

Central government social service departments and the search for efficiency

The period since the early 1980s has seen a series of initiatives to improve the efficiency of central government social service departments. Not surprisingly, in view of the amount of government expenditure involved and the range of services provided, the department responsible for the delivery of the massive social security programme (through the DHSS, then DSS, and now DWP) has been at the forefront of such initiatives. In addition to large cuts in civil service staffing (which in the 1980s fell particularly heavily on the DHSS and the two other social service departments of the DoE and the DES: see Drewry and Butcher 1991: 200), social service departments have been affected by a series of other initiatives designed to improve the efficiency of government departments.

One important initiative introduced in the early 1980s was the programme of detailed scrutinies of government departments designed to improve efficiency and eliminate waste, and undertaken by Sir Derek Rayner, the then managing director of Marks and Spencer, who was appointed as head of the prime minister's Efficiency Unit following the 1979 election. The Rayner scrutinies investigated a broad range of mainstream functions in the DHSS and uncovered a number of areas of waste and inefficiency, including the arrangements for the payment of social security benefits (see Warner 1984), the payment of benefit to unemployed people, and the arrangements for checking national insurance contributions. In the mid-1980s, the then DHSS estimated that the Rayner scrutiny recommendations accepted for implementation would ultimately result in annual savings of over £53 million (National Audit Office 1986: 16). Improvements in the operational efficiency and administrative costs of the social security benefits system were also expected to result as a consequence of the massive computerization programme, the Operational Strategy (OS), first announced in 1982 (Department of Health and Social Security 1982). We shall have more to say on the impact of the OS in Chapter 9.

The search for efficiency in the operations of central government in the early 1980s also required departments to improve their financial management. The year 1982 saw the launching of the Financial Management Initiative (FMI), involving moves towards the devolution of budgetary authority within departments, with middle and junior managers being held accountable for the management of the costs under their control and for the results achieved. The response of the DHSS was to establish a system of management based upon the principles of the FMI throughout its regional organization and central offices, based on cost centres with devolved budgetary responsibility. Speaking about the consequences of the introduction of the FMI at Newcastle Central Office (which included the operations later delivered by the Contributions Agency) one DHSS senior civil servant stated that managers at all levels had become more cost-conscious and able to work in 'a much more systematic fashion' (Thorpe-Tracey 1987: 335). The other government department responsible for the delivery of social security benefits (the then DEmp) also devolved budgetary responsibility to line managers.

The most dramatic change in the organization of the arrangements for the delivery of social security benefits since the early 1980s has been the establishment of executive agencies as a result of the Next Steps programme, a reform package associated with the Ibbs Report of 1988 (Prime Minister 1988), and reflecting the devolved budgeting principles of the FMI. Concerned by what it saw as an insufficient focus within central government departments on the delivery of services, Ibbs recommended that there should be a quite different way of delivering services, involving the hiving-off of the service delivery functions of departments from their policymaking core. The Next Steps programme involved the transfer of most of the service delivery functions of departments to semi-autonomous executive agencies. The managers of executive agencies are given certain managerial freedoms, but operate within the terms of framework documents set by the parent departments, which set out policy, the agency's budget and specific targets.

As a result of the agency programme, the day-to-day delivery of social security benefits is the responsibility of executive agencies. In the 1990s the Employment Service agency was set up within the DEmp, with responsibility for the administration of unemployment benefits and the running of the jobcentre network. The massive social security benefits delivery operations of the then DSS were transformed into the Benefits Agency in 1991 to become the flagship of the whole Next Steps programme.

The launching of the Benefits Agency followed on from the creation of the DSS's Information Technology Services Agency the previous year and the Resettlement Agency in 1989. The Conservative government also established the Contributions Agency, the CSA and the War Pensions Agency. As we saw in Chapter 2, following rationalization by the Blair government, what is now the DWP has four executive agencies, the Employment Service and part of the former Benefits Agency having been merged to form Jobcentre Plus.

The establishment of executive agencies transformed the structure and culture of the arrangements for the delivery of social security benefits. The delegation of important managerial freedoms to the chief executives of the Benefits Agency and the Employment Service, together with the setting of financial and quality targets, led not only to an emphasis on greater efficiency and value for money, but also to greater customer responsiveness (see Chapter 9). The Benefits Agency achieved or exceeded over 70 per cent of the secretary of state's targets, and 80 per cent of its internal management targets, in eight of the nine years following its establishment in 1991 (National Audit Office 1998: 1). But, although figures show that the Benefits Agency and other executive agencies normally met, and in many cases exceeded, their performance targets, this does not necessarily mean that there had been improvements in the overall efficiency and effectiveness of these organizations. As James (2001: 40–1) observes, in the case of the Benefits Agency the performance target system led managers 'to pay insufficient attention to the performance of activities that were not the main focus of targets'. For example, the agency's concern with budgetary targets resulted in less emphasis on redressing errors.

Indeed, there has been some concern about the efficiency of some aspects of the delivery of social security benefits by executive agencies. The CSA has been the subject of much complaint since its creation in 1991, being heavily criticized for its repeated failure to deliver an acceptable standard of administrative performance. One study of the CSA's operations referred to 'a catastrophic administrative failure' (Davis and Wikeley 1998: v). By the end of 1994, complaints against the CSA made up over one-third of the total of complaints against government departments made to the PCA, and the agency's chief executive, Ros Hepplewhite, resigned in the same year (see Harlow 1999). In 1999, the Blair government promised reforms, with a new and more efficient scheme to be introduced in 2002. In March 2002, the government announced that the planned start date for the reform of the CSA had been deferred owing to the fact that testing of the new computer system had not been completed (*Hansard* 2002). Neither did the Benefits Agency, the flagship of the whole executive agency initiative, escape criticism, being reprimanded soon after its creation by both the Parliamentary Commissioner for Administration and the House of Commons Social Security Committee over the chaotic introduction of the new disability living allowance in 1992. In 1998, the Comptroller and Auditor

General qualified his opinion on the social security accounts for the tenth successive year, pointing to fraud and errors in the payment of benefits (Public Accounts Committee 2000: para. 3).

Critics of the agency initiative have also maintained that there has been insufficient attention paid to the implications for accountability, especially with regard to the sensitive area of social security benefits payments. Particular concern has been expressed about the possible undermining of ministerial responsibility as a consequence of questions from MPs being referred directly to the chief executives of executive agencies (see Chapter 5). However, the troubled history of the CSA shows that in sensitive areas like child maintenance payments, an arm's-length relationship cannot be maintained between the responsible minister and the agency's chief executive.

The next stage in the Conservative government's attempts to improve efficiency and value for money in its delivery of social (and other) services was the introduction in 1992 of the market testing programme, whereby government departments and executive agencies were required to test the cost of providing services in-house against the cost of purchasing them from a private contractor, an extension of the CCT initiatives introduced in the NHS and local government in the 1980s (see Chapter 7). The market testing programme was seen by government as part of the increasing movement of public services to a culture in which relationships are 'contractual rather than bureaucratic' (HM Treasury 1991: 2). Although the early rounds of testing, like that in local government and the NHS, were confined to ancillary and support services (examples included the DSS's accommodation and audit services, and DoH office services), it was intended that the initiative should eventually proceed to areas 'closer to the heart of government'.

Market testing raised important issues. Thus a Benefits Agency feasibility study warned that the contracting out of the agency's social security fraud division, being considered as a candidate for contracting out under the market testing programme, could lead to blackmail and abuse of the system by unscrupulous employees of private firms (Travis 1993). Some observers saw the programme as a stepping stone to the eventual privatization of services currently delivered by government departments and their executive agencies. The crucial question was how far the contracting process would bite into the heartlands of service delivery in such areas as social security, once the obvious support services had been market tested (Stott 1994: 46). One commentator observed that private insurance companies, or even management teams of Benefits Agency staff, might eventually be able to tender for the delivery of parts of the social security system to the public (Hill 1994: 251). Although the Labour Party was initially critical of market testing, concerned about the principle of public provision and the accountability of private contractors, by the time of the 1997 general election, it was clear that under a Labour administration, some form of contracting out would remain a managerial tool available to the civil service. In office, the

Blair government replaced market testing with the Better Quality Services (BQS) initiative in 1999. Under this initiative, the best supplier of a service was to be identified through a process that considers the possibility of competition, but tendering was not to be compulsory (Cabinet Office 1998a).

Under the Conservative governments, central government departments were also affected by the Private Finance Initiative. One major contract awarded under the Major administration was that signed with the Contributions Agency by Andersen Consulting to develop and operate a replacement for the existing national insurance recording system. The Major government also awarded a contract to Pathway, a subsidiary of ICL computer services group, to deliver the Benefits Payments Card (although this was cancelled in 1999). The potential role of private sector involvement in improving the efficiency of service delivery has also been recognized by the Blair government. In 1998, in a project known as Private Sector Resource Initiative for the Management of the Estate (PRIME), the then DSS transferred the ownership and management of almost all its estate to a private sector consortium. It was estimated that the deal would save the department over £500 million over 20 years. The DSS also awarded PFI contracts for information technology services.

The search for efficiency in local government

The concern with efficiency, cost-consciousness and value for money associated with developments in central government departments has also been a feature of parallel developments in the field of local government. Attempts to improve the efficiency of local authorities are, of course, not new. Inefficiency and financial waste were identified as important consequences of local authority departmentalism in the mid-1960s by the Maud Committee (1967: para. 108). As Elcock et al. (1989: 139, 146) remind us, the introduction of corporate management in the 1970s – stimulated by the Bains Report of 1972 – was seen partly as a means of improving value for money in local authorities, being linked to the idea that failures of coordination between local authority departments led to 'sub-optimal expenditure'.

The attacks on inefficiency in local government by the Conservative government 1979–97, and its attempts to encourage a more business-like approach to the affairs of local authority services like education, housing and the personal social services, manifested themselves in a number of ways. The 1980s saw the introduction of a series of measures designed to tighten central government's control over local authority spending, notably the new system of distributing central government funding through block grant introduced in 1980, the system of spending targets for individual local authorities, rate capping, and the introduction of the controversial community charge, itself replaced by the council tax in 1993 (see Chapter 6).

One result of these initiatives was to put pressure on individual local authorities to make financial economies and to encourage the more efficient use of resources.

The Conservative government also attempted to introduce market disciplines into the operations of local authorities by requiring them to apply competitive tendering to a range of services previously provided in-house. Although, as we saw in Chapter 7, CCT did not bite deeply into the delivery of local authority social services, the development of the concept was a significant marker for the future. The reforms in community care which separated the assessment of need from the commissioning of care by local authority social services departments were also part of the 'new managerialism' which now characterized the local government welfare state, and were seen as setting in motion a process of change which would 'turn organisations upside-down' (Audit Commission 1992: para. 45).

Initiatives aimed at increasing efficiency were also introduced into the education and housing services. Thus the introduction, following the Education Reform Act 1988, of local management of schools, which devolved responsibility for at least 75 per cent of a school's budget to school governing bodies, was an attempt to increase management efficiency through the clear identification of responsibility for the delivery of educational services (McVicar 1993: 197). In the case of housing, in 1990 the Thatcher government introduced a new financial regime for local housing authorities in England and Wales which put a 'ring-fence' around the housing revenue account so as to prevent contributions from the local authority's general fund. The aim of this new regime was to ensure that the cost of housing services not met by subsidy would be covered by rents, the previous system having been criticized as providing a 'cover for inefficiency' in the management of local authority housing (Malpass and Murie 1990: 186–7; Forrest 1993: 46).

Probably the most important attempt to improve efficiency in local government under the Conservatives was the creation of the Audit Commission in 1983, established as a result of the Local Government Finance Act of the previous year. In the words of one commentator: 'While central government applied the resources brake, the Audit Commission stepped on the managerial accelerator' (Kelly 1991: 179). The Audit Commission has had a major impact on the management of the local authority departments responsible for the delivery of social services.

The Audit Commission is responsible for the external auditing of local authority accounts (and since October 1990 the accounts of NHS bodies), either by the Commission itself or by private accountancy firms appointed by it, a task which had previously been carried out by the DoE's District Audit Service, a body which had its origins in the mid-nineteenth century. The original concept of local authority audit focused on the narrow concern with legality and regularity, ensuring that proper accounting practices had been observed and that spending had been in accordance with the law. Although the 1982 legislation retains the concept of legality, it also requires individual auditors and the Audit Commission to promote value for money in local authorities. Thus individual auditors are responsible for ensuring that local authorities have made proper arrangements for securing economy, efficiency and effectiveness (the 'three Es') in their use of resources. The Commission is required to undertake studies leading to recommendations for improving the 'three Es' in the delivery of local authority services. Thus, one consequence of the Audit Commission's work has been a move away from the traditional concern with legality and regularity towards what has been described as a management consultancy style approach (Radford 1991: 930).

Value for money in local authorities is therefore directly linked with the 'three Es'. Each year, the Audit Commission produces a statistical profile for each local authority that looks at each of the services provided by that authority and tells it how its levels of service compare with similar authorities. The Commission also undertakes national value-for-money studies of individual services or areas of expenditure designed to identify what is working well and disseminate best practice. National studies have included reports on the housing aspects of community care, local education authorities, and mental health services for older people (Audit Commission 1998, 1999, 2000a).

Thus the Audit Commission acts as an important body in promoting management change in local authorities and in identifying possible savings in the cost of local social services. In the words of one study of local government budgeting (Elcock et al. 1989: 164), the Commission has been 'the external muscle behind VFM in local government'. It has identified substantial savings in the cost of the social services delivered by local authorities. For example, a report on the care of elderly people claimed that many local authorities might be able to provide 15–20 per cent higher service levels of residential care for elderly people at no extra cost (Audit Commission 1985: 3). The Commission's VFM studies have also played an important role in enabling local authorities to learn from good practice in other authorities (Environment, Transport and Regional Affairs Committee 2000: AC 13).

The Audit Commission's emphasis upon the potential for savings and its use of league tables is seen by Stoker (1991: 242) as an attempt to provide a 'countervailing force' to what public choice theorists see as the budget maximizing tendencies of local authority bureaucrats. Doubts, however, have been expressed about the methodology employed by the Audit Commission (see McSweeney 1988), and it has also been suggested that there is an 'effectiveness gap', the Audit Commission having placed too much emphasis on the first two 'Es' of economy and efficiency, at the expense of the third 'E' of effectiveness. Certainly, in its early years, the commission did concentrate on encouraging efficiency, though in the late 1980s there was a shift of emphasis towards the promotion of effectiveness (Henkel

1992: 75–6). One manifestation of this change was the introduction of the idea of 'service effectiveness': thus the key questions for local authorities identified in the Audit Commission's 1988 action guide included: 'Is the service getting to the right customers, in the right way, with the right services, in keeping with its stated policies?' (Audit Commission 1988b: 5). The Commission's growing concern with the users of services – increasingly described in the 1990s as customers – is highlighted by its statement that one of the key factors which characterize a well-managed local authority is that it 'understands its customers' (Audit Commission 1988a: para. 27).

Under the Blair government, the powers of the Audit Commission have been extended to include the monitoring of the Best Value initiative, the successor to CCT (see Chapter 7), and a key element in Labour's approach to improving the economy and efficiency of local authority services. With effect from April 2000, local councils were given the duty to secure the best value in the provision of services, and to undertake performance reviews of all their services. The initiative is monitored by the Best Value Inspectorate (which incorporates a Housing Inspectorate) under the auspices of the Audit Commission. Acting alongside other service inspectorates, including Ofsted and the Social Services Inspectorate, the Best Value Inspectorate ensures that local authorities have set challenging and realistic performance targets, and carries out special inspections where there is evidence of a failing service. The aim of the Best Value initiative is to ensure that, within a period of five years, all local authority services achieve the performance levels achieved by only the top quarter of councils at the start of the period. Each local council is given a star rating depending on how it performs, ranging from three stars for excellent performance to no stars for poor performance. If performance does not improve, the government has the power to transfer the control of a service to another service provider. A key feature of the Best Value initiative is the requirement that local authorities consult with service users about how services can be improved. We shall discuss the increasing customer orientation of local authorities in Chapter 9.

Towards a more efficient National Health Service

Management has been on the agenda of the NHS since it was first established, but it is a concern which has been characterized by changing ideas. Thus, from the creation of the NHS in 1948 to the early 1980s, health service managers were what Harrison (1988: 30) has described as 'diplomats', concerned with minimizing conflicts within the service and facilitating the work of the medical profession, rather than with attempting to bring about major change in the organization and delivery of health care.

Management as 'diplomacy' was reflected in the tradition of consensus management that was a major feature of the NHS during its first three and a half decades. There was shared managerial responsibility between senior medical and nursing staff and health administrators. A key feature of the reorganization of the NHS in 1974 was the institutionalization of this concept: in the words of Strong and Robinson (1990: 18), the NHS was to be managed 'not by a boss, but by a group of equals'. The idea of a chief executive responsible for the management of the new health authorities was specifically rejected, the DHSS stating that professionals were 'most suitably managed by members of their own professions' (Department of Health and Social Security 1972a: 57). Instead, the management structure of health authorities was based on a multidisciplinary management team, which brought together senior medical, nursing, administrative and financial staff. The management style was one of consensus, with the members of the management team taking decisions as 'a consensus-forming group', each of them having a veto over any particular decision (Department of Health and Social Security 1972b: para. 2.42). Consensus management undoubtedly had its strengths, including the wider dimension that it brought to decision-making and the commitment of management team members to the implementation of particular decisions. But the system also had its disadvantages, notably the fact that it often led to delays in the decision-making process as well as encouraging management team members to avoid difficult decisions (see, for example, Merrison 1979: paras 20.13–20.15).

Up to the early 1980s central government showed little interest in placing the medical profession in the NHS under managerial control (Harrison 1988: 22). As a result, the profession was able to exercise a large degree of discretion in the allocation and management of resources within the service. With the election in 1979 of the first Thatcher government, however, with its commitment to improving the efficiency and cost-effectiveness of the public sector, the NHS became dominated by what has been described as a 'managerialist agenda' (Wistow 1992a: 103). The Conservative government inspired a series of initiatives in which the manager was viewed as 'scapegoat' rather than as 'diplomat' (Harrison 1988: 56). Drawing upon practices in the private sector, these initiatives were designed to encourage efficiency and the better use of resources by health authorities. As Robinson (1988: 9) has observed, the NHS served, in many ways, as a 'testing ground' for the injection of an 'enterprise culture' into the public sector.

The starting point for these initiatives was 1982, a year identified by Davidson (1987: 43) as when 'management and managerial preoccupations took over the NHS'. Area health authorities were abolished in 1982 as part of the 'slimming down' of the NHS, and annual accountability reviews of RHAs by the DHSS were introduced, a process which was later extended downwards to include reviews of DHAs by the appropriate RHAs and reviews of individual units by DHAs. In the same year, drawing upon the experience of the efficiency scrutinies pioneered in central government departments, the DHSS also adopted the concept of Rayner-type scrutinies. These scrutinies have involved in-depth studies of particular areas of the

NHS where savings are thought to be possible – including such areas as residential accommodation, ambulance service control systems and catering costs.

Cost improvement programmes requiring DHAs to save money by operating more efficiently were introduced in 1984. Two years later, following a number of experiments in management budgeting, the Resource Management Initiative (RMI) was launched in order to develop systems which would provide senior medical and nursing staff with information enabling them to make better informed decisions about resource allocation (see Packwood et al. 1990). Other measures introduced during this period designed to improve efficiency included compulsory competitive tendering (see Chapter 7) and performance indicators (see pp. 153–4). All of these initiatives were based on the assumption that they would lead to improvements in efficiency within the NHS (Harrison et al. 1990: 86).

The high point of Conservative government-inspired initiatives to improve efficiency in the delivery of health care during this period was the Griffiths Report of 1983. Concerned by what it saw as a lack of management in the NHS, the Conservative government appointed a team of business people, led by Roy Griffiths (deputy chairman and managing director of Sainsbury's, the retail supermarket company), to give advice on 'the effective use and management of manpower and related resources' in the NHS. The inquiry's report was highly critical of consensus management, arguing that 'if Florence Nightingale were carrying her lamp through the corridors of the NHS today she would almost certainly be searching for the people in charge' (Griffiths 1983: 12). The report's diagnosis was that the NHS lacked general management support, with the result that there was 'no driving force seeking and accepting direct and personal responsibility for developing management plans, securing their implementation and monitoring actual achievement' (Griffiths 1983: 12).

Although recognizing that the NHS was not concerned with the profit motive, Griffiths argued that there were clear similarities between NHS management and business management, and, in particular, the level of services, the quality of products, meeting budgets, cost improvement, productivity, and motivating and rewarding staff. The inquiry said that it was surprised to find that there was no real continuous evaluation of performance in the NHS: precise management objectives were rarely set; there was little measurement of health output; clinical evaluation of particular practices was not common; and economic evaluation of these practices was very rare (Griffiths 1983: 10).

Griffiths' recommended cure for these perceived ills of NHS management was the appointment of general managers at the regional, district and unit levels of the service. General managers would be the best persons for the job regardless of discipline, with responsibility for the planning, implementation and control of performance at their particular level of the service. Griffiths also recommended the streamlining of the central management of the NHS through the establishment of supervisory and management boards (the management board subsequently became the NHS Executive: see Chapter 3). As Day and Klein (1983: 1813) put it, the management of the NHS was to change from a system that was based on 'the mobilisation of consent' to one based on 'the management of conflict', from a system that had 'conceded the right of groups to veto changes' to one that 'gave the managers the right to override objections'.

The Griffiths Report was accepted by the government in 1984, and two years later most regions, districts and units had appointed general managers on short-term contracts. The introduction of this 'new managerialism' was followed by the incorporation of such private sector practices as cost improvement programmes and management budgeting (see above), the introduction of individual performance review and performance-related pay for general managers, and the development of improved performance indicators enabling health authorities to compare their performances (Moon and Kendall 1993: 180; Pollitt 1993: 64).

The Griffiths Report, and the developments that followed it, was a radical change in the organization and culture of health care delivery. In the words of one observer, the NHS was transformed from a classic example of 'an *administered* public sector bureaucracy into one that increasingly is exhibiting the qualities that reflect positive, purposeful *management*' (Best 1987: 4, original emphasis). The Griffiths Report pushed management to the heart of the NHS: 'Where once there had been administration, now there was management from the top to the bottom of the service' (Strong and Robinson 1990: 27).

For critics of this 'new managerialism' (Townsend et al. 1988: 25), Griffiths represented 'the triumph of a set of beliefs about what was important and how things should be done':

> It thrust management and management preoccupations to the very centre of NHS thinking, pushing aside, or at least subordinating, the arguably less clearly formulated collection of ideas about service and the public good which had hitherto provided the dominant ethos.
> (Townsend et al. 1988: 25)

The management revolution in the NHS during the 1980s was the subject of much criticism, particularly the concern that the culture of private sector management was inappropriate for a public sector organization that had traditionally had a consensus style of management. Anxieties were also expressed that the search for efficiency in the NHS constituted a threat to the traditional values of the service. Thus for some critics, the developments of the 1980s constituted a change of direction from a concern with the overall quality of the service being delivered to 'a preoccupation with how resources can best (most productively) be used' (Townsend et al. 1988: 26). It was argued that the focus of attention had turned from questions of need to questions of efficiency. In the view of Townsend and his colleagues

(1988: 26), 'in substituting efficiency for need', the NHS was 'turning in on itself' and away from the social context within which it was operating.

On the other hand, other observers argued that the search for efficiency in the NHS in the 1980s did not go far enough, and that more radical initiatives were required. As one assessment of general management concluded, Griffiths was only a beginning (Strong and Robinson 1990: 182). Despite its radicalism,

> Griffiths . . . was only a partial break with the past . . . the service was still trapped, for general managers at least, within a national straitjacket. Local initiative was frustrated by ministers, by civil servants, by supervisory management tiers and by powerful professional bodies.
>
> (Strong and Robinson 1990: 164)

The real attempt to break with the past came in 1991 with the introduction of the NHS internal market. This was an idea very similar to one suggested a few years earlier by Alain Enthoven (1985), who argued that an approach to health care delivery in which market forces operated within the NHS would improve efficiency in the use of resources. The internal market was the centrepiece of the package of NHS reforms contained in the 1989 White Paper *Working for Patients* (Department of Health 1989a) and given legislative effect a year later by the National Health Service and Community Care Act. As we saw in Chapter 7, this involved the separation of the purchaser and provider roles of DHAs, who (along with fund-holding GPs) purchased health care services from their own hospitals, hospitals in other districts, the new self-governing hospitals run by the NHS trusts, or the private sector. The theory behind the internal market was concisely put by Perrin (1992):

> well-managed providers will have incentive to improve efficiency and performance quality in order to attract more 'sales' of services to purchasers, thus increasing their share of funding but also consequently exerting pressure on less successful competitors to, in turn, improve their own efficiency and quality so as to avoid cut-backs or possible redundancies or closures.
>
> (Perrin 1992: 266–7)

Thus a key objective of the Conservatives' NHS reforms was to improve value for money in the delivery of health care by introducing systems and incentives designed to achieve greater efficiency (King's Fund Institute 1989: 5). The reform package included other measures designed to strengthen management and the control of spending, such as the extension of the RMI, the introduction of medical audit, and the inclusion of a management element in the criteria for consultants' merit awards (see Department of Health 1989a). According to Wistow (1992b: 71), this was a set of reforms that seemed to represent a government commitment to the achievement of 'a substantial transfer of power and influence from medicine to management'.

The Conservative government's introduction of the internal market was 'the most radical reform of the NHS' since its creation in 1948 (Baggott 1998: 188). In the event, it has been suggested that the internal market had 'a rather ambiguous impact' on the efficiency of the NHS. Recorded improvements related to statistics that were the subject of criticism, and efficiency gains were offset by the operating costs of the new system (Baggott 1998: 198).

Although, in opposition, the Labour Party was committed to abolishing the internal market, in office the Blair government accepted the purchaser–provider split, although it used the term commissioning rather than purchasing. Fund-holding was abolished, and contracts were replaced by long-term service level agreements, with PCGs commissioning health services (see Chapter 3). Primary care groups were given devolved responsibility for a single unified budget, the intention being that this would provide family doctors and community nurses with the maximum flexibility and efficiency in the use of resources. As seen in Chapter 3, PCGs were replaced by PCTs in April 2002.

The Blair government also introduced a number of other measures designed to improve the efficiency of the NHS. It established the National Institute for Clinical Excellence to issue guidance on cost-effectiveness and clinical effectiveness, together with a Commission for Health Improvement, with responsibility for scrutinizing standards and providing advice on the action required to improve quality. Under legislation passed in 2002, the Commission is to be turned into an independent body (with an Ofsted-style inspection role), allowing it to recommend that the Secretary of State for Health impose special measures on failing NHS bodies. As we shall discuss in the next section, one of the key principles behind the Blair government's approach to driving efficiency in the public sector has been through a more rigorous approach to performance.

Performance indicators and welfare delivery

A key element in attempts to improve efficiency and encourage value for money in all three major delivery agencies of the welfare state has been the development of performance indicators, a concept described by one Conservative minister in the mid-1980s as having a vital part to play in ensuring that public money is being spent as efficiently as possible (Pollitt 1985: 4). More recently, the use of performance indicators has been seen as a way of monitoring the achievement of corporate objectives, holding organizations accountable, identifying opportunities for improvement, and encouraging service improvement by publicizing performance (Audit Commission 2000b: 6). Yet another technique that has been transplanted from the private sector, performance indicators in the public sector draw heavily on the private sector concept of management accounting (Greenwood and Wilson 1989:

10–11). Performance management was widely used under the Thatcher and Major administrations, and, if anything, has become even more prominent under the Blair government (Rouse 1999: 89).

The central government department responsible for the massive social security system has used performance indicators for many years. Indicators designed to compare the performance of local social security offices through the regular monitoring of such aspects as work done and the accuracy of payments, were introduced in the then DHSS as long ago as the mid-1970s (Garrett 1980: 124). In the late 1980s, the department introduced a nation-wide Quality Assessment Package (QAP), measuring quality of services indicators such as caller waiting times, the quality of interviews, and the quality of correspondence within local social security offices (see Carter et al. 1992: 96–100). The setting of annual performance targets has been central to the operations of the agencies responsible for delivering social security benefits, although there have been criticisms that targets have con-centrated on quantitative efficiency indicators such as clearance times for the handling of benefit queries and benefit assessment accuracy, rather than on effectiveness indicators, especially those regarding quality and customer satisfaction (Carter and Greer 1993: 412; Greer 1994: 74).

An important development in central government performance meas-urement under the Blair government has been the introduction of PSAs for each government department and some cross-cutting areas (for example, care and support for older people, and the *Sure Start* programme), showing aims, objectives and related performance targets, and the progress they are expected to make over a three-year period (see Chapter 4). Just over half of the 1998 targets for the then DSS were performance targets – for example, to simplify the child support scheme. The rest were productivity targets, concerned with the efficiency of delivery (Department of Social Security 2001: 13). Since 2000, PSA targets have been much more orientated towards desired outcomes rather than the outputs of departmental activities.

Performance indicators have also become an important factor in the work of local government. Many local authorities introduced performance indicators during the 1980s, a leader in the field being the London Borough of Bexley, which introduced targets for each of its services, together with comparisons of performance in previous years (Bexley 1984). The National Consumer Council (1986) helped to develop performance indicators for local authorities for housing and services for the under-fives. Local housing authorities were required by the Local Government and Housing Act 1989 to publish the results of their performance in the form of a list of specified indicators. Evidence showed that performance indicators in local authorities – like those used in social security agencies – concentrated on economy and efficiency rather than on issues of effectiveness and quality (Burningham 1992: 89).

Further developments in the measurement of local authority perform-ance took place as a result of the Citizen's Charter (see Chapter 9), which emphasized the importance of providing the public with comparative information on how public services perform, partly as a way of pressurizing delivery agencies to emulate others. One important manifestation of this approach introduced in 1993 was the requirement that local authorities measure their performance in individual services against indicators drawn up by the Audit Commission, and publish details of their performance. Examples of such indicators have included the success of housing authorities in collecting rent, the numbers of under-fives receiving education, and the number of people cared for in residential homes. The Audit Commission did not specify statutory performance indicators for 2001–02, focusing instead on the development of voluntary indicators that address cross-cutting issues and the quality of life for local people. Another spin-off from the Citizen's Charter has been the publication since 1992 of annual statistics for examination results for secondary schools, which appear as 'league tables' in the national press. Annual statistics for examination results for further education colleges and sixth form colleges, as well as statistics for primary school tests, are also published.

Performance indicators are at the heart of the Best Value regime introduced by the Blair government, with the Best Value performance management framework requiring local authorities to report within a national framework of performance measures, designed to enable comparisons to be made between the performance of different local authorities. Key indicators reflect the effectiveness and quality of local services for each of the major services; strategic objectives; cost/efficiency; service delivery outcomes; quality; and fair access. For example, local education authorities have to indicate adult education expenditure per head of adult population, housing authorities have to indicate the satisfaction of tenants of council housing with the overall service provided by their landlord, and local authorities responsible for personal social services have to indicate the percentage of people receiving a statement of their needs and how they will be met (Department of the Environment, Transport and the Regions 2001a). Each local authority is expected to set targets for service improvement in respect of these indicators and to publish those targets, and subsequent performance against them, in annual local performance plans.

Performance indicators have also become an important feature of management in the NHS, enabling comparisons to be made between different health authorities and assisting DoH ministers and officials in their attempts to assess the performance of health authorities in the efficient use of resources. Developed in response to parliamentary criticism of the then DHSS's failure to ensure effective financial control over health authorities (see Public Accounts Committee 1981), the first set of NHS indicators was introduced in 1983 and consisted mainly of the repackaging of existing statistics, such as the average length of stay in bed by hospital speciality. As Carter and his colleagues (1992: 107) graphically observed, statistics that had been available in the NHS for decades 'suddenly emerged re-born and re-christened as performance indicators'. Following criticisms that too many of the indicators referred to costs and not health care outcomes, subsequent sets of indicators became more sophisticated, but they were still criticized for being too concerned with efficiency rather than effectiveness, thereby reinforcing a cost containment approach to management (Long 1992: 64).

In 1998, the NHS Executive (1998: 3) concluded that the old approach to performance measurement gave health authorities and trusts 'an incentive to focus more on counting the number of patients treated rather than what the treatment meant for the health and wellbeing of patients'. The Blair government introduced a broader based approach to looking at performance in the NHS, designed to evaluate the quality of care and the outcomes that patients expect from NHS treatment. In 1999 the government published the NHS Performance Assessment Framework assessing performance across the six areas of health improvement, fair access, effective delivery of appropriate health care, patient and carer experience, health outcomes, and efficiency. The framework was later underpinned by 49 high level performance indicators covering the six areas, and clinical indicators focusing on certain specific issues of clinical care.

In 2001, in what the Secretary of State for Health described as 'a significant step towards developing a new public sector enterprise culture in the NHS', the DoH published league tables showing the performance ratings of every major hospital trust in England (Batty 2001). Trusts were ranked on the basis of nine core indicators such as waiting times, cancelled operations, patient satisfaction and cleanliness. Each hospital was given a star rating. The top 35 performers received three stars and were given greater freedom to spend their share of money from a NHS performance fund. The worst performers received no stars, and were given a short period of time to improve their services, with management teams from the best-performing trusts being sent in if they failed to raise their standards. The star system was introduced for local authority personal social services in 2002 (Social Services Inspectorate 2002).

Although the use of performance indicators has become an increasingly important feature in the operations of all the delivery agencies of the welfare state, both their design and use has been seen as 'highly problematic' (Carter 1989: 136). Initially, performance indicators concentrated primarily on the criteria of efficiency and economy rather than broader questions of effectiveness and quality. Not surprisingly, it was suggested that this emphasis might be a reflection of the concern of Conservative governments with cutting public expenditure and attacking inefficiency (Pollitt 1986: 159). More recently, there has been a greater emphasis on the measurement of outcomes, with the appropriateness of services to the needs of their users being incorporated into some performance measurement systems. As we saw earlier, both the NHS Performance Assessment Framework and the Best Value performance indicators have incorporated the category of 'fair access'.

There has been particular debate about the government's comparative tables on school examination performance and the performance of NHS hospitals and trusts. Concern has been expressed that what appear in the tables to be low-performing schools are, in fact, performing very well in terms of apparently unpromising academic material, and it has been suggested that value-added tables measuring how much individual schools add to the performance of their original intakes would be a much better indication of performance. Following a pilot project involving 200 schools in 2001, league tables intended to assess the value added by each school for 14-year-olds was introduced nationally in 2002. Doubts have also been expressed about the value of hospital tables that compare different sized hospitals with different kinds of caseloads and located in different areas.

As Carter (1989: 133) points out, the use of performance indicators in the social services is also complicated by the problem of determining who actually 'owns' performance. Performance is often constrained by the interdependence of different units or activities within a delivery agency. He cites the NHS as an example of such interdependence, involving as it does the involvement of a number of different staff – radiologists, anaesthetists, surgeons, nurses, social workers and others – whose individual contributions to the care of a patient may be difficult to disentangle. It is also difficult to unravel the effects of outside influences on performance. Thus critics of school league tables argue that they fail to take account of social class on the performance of school children (Carter et al. 1992: 32).

There is also the danger that the use of performance indicators will have unintended consequences, including putting undue pressure on the managers of welfare delivery agencies. A critical report by the National Audit Office (2001) published in December 2001 listed six NHS trusts where waiting lists had been 'inappropriately adjusted'. Investigation reports that followed allegations of inappropriate adjustments said that the adjustments were made in the context of pressure on the trusts to meet departmental performance targets.

Despite such concerns, performance indicators, and the league tables that often accompany them, have become a valuable tool in the drive by successive governments to improve standards in the major social services. As we have seen, there has been a greater concern with outcomes in the use of such measures. As we shall discuss in Chapter 9, the delivery agencies of the welfare state are also making use of user surveys and other mechanisms to evaluate the performance of services.

From welfare administration to welfare management

Thus there have been a series of developments under both Conservative and Labour governments since the early 1980s designed to ensure that the various delivery agencies of the welfare state adopt a more business-like

approach to their operations. The guiding principles behind these developments have been the search for efficiency and value for money. Such
initiatives have introduced 'a world where bureaucrats . . . are redefined as
accountable managers, public sector operations sub-divided into *businesses*,
and the public seen as the *customer*' (Gray and Jenkins 1986: 171, original
emphasis).

Critics have argued that attempts to introduce managerialism into
the delivery agencies of the welfare state are incompatible with the values
of the public administration model that has traditionally underpinned the
organization of the delivery of welfare. Discussing developments in central
government departments during the Thatcher era, Greenwood and Wilson
(1989: 141, original emphasis) argued that the attitudes and practices of the
private sector 'cannot *easily* be transplanted' into the public sector. In particular, concerns about accountability and equity – two of the traditional
features of the public administration model of welfare delivery – are seen as
obstacles to the wholesale introduction of such techniques. Thus the decentralization of responsibility to line managers may conflict with traditional
notions of accountability (Greenwood and Wilson 1989: 139), while the
search for value for money may lead to the downgrading of the imperative
of equity of treatment (Gray and Jenkins 1985: 157).

As we have seen, the search for efficiency has also been criticized
for its narrow concern with cost cutting and inputs, the first two 'Es' of
economy and efficiency. The 1990s and early years of the twenty-first
century, however, have been characterized by a greater concern with the
third 'E' of effectiveness and there has been a greater emphasis on customer
responsiveness and issues of quality within the delivery agencies of the
welfare state, what has been referred to as 'managerialism with a human
face' (Pollitt 1991: 3). We turn to these developments in Chapter 9.

Further reading

Pollitt (1993) provides an analysis of the ideas behind the 'new managerialism'
of the late 1980s and early 1990s, while Taylor-Gooby and Lawson (1993)
examine the emergence of the managerialist perspective in the delivery of
welfare in the 1990s. Developments in government departments under the
Thatcher government are discussed in Drewry and Butcher (1991), while
Butcher (2000) provides a discussion of more recent developments. James
(2001) discusses the important Next Steps initiative, including the Benefits
Agency. For a discussion of managerial developments in local government,
see Elcock (1996) and Painter and Isaac Henry (1999). Corby (1999) provides a survey of management changes in the NHS since 1979.

9

The customer orientation

In addition to the challenges posed to traditional methods of welfare delivery by such developments as privatization, in its various manifestations, and the search for efficiency and value for money, the period since the early 1980s has been characterized by a growing concern with the encouragement of greater consumer responsiveness. Under successive governments, the delivery agencies of the welfare state have been expected to become more sensitive to the demands of their service users or customers, as they are increasingly described by government. There has been a recognition that the delivery of welfare involves much more than value for money, and one commentator has even extended the 'three Es' of economy, efficiency and effectiveness associated with the managerialist approach discussed in Chapter 8 to include the fourth 'E' of 'excellence' (Gunn 1988: 21).

Central to this concern with 'excellence' has been the recognition that the consumers of services – the customers – should be at the heart of the arrangements for delivering welfare. Like most of the initiatives associated with the managerialist approach discussed earlier, the concept of consumerism and customer care is an idea which has its origins in the literature of private sector management. The importance of being close to the customer is particularly associated with the ideas of two influential North American writers on organizations, Tom Peters and Robert Waterman, the authors of the best-selling book, *In Search of Excellence* (1982). Written when the authors were both partners in a leading management consultancy firm, McKinsey & Company, the book developed a set of basic principles shared by what Peters and Waterman describe as the United States' 'best-run' companies. One of these principles was being 'close to the customer'. Peters and Waterman concluded that 'excellent' companies were dominated by an organizational culture that focused on customers, learning their preferences and catering to them. Customers were not regarded as a nuisance or ignored, but were regularly listened to, with companies often getting some of their best product ideas from them. 'Excellent' companies had what amounted to an 'obsession' with customer service (see, for example, Peters and Waterman 1982: 156–7).

Closeness to the customer is part of what Connelly (1992) has described as the weak version of consumerism. It is a view of consumerism that is

> an orientation towards the consumers of goods/services rooted in a sense of public service with its concomitant moral obligations towards the public. It is simply the desire to make things better for the consumer by taking the consumer's point of view and attempting to improve service in the light of that standpoint.
>
> (Connelly 1992: 30)

A second, and stronger, version of consumerism is rooted in the notion of customer sovereignty. In this sense of the concept, consumerism leads to the situation in which an organization 'provides the goods and services that customers want in the quantity, quality and manner in which they want them' (Connelly 1992: 30). It is a concept derived from the private sector, where if customers cannot obtain high quality goods and services from a particular supplier, then they will go elsewhere for them. Although Connelly (1992: 31) argues that consumerism in this strong sense of the concept cannot apply to the NHS and the other social services, as we saw in Chapter 7, market mechanisms were introduced into welfare delivery by Conservative governments in the late 1980s and early 1990s through such initiatives as the contracting out of local authority services and the creation of quasi-markets in the NHS and community care.

Consumerism in the weaker sense of the concept – closeness to the consumers of services – is an approach which has increasingly been taken on board by welfare delivery agencies in Britain, especially local authorities. Thus a report published by the Association of County Councils (ACC) in the early 1990s argued that improving closeness to the customer was one of the main challenges facing local government. The customer-orientated council was seen as one which puts the needs, wants and priorities of the public 'at the centre of everything it does' (Webster 1991: 7). The customer orientation in local government has also been emphasized by the Audit Commission, the watchdog of local government efficiency and value for money, which has stressed the importance of local authorities 'understanding customers', rather than simply assuming what the needs of those customers ought to be (Audit Commission 1988a: para. 27).

Beyond the local government welfare state, other welfare delivery agencies, such as NHS bodies and the central government executive agencies concerned with the delivery of social security benefits, have also recognized that customer care should be at the heart of the delivery of services. Thus the architect of general management reforms in the NHS, Sir Roy Griffiths (1988b: 196), maintained that the consumer dimension must 'be seen as part of a total management and organizational philosophy', while the former Benefits Agency identified 'customer service' as one of the core values paramount to its business. The customer orientation was also manifested in the Citizen's Charter programme begun by the Conservative government in the early 1990s, and developed by the Blair government, with its emphasis on greater sensitivity to consumer needs.

In the words of one writer on developments in this field, by the late 1980s, consumerism in the arrangements for delivering social services had become 'an officially-approved fashion' (Pollitt 1987: 43). The customer orientation became a key feature of arrangements for the delivery of welfare under the Major government. This approach has been continued by the Blair government, which has argued that citizens should 'come first', declaring that it wants 'public services that respond to users' needs and are not arranged for the provider's convenience' (Cabinet Office 1999: 23). The remainder of this chapter will critically examine some of the ways in which the customer orientation has manifested itself in the organization and workings of the delivery agencies of the welfare state.

Consumerism in local government: the public service orientation

An important approach which transfers Peters' and Waterman's concept of being 'close to the customer' to the public sector in Britain, an 'anglicised version' of their philosophy (Cole and Furbey 1994: 227), is the 'public service orientation'. A term originally devised by Michael Clarke and John Stewart (1985), the public service orientation is an approach which is associated primarily with local authorities, although, as we shall discuss later, elements of its philosophy can also be found in initiatives undertaken by the NHS.

The emphasis of the public service orientation is on 'service *for* the public' and not 'service *to* the public' as the major organizational value of local authorities (Stewart and Clarke 1987: 167). It argues for greater responsiveness to the public as customers of local services, arguing that local authorities should look at their services from the viewpoint of the public, rather than simply from the viewpoint of the local authority. The public service orientation argues that local authorities should get closer to the customer by seeking views and opinions on services, maximizing customer choice, and providing customers of services with standard of service statements, as well as making services more accessible. Thus, the public service orientation stresses delivery agencies which are outward looking and proactive, rather than inward looking and reactive (Elcock 1991: 104).

Since the early 1980s, the concept of the customer orientation and customer care has gained increasing prominence in local government. Typical is Kent County Council Social Services Department's mission statement, which stresses one of its values as 'Putting the service user first'. Another local authority which is at the forefront of such initiatives is York City Council, which states that involving customers is at the core of the council's approach to policy creation (Public Administration Committee 2000: App. 36). Local authorities have undertaken a range of initiatives in an attempt to become more consumer responsive in the delivery of welfare (Fenwick 1989; Webster 1991; Lowndes et al. 1998). These initiatives have included discovering more about customers' views; providing the public with more information about services; improving access to services; using performance indicators; increasing public participation and accountability; and developing a customer culture. Performance indicators and issues of public participation and accountability were discussed in Chapters 5 and 8. This section therefore concentrates on the other types of initiatives designed to improve consumer responsiveness. (Much of the discussion in this section draws upon information available on the web sites of the local authorities cited.)

Finding out what the public need and want from local authority services is 'at the heart' of getting closer to the public (Webster 1991: 16). Thus local authorities, a notable example being Kent County Council, have undertaken surveys in an attempt to obtain information about what the public wants from education and the personal social services. Thus, Kent's Social Services Department issues consultation papers on such issues as its proposals for developing services for people with learning difficulties. York City Council's Community Services Department employs sophisticated research techniques to ensure thorough and inclusive consultation on housing issues, with tenants being consulted about all major projects, and panels and focus groups also being used for consultation. Cumbria County Council has a Discussion Forum where local residents can contribute to discussion on such issues as social services through the internet. Local authorities have actively sought complaints and comments from the public as a means of discovering what customers think about services. For example, having discovered that customers wanted a range of services delivered from one point, the London Borough of Lewisham introduced 'Access Point', offering services such as housing benefit, education, pupil benefits and general information and advice. Weekly exit surveys and a range of customer focus groups assist Lewisham in finding out what service users require.

Making more information available about services is another important element of the customer orientation. Thus Kent Social Services Department provides information fact sheets on the services that it provides, while York's Community Services Department has produced a housing information handbook setting out the rights and responsibilities of council tenants. As we saw in Chapter 1, one criticism that has been made of local authorities has been the lack of attention given to providing access to services. The barriers to access have included geographical inaccessibility, inconvenient opening hours, language restrictions and unwelcoming reception areas. As will be discussed later, many local authorities have reorganized their delivery of the key welfare services of housing and social services on the basis of decentralized offices to ensure that services are geographically accessible to consumers. Other attempts to improve access for the public include improved reception areas in social services departments in attempts to create more welcoming atmospheres for the consumers of their services. Lewisham's local housing offices are equipped with induction loops to assist people with hearing aids, and provide face-to-face interpreter services. The translation of social services departments' leaflets and other information about services into ethnic minority languages is a feature in many local authorities. Local authorities have also recognized that training has an important part to play in getting front-line staff to be more customer sensitive.

Another important manifestation of the customer orientation in the delivery of welfare by local authorities has been the increasing use of users' charters and customer contracts giving local residents specific guarantees of certain standards of service, an approach which was taken up at the national level by all three major political parties in the early 1990s and manifested in the Conservative government's Citizen's Charter (see pp. 169–75). Such charters were pioneered by York, whose Labour-controlled council intro-duced a Citizen's Charter in 1989. Newcastle-upon-Tyne City Council has a Customer Service Charter setting out the standards of customer care that can be expected from its Community and Housing Directorate and other directorates. Its Social Services Directorate has a charter for long-term care that sets out standards of care.

Thus, the customer orientation has become 'a familiar part of the vocabulary of local government' (Fenwick and Snape 1996: 45). The culture of many local authorities has changed dramatically since the early 1980s: local authorities have placed the customer at the centre of their arrangements for welfare delivery. A survey commissioned by the DETR, and carried out in the late 1990s, indicated that most local authorities made use of service satisfaction surveys, and complaints and suggestion schemes. It was clear that local authorities had responded to the consumerist agenda that had developed under the Conservative governments in the 1980s and early 1990s. Growing numbers of local authorities have also been making use of new methods such as citizens' panels and citizens' juries (Lowndes et al. 2001: 207–8).

Going local: the decentralization of welfare delivery

An important element of the customer orientation within local authorities is the attempt to make local services more accessible to the public. One aspect of this approach has involved the transfer of managerial responsibility for service delivery to decentralized offices. As a result of developments since the 1980s, locally based offices are now almost the norm in local authority housing and social services departments (Lowndes 1992: 53). By the end of the twentieth century, decentralization had become a 'main-stream concept' (Fenwick and Bailey 1998: 27).

The decentralization of local services like housing and the personal social services is not a completely new phenomenon. Decentralization initiatives can be traced back to the area management experiments under-taken in such authorities as Stockport and Newcastle-upon-Tyne in the mid-1970s (see, for example, Harrop et al. 1978), but the real starting point for more recent developments is the metropolitan district of Walsall, which set up a network of 32 neighbourhood housing offices in the early 1980s (see Fudge 1984). Although closely associated with what were described as New Urban Left local authorities (Hackney, Islington, Manchester, Birming-ham and others) and their criticisms of paternalistic and unresponsive local authority bureaucracies (Gyford 1985), the decentralization of services has been introduced by local authorities of all political complexions, including the formerly Liberal Democrat controlled London Borough of Tower Hamlets and Conservative-controlled East Sussex. As one commentator argues, decentralization has been seen as a new 'managerial paradigm', which is accompanied not only by increased customer responsiveness, but also by increased efficiency (Lowndes 1992: 53).

Individual local authorities have approached the decentralization of housing and the personal social services in a number of different ways. Many schemes involve what Elcock (1996: 189) describes as 'departmental decentralization', where a single local authority department decentralizes its delivery of services to local offices. Housing has been at the forefront of such initiatives, with London boroughs like Hackney and Lambeth decentralizing housing management, partly as a response to the challenges directed at the local authority housing service by the Thatcher government during the 1980s. County councils like East Sussex have decentralized the personal social services through 'patch' systems in which small teams of social workers and other social care staff are responsible for particular neigh-bourhoods (see, for example, Elcock 1986b). By contrast, other local author-ities have developed decentralization across departmental boundaries, what has been termed 'corporate decentralization' (Elcock 1996: 189). A notable example of this latter form of decentralization is the London Borough of Islington, where, in the mid-1980s, housing services, personal social services, environmental health services, welfare rights and community work were all decentralized to 24 neighbourhood offices serving average populations of 6500 (Burns et al. 1994: 112–14). In more recent years, some local author-ities have set up 'one-stop' offices that provide access to a range of services (Fenwick and Snape 1996: 47).

An even more radical form of decentralization was introduced in the mid-1980s in another inner London borough, Tower Hamlets, which,

under a Liberal Democrat council, combined administrative decentralization
with political decentralization, involving political input into decisions about
service delivery. Tower Hamlets was divided into seven neighbourhoods,
each of which had a Neighbourhood Committee, consisting of councillors
from wards in those neighbourhoods, which was given an annual budget
and responsibilty for the delivery of the council's services in their area.
Managerial responsibility in each neighbourhood was in the hands of a team
of six neighbourhood managers, headed by a chief executive who reported
to the Neighbourhood Committee, who were each responsible for particular
functions, including housing and the personal social services (Lowndes and
Stoker 1992). Other local authorities, including Middlesbrough, Islington
and York, have experimented with neighbourhood councils and neighbourhood forums (see, for example, Burns et al. 1994).

One advantage of decentralization is that, because they are smaller
and closer to local residents, neighbourhood and area offices are more
accessible to local people. Corporate decentralization is also seen as enabling
local people to be able to identify more with a single multi-service neighbourhood office than with a range of individual service offices. Decentralization is also said to generate a greater responsiveness to the needs of local
areas by the deliverers of services, who are able to acquire information about
the needs and priorities of the people in their particular neighbourhood.
The staff of neighbourhood offices can also build up contacts with local
community associations and voluntary organizations (Lowndes 1992: 54–5;
see also Elcock 1986b: 46; 1988: 47). The closeness of the deliverers of local
social services to the customers of their services may also lessen the risk
of the 'accountability outwards' of welfare professionals to professional
colleagues becoming too dominant compared with their 'accountability
downwards' to users (Elcock 1986b: 36).

Despite such advantages, the decentralization of local services like
housing and the personal social services has met with a certain amount
of resistance. Decentralization challenges the principles of bureaucratic
structure and professionalism which have traditionally underpinned the
organizational arrangements for delivering local authority services, and which
have been key features of the public administration model of welfare
delivery (see Stewart 1987: 50). It involves an increase in the powers of
the front-line staff of local social services and housing departments, the
so-called 'street level bureaucrats', responsible for the actual delivery of
services at the area or neighbourhood level, thereby weakening the roles of
senior staff at the centre. In addition to resistance from senior managers,
there has also been opposition from local authority trade unions, concerned
with the implications of service decentralization for the employment conditions of their members (Elcock 1996: 189–90). Inevitably, decentralization
also involves considerable capital and staffing costs (Stoker 1988: 205).

The decentralization of local services has been criticized as being
essentially a managerialist exercise. Thus it has been suggested that the

decentralization of the personal social services in East Sussex was a means of resolving the problem of controlling field units in the county's social services department (see Chandler 1996: 147). A study of the decentralization of housing services has concluded that local councillors have supported an approach to decentralization which has been stronger on such qualities as convenience and accessibility than on council tenant control or empowerment (Cole 1993: 164). Although many local authorities have introduced decentralization, few have decentralized political authority in order to allow local communities to make political decisions – British experience 'remains piecemeal and limited' (Fenwick and Snape 1996: 51). As Jeffrey (1997: 25) has concluded, most local councils have not involved people in decision-making: decentralization stops short of 'democratization'.

Decentralization has been predominantly a consumerist approach to the problems of delivering welfare at the local authority level, rather than a collectivist approach which focuses upon such issues as the empowerment of service users through control by user groups and other approaches (see also Hambleton and Hoggett 1988). Decentralized structures for local authority decision-making have been suggested by the Blair government as a way of bringing decision-making 'closer to the people' (Department of the Environment, Transport and the Regions 1998: paras 3.48–3.52); the Local Government Act 2000 includes the option of some local authority functions being performed by area committees, which may be advisory or decision-making bodies. Evidence indicates, however, that, although area committees are a feature of many local authorities' new decision-making processes, such bodies tend to be consultative rather than decision-making bodies (Environment, Transport and Regional Affairs Committee 2001: LAG 17).

Consumerism in the National Health Service: rhetoric and reality

The importance of 'getting closer to the customer' has also been a key theme in the restructuring of the NHS since the mid-1980s. As we saw in Chapter 1, the NHS has been criticized for being 'producer orientated' rather than 'consumer orientated'. The subject of consumerism was placed firmly on the agenda by the Griffiths inquiry into NHS management in 1983. Echoing Peters and Waterman (1982), Griffiths (1983) stressed the importance of customer opinion in the management of the NHS. Griffiths was critical of the NHS's failure to look after what it described as its customers, stating that:

> Businessmen have a keen sense of how well they are looking after their customers. Whether the NHS is meeting the needs of the patient,

and the community, and can prove that it is doing so, is open to question.

(Griffiths 1983: 10)

Griffiths (1988b) later argued that consumerism must be centre stage in the NHS:

It is central to the approach of management, in planning and delivering services for the population as a whole to ascertain how well the service is being delivered at local level by obtaining the experience and perceptions of patients and the community: these can be derived from Community Health Councils and by other methods, including market research and from the experience of general practice and the community health services.

(Griffiths 1988b: 196)

Consumerism had, of course, not been completely neglected in the NHS before the Griffiths Report. Community health councils were set up in the mid-1970s with the specific task of representing the interests of the local community to those responsible for the management of local health services, while a Health Service Commissioner was appointed to supplement the procedures available for the redress of grievances within the NHS (see Chapter 5). However, neither of these two developments was the result of a deliberate decision to give greater priority to the interests of the NHS's consumers: they were both ad-hoc reactions to particular problems within the service (Harrison 1988: 28).

Following the Griffiths critique, there was an increased awareness by NHS managers of the importance of consumerism. A number of techniques were introduced in the 1980s in an attempt to improve the responsiveness of the NHS to its users. Health authorities attempted to discover what the public thought of hospital services through the use of patient satisfaction surveys and questionnaires, often in conjunction with CHCs. Other initiatives included the development of improved patient literature and information, such as the newspapers circulated by some DHAs, and the establishment of staff development programmes for dealing with the public. In addition, all RHAs designated a member of staff with responsibility for either quality assurance or customer relations (Carr-Hill et al. 1989: 5). On a broader level, some health authorities also published mission statements focusing on the consumer.

Despite such developments, however, these initiatives were criticized for being part of what has been described as the 'customer relations movement'. Echoing the concerns expressed about consumerism in local government, critics argued that consumerism in the NHS was about customer relations, rather than about empowering the consumer. Consumerism in the NHS was described as a 'supermarket model' of health care, denying patients the right to be consulted about what should be 'on the shelves' and failing to encourage them to seek redress if the goods are faulty (Scrivens 1988: 184). According to Winkler (1987: 1), consumerism in the NHS was a 'harmless version' of consumerism, an approach that required 'little serious change, but much public visibility'. It was 'about the appearance, not substance, of change'. Other critics argued that while consumerism might well lead to better communication and feedback, it did not contribute very much to solving the problems of scarce resources and staff shortages which might lie behind the poor quality of many social services – 'a smiling doctor or nurse is not contributing much to effectiveness when telling a patient that he or she has to wait months for an operation' (Harrow and Willcocks 1990: 295).

Nevertheless, the NHS has continued with its consumerist approach. Health authorities have employed such approaches as focus groups, panels of local people that meet on a regular basis to discuss health service issues, with background information provided by the health authority (see, for example, Bowie et al. 1995). Another approach has been the use of citizens' juries (12 to 16 randomly selected local people chosen to match a profile of the local community) by a number of health authorities. Thus, Kensington, Chelsea and Westminster Health Authority used a citizens' jury to consult local opinion on the standard of mental health care provision (Coote and Mattinson 1997).

Consumerism is an important part of the Blair government's approach to the delivery of health care, emphasizing that NHS care 'has to be shaped around the convenience and concerns of patients' (Department of Health 2000a: para. 10.1). The government is committed to providing far greater information about local health services (Department of Health 2000a: para. 10.2). Its NHS Direct service, introduced in 1999, enables people to telephone, 24 hours a day, for health care advice and information from experienced, qualified nurses. The government is also introducing patient surveys countrywide to enable members of the public to feed back their views on NHS services, with every NHS organization being required to publish an annual account of the views received and the action taken as a result. As we saw in Chapter 5, a national patients' organization, the Commission for Patient and Public Involvement in Health, is to be set up to promote public involvement in the NHS. Echoing the words of Roy Griffiths 13 years earlier, one Labour government health minister stated that the patient 'must be at the centre of everything the NHS does' (Department of Health 2001e).

Consumerism in central government

The growing attention given to the customer orientation has also been taken on board by the central government department directly responsible for the delivery of welfare – what is now the DWP. The DWP's predecessors, the DSS and the DHSS, had not scored well on the criterion of 'closeness to the customer', having long been the subject of complaints regarding the quality of service delivery (see Chapter 1). The importance of the customer orientation was forced to the top of the DHSS's agenda in 1988 following critical reports on the quality of service it delivered to members of the public from both the House of Commons Public Accounts Committee and the body which provides its supporting professional assistance and information, the National Audit Office. The report by the National Audit Office (1988) on the quality of service provided by the DHSS's nation-wide system of local offices revealed that there was a significant amount of dissatisfaction with the services provided, notably over high levels of inaccurate or late payments, delays in processing claims, long waiting times, and the poor accommodation and facilities provided for both staff and claimants. Such concerns were reinforced by the Public Accounts Committee (1988), which concluded that there were a number of local offices providing a poor standard of service.

Criticisms about the quality of the delivery of social security benefits were repeated in a report by a group of DHSS civil servants, who were given the task of examining the organization and location of social security work and advising on a new structure for the department's local office network. The new structure was expected to maximize the opportunities to improve the quality of services delivered to the public. Known as the Moodie Report, after its principal author, and published in 1988, the group's findings concluded that the service provided for the DHSS's customers varied enormously 'from the quite outstanding to the quite appalling' (Moodie et al. 1988: para. 6). Like the Public Accounts Committee and the National Audit Office, the group highlighted examples of poor quality service, including the time taken to process claims, waiting times in local offices and accuracy in the making of payments. One of the group's main conclusions was that the social security system had to project a consistent and recognizable image which transmitted 'positive messages' to its customers (Moodie et al. 1988: 2). As the group's report put it: 'Social security is in the business of service. Its product is good quality service' (Moodie et al. 1988: para. 2).

Thus the Moodie Report put the customer at centre stage. Speaking of the social security system, it said:

> Few organisations can have greater claims to be a consumer organisation. Social security is a service which at some point or another, in some form or another, touches the whole population in ways which are uniquely personal and intimate.
>
> (Moodie et al. 1988: para. 3)

One immediate manifestation of this new customer orientation emerged the following year in the form of a set of 'principles of good service' that the staff of what was now the DSS had to adopt, including efficiency, responsiveness to the public's needs, and fairness, and which emphasized that the new department aimed 'to provide a good service to the public – a professional service that is fair, impartial, prompt, courteous and accurate, and which recognises each one of our customers as an individual' (Department of Social Security 1989). The commitment to improving the quality of service to its customers had been further reflected in the introduction of a Quality Assessment Package in the late 1980s (see also Chapter 8), which involved the monitoring of the quality of the service provided to the public (National Audit Office 1988: para. 2.3; see also Carter et al. 1992: 99–101).

Improving the quality of service delivery to the public was also one of the objectives of the massive computerization of the social security system, known as the Operational Strategy and completed in the early 1990s. One of the objectives of the OS was to improve the quality of service delivery by treating individual claimants as 'whole people' rather than according to the particular benefit being claimed (Margetts 1991: 327– 8). Unfortunately, the project, which was the largest civil computerization programme ever installed in Europe, was beset with problems and critics claimed that not all of the hoped-for benefits were achieved. Margetts (1991: 341) concluded that the OS was characterized by top-down design and implementation, and that although social security claimants might have been renamed 'customers', their needs had remained a low priority. According to Bellamy and Taylor (1998: 43), the OS 'did little to simplify the DHSS's relationship with "customers"'. Indeed, it proved 'a handicap rather than a help in developing a more consumer-sensitive approach to benefits delivery'.

Despite these developments, the most significant manifestation of the recognition of the customer orientation in what is now the DWP has been the creation of executive agencies as a result of the Next Steps programme launched in 1988 (see Chapter 2). A major aim of the Next Steps initiative was to deliver services in a way that is more responsive to the needs of customers. As one senior official of the then DSS told the House of Commons Select Committee investigating the whole Next Steps initiative, the Benefits Agency stood to be judged by 'the extent to which there is an observable and, indeed, a measurable difference in the quality of service we give'. In his opinion, if the Benefits Agency did not improve service, 'we shall have wasted our time' (Treasury and Civil Service Committee 1989: para. 48).

The Benefits Agency, along with the CSA and the Employment Service, developed a clear customer orientation. The main way in which service to the customers of executive agencies is measured is by the setting of performance targets. For instance, in 2000–01, the Benefits Agency was required to improve the performance of the lowest performing offices, and to contact at least 2 million pensioners encouraging them to claim the pensioner Minimum Income Guarantee. In the same year, the CSA's performance targets included reducing the number of complaints compared with its caseload to less than 0.15 per cent. Given that, unlike customers in the private sector, the customers of the CSA and what is now Jobcentre Plus cannot 'shop around for the best deal', the use of such performance targets is clearly important in helping to provide incentives for improved service to the public (Treasury and Civil Service Committee 1990: para. 54).

As part of its attempts to develop an efficient and customer related delivery service, the Benefits Agency also undertook nationwide, representative customer surveys, and consulted customers' representative groups. The Employment Service also carried out customer satisfaction surveys, testing views on the quality of service being provided. As we shall discuss in the next section, both the Benefits Agency and the Employment Service, along with other key delivery agencies of the welfare state, published customers' charters setting out the standards of service which the users of their services were entitled to expect.

The customer orientation has continued under the Blair government, with the DSS, and its successor, the DWP, responding to the agenda laid out in the *Modernising Government* White Paper (Cabinet Office 1999). The DWP is pursuing ways of bringing consumer views more directly into the delivery of services, including the development of customer strategies for each of its client groups. From 1999 to 2002, the Benefits Agency worked with the Employment Service, and local authorities, in 12 pilot areas for the 'One Service' – aimed at delivering a more integrated benefit service for people of working age (see Education and Employment Committee 1999b). As we saw in Chapter 2, in April 2002 parts of the Benefits Agency were merged with the Employment Service to create a new agency, Jobcentre Plus, which offers an integrated service to people of working age. The DWP's new Framework setting out its arrangements for managing the department from April 2002 emphasized that the department would 'have a clear focus on its customers' (Department for Work and Pensions 2002: iii).

The Citizen's Charter: focusing on the customer

The late 1980s witnessed the publication by several pioneering local authorities (mainly Labour controlled) of charters and customer contracts informing the users of local services about the standards which their councils hoped to achieve in those services and explaining the arrangements for redress if these promises were not met. The early 1990s also saw the publication of proposals for national charters by the Labour Party (1991) and the Liberal Democrats (1991).

Following his appointment as prime minister in late 1990, John Major announced that the Conservative government was developing 'the most comprehensive quality initiative ever launched', which would offer nothing less than 'a revolution in the way public services are delivered' (Hetherington 1991). The initiative was officially launched as a White Paper entitled *The*

Citizen's Charter in July 1991 (Prime Minister 1991). The stated purpose of the Citizen's Charter was to improve the quality of public services and to make them more responsive to their users (Prime Minister 1991: 2).

The underlying aim of the charter was described by the then Treasury minister responsible for its implementation, Francis Maude, as being 'to encourage those who work in public services to think about what they do in relation to how it affects the customer, the user of services'. He indicated that one of the most important principles underlying the Charter was the orientation of public services towards their users, in contrast to the preoccupations of the conventional bureaucratic structure, in which people 'tend to think about their own role in relation to others within the organisation rather than in relation to those outside.' The important relationship was seen as that which exists between the organization and the user of its services (Parliamentary Commissioner for Administration Select Committee 1992: Q.3).

Echoing this description of the philosophy behind the Charter, the deputy director of the government's Citizen's Charter Unit later stated that the Charter was about 'the outward face of the organisation: the relationship between public services and their users' (Goldsworthy 1993: 140). According to her, the Charter put itself 'in the shoes of the recipient of services', asking such questions as: 'What can I as an individual expect from this organisation?' 'Does this represent my full and fair entitlement?' 'Have I received what I was told to expect?' 'What is the organisation going to do for me if it fails to deliver the standards that I as an individual have been told I can expect?' Thus the aim of the Citizen's Charter was to raise the standard of public services and to make them more responsive to their users. It attempted to make the idea of the customer 'a reality' (Goldsworthy 1993: 141).

In attempting to emphasize the customer orientation, the Citizen's Charter, like other developments in the arrangements for the delivery of welfare introduced since 1979, was based upon the assumption that the public sector can learn from the private sector (see, for example, Connolly et al. 1994: 27). The Major government itself stated:

> Through these Charters the citizen can increasingly put pressure upon those responsible for providing services to deliver them to a high standard, rather as commercial competition puts consumer pressure on the performance of private sector organisations.
>
> (Prime Minister 1992: 1)

The Citizen's Charter had four main themes:

- to improve the quality of public services
- to provide choice, wherever possible, between competing providers
- to tell citizens what service standards are and how to act where service is unacceptable
- to give full value for money within a tax bill the nation can afford.

The Charter's principles applied to all the public services, including the wide range of social services delivered by the Benefits Agency, the Employment Service, local authorities and the NHS. Its publication was the prelude to the publication of a number of specific charters in a range of public services, including those for parents of school-age children, students in further and higher education, NHS patients, council house tenants, jobseekers and people receiving social security benefits.

Described by the Conservative government as the beginning of a long-term programme, 'a programme for a decade', the Citizen's Charter was only a starting point, being seen as 'a toolkit of initiatives and ideas to raise standards in the way most appropriate to each service' (Parliamentary Commissioner for Administration Select Committee 1992: Qs. 1, 17). The means by which the Charter was to be implemented covered a range of different initiatives and ideas, including more privatization; increased competition; further contracting out; greater emphasis on performance-related pay; the publication of local and national performance standards; comprehensive publication of information on the standards achieved; more effective complaints procedures; tougher and more independent inspectorates; and better redress for the citizen when things go wrong (Prime Minister 1991: 5). The Charter was seen as John Major's 'big idea', the prime minister's attempt to put his own stamp on the reform of the public sector, what one commentator described as 'a vehicle for symbolically differentiating him from his predecessor' (Doern 1993: 20). As we have seen in previous chapters, however, some of the initiatives involved in the implementation of the Charter's principles, especially privatization, contracting out and performance indicators, were not new. They were clearly extensions of initiatives introduced by the Thatcher government in the 1980s.

Although part of a wider consumerist movement to bring such services as social security benefits, the NHS and the various social services delivered by local authorities closer to the customer, the Citizen's Charter also included initiatives which fitted in with the stronger version of consumerism discussed in the early part of the chapter. Thus part of the solution to what were seen as the problems of consumer choice was seen as lying in the introduction of increased competition and choice, and the development of contracting out through the government's plans for market-testing. The Cabinet minister originally responsible for ensuring that the public services were implementing the Charter principles stated that the introduction of competition into public provision 'cannot . . . properly be done without one key organisational reform, namely the separation of purchaser from provider' (Waldegrave 1993: 17). Hence, as we have seen in previous chapters, the new arrangements for welfare delivery included the introduction of market-type conditions through such mechanisms as quasi-markets in the NHS and community care. This particular approach emphasized the importance of the consumer, in that markets are expected to offer consumer choice, a key principle of the Citizen's Charter. However, as we saw in our earlier discussion of these developments, these changes did not really empower the consumer at all. Under these new arrangements, patients and users of community care were represented by fund-holding GPs and care managers in decisions about the choice of hospital or residential home.

Thus the Citizen's Charter was an official recognition of the importance of quality and consumerism in the public services: what has been described as 'an original and radical approach' to public sector reform (Farnham 1992: 79). But as Drewry (1993: 250) observed, the Charter's invocation of 'citizenship' was 'highly misleading'. The Charter was about promoting the responsiveness of public services and not about enhancing people's rights as citizens. In the words of two observers:

> The emphasis is upon individual rights to choice and to quality, with little reference to citizens' duties. Accountability is seen as market based . . . The public is seen as having acquired rights to services through the payment of taxes rather than community membership.
>
> (Stewart and Walsh 1992: 507)

Or as another commentator observes, the Citizen's Charter appeared to have a view of citizenship that was

> stunted and uni-dimensional. It is rooted in the assumption that the citizen is primarily an economic person, a consumer and a tax payer who is concerned largely with economic and market rights rather than with any non-economic rights.
>
> (Farnham 1992: 80)

The contemporary concept of citizenship has conventionally been associated with the writings of T.H. Marshall, the British sociologist. Marshall (1963: 87) defined citizenship as 'a status bestowed on those who are full members of a community', and identified three rights with which it was associated – civil rights, political rights and social rights. Civil rights consist of the rights necessary for individual freedom, such as liberty of the person, freedom of speech, freedom of religion, and equality before the law. Political rights involve the right to take part in the exercise of political power through either voting in elections or serving as an elected member of Parliament or as a local councillor. These civil and political rights were supplemented by the social rights introduced by the welfare state in the post-war period, such as rights to health care, education and a basic income (Marshall 1963: 74).

According to Barron and Scott (1992: 533–4), the Citizen's Charter appeared 'to contain little that Marshall might have acknowledged to be an enhancement of citizenship'. As they pointed out, the Charter suggested no new initiatives for the protection of civil liberties, said nothing on political rights and promised no new entitlements to social welfare. What they referred to as 'the novelty' of the Charter lay more in its language and ideology than in the policies that it set out. The conception of the citizen as 'entitlement based on need' was reconceived as the conception of 'a paying customer, who as such is entitled to receive the level of quality which could be guaranteed were the provider constrained by the pressure of competition in the marketplace' (Barron and Scott 1992: 535, 543).

The Citizen's Charter was essentially a consumer's charter, and, as we shall discuss below, was the subject of the same kind of criticisms that have been made of other attempts to enhance consumerism in the delivery agencies of the welfare state. Its critics accused it of adopting a 'simplistic approach' to the public services, concentrating on the 'repackaging' of existing services, and ignoring the more complicated considerations that are essential for the development of quality services in the public sector (Local Government Information Unit 1991: 4). The charter was also criticized for involving no extra resources for the development of those services. Thus the Patient's Charter, for example, pointed out that the 'rights' which it outlined were 'not legal rights but major and specific standards which the Government looks to the NHS to achieve, as circumstances and resources allow' (Department of Health 1991b). As the Citizen's Charter (Prime Minister 1991: 6) itself emphasized, the charter programme was about 'finding better ways of converting the money that can be afforded into even better services'. This particular feature of the charter programme aroused much criticism, an assistant manager in the Benefits Agency being quoted as saying that 'most of us see it as quite a cynical exercise to paper over the cracks in the service' (Willmore 1992), while another critic argued that it would be no consolation to people who went to a local authority housing department 'to be told politely, quickly, efficiently and courteously that there [were] no houses available and it [was] unlikely that there [would] be any available to meet their demands' (*Hansard* 1991).

The Citizen's Charter was relaunched by the Blair government in 1998 under the new title of *Service First*, a label that was thought to better reflect the revamped programme's emphasis on delivering services that meet people's real needs. Underlying the new approach was the criticism that the Charter had been a top-down system, with particular initiatives 'owned' by the service providers rather than the users of services. *Service First* was to employ a bottom-up approach driven by the needs of service users (Cabinet Office 1998b: 1). All existing charters were to be reviewed after consultation with service users (see Table 9.1). The *Service First* programme included a People's Panel (5000 randomly selected men and women) to provide the public's views on the delivery of public services. Critics of this particular initiative argued that it was difficult to keep a fixed group of people on such a large body, and, following an evaluation carried out by the Office of National Statistics, the People's Panel was wound up in early 2002 (Wintour 2002).

The Charter's principles of public service were expanded to nine principles of public service delivery (see Table 9.2). One of the principles

Table 9.1   Main social services charters 2002

Benefits Agency Customer Charter
Charter for Further Education
Charter for Higher Education
Child Support Agency Charter
Council Tenant's Charter
Jobseeker's Charter
Your Guide to the NHS

Table 9.2   Principles of public service delivery

- Set standards of service
- Be open and provide full information
- Consult and involve
- Encourage access and the promotion of choice
- Treat all fairly
- Put things right when they go wrong
- Use resources effectively
- Innovate and improve
- Work with other providers

Source: Cabinet Office 1998b

of public service emphasized by *Service First* is the setting, monitoring and publication of service standards, so that the users of services know what to expect from those services. Thus the Jobseeker's Charter specifies that jobcentres will display up-to-date and available job vacancies, the time a jobseeker has to wait to be seen in a local office, the time taken to answer the telephone, and the time taken to give a full reply to a letter. Quality standards and maximum waiting times are also included in *Your Guide to the NHS*, the successor document to the Patient's Charter.

Another major theme highlighted by *Service First* is the provision of information – about how services are run, how much they cost and how well they perform. Thus *Your Guide to the NHS* gives NHS patients the right to be given detailed information on local health services. The Jobseeker's Charter sets out the services that the jobcentre network of Jobcentre Plus offers to its clients in helping to get them a job and information on the benefits that can be claimed while working. The importance of information is also emphasized by the Council Tenant's Charter, which sets out the right of council tenants to expect information from the local council.

Service First also emphasizes the importance of consulting and involving the users of services, and using their views to improve services. Thus, as we have already seen, the former Employment Service regularly surveyed the views of its customers. The Council Tenant's Charter states that a council must consult tenants about important changes. The former Benefits Agency talked to organizations that represented its customers, and suggestions could also be made to the customer service manager of the local office.

As befits a document that emphasizes the interests of the consumers, and not the providers, of services, a central theme of *Service First* is the promise to put things right when they go wrong. Thus *Your Guide to the NHS* promises that complaints about NHS services will be investigated, and that complainants will receive a full reply within four weeks. If a patient is not satisfied, they can ask for an independent review (see Chapter 5). The Benefits Agency's Customer Charter, inherited by Jobcentre Plus, informs people that if they are not happy about the way a complaint has been dealt with, then they can ask for it to be looked at by an independent complaints panel for that area.

Consumerism or citizenship?

The 1980s and the 1990s saw a growing concern with consumer responsiveness in the operations of the delivery agencies of the welfare state. Critics, however, have argued that these kinds of developments have not been sufficient. As one commentator put it: 'Consumerism is fine as far as it goes, but it does not go far enough to affect a radical shift in the distribution of power' (Potter 1988: 157).

Thus, for observers like Rhodes (1987), the public service orientation within local government needs to be set in a wider context than service delivery. As we have seen, a major criticism of consumerist approaches in local government has been that they are essentially managerialist. While such approaches enable the consumers of services to have a greater say in informing the deliverers of services about their needs, they do not normally involve consumers in meeting those needs. Thus consumerism in local government has tended to see the public as customers rather than as citizens. Critics argue that reforms to the delivery of welfare services need to go beyond the consumerist approach. As Rhodes (1987: 66) observes, the consumers of public services are also citizens, defined by the Greeks as those who shared in decision and office. Thus the arrangements for the delivery of services need to recognize this duality of roles through, for example, a greater concern for citizens' rights of participation and representation.

Similar criticisms have been made of attempts to increase the responsiveness of local services through decentralizing the delivery of such services as housing and the personal social services, it being argued that decentralization has been mainly a modification to traditional ways of delivering services rather than a radical change in the workings of local authorities (Stewart 1987: 51). While there have clearly been important gains, improved public access and more responsive local services, the decentralization of welfare delivery has not led to any fundamental change in the distribution of managerial – let alone political – power. Decentralization has been essentially concerned with the reform of the administrative arrangements for the delivery of local authority services. Critics of these initiatives emphasize the importance of the democratization of services, as well as the localization, of services (see, for example, Hambleton and Hoggett 1988). Such an approach includes the devolution of power to local communities through such mechanisms as user group participation and forms of local decision-making which involve both elements of local representative democracy and community groups.

The argument that the concept of the citizen has been defined too narrowly has also been a criticism of the development of user charters for the major social services. Thus, in the Major government's Citizen's Charter, elected local authorities, traditionally the major delivery agencies of the welfare state, were seen solely as agencies for the efficient and responsive delivery of services. Despite the fact that local government had traditionally been justified, in part, on the basis of its contribution to local democracy and accountability, local authorities were viewed as organizations that arrange for the delivery of services. There was no recognition of the role of local authorities as the representatives of local communities, nor of the importance of local democracy as a means of 'resolving conflicting aspirations for services' (Local Government Information Unit 1991: 4). As Stewart (2000: 259–60) points out, an emphasis on the public as customer reflects the dominance of the view of local authorities as providers of services. 'If the local authority is seen as a political institution constituted for local government, then the emphasis will be on the public as citizen'. The traditional conception of a local authority as a political institution is through representative democracy. A different conception of representation is as 'an active and continuing process'. Such a conception requires innovation in democratic practice, including such initiatives as the greater use of citizens' juries (see, for example, Hall and Stewart 1997).

The Blair government's relaunched charter initiative – *Service First* – has also been criticized as failing to enhance citizenship rights. According to one observer, the 'only way to strengthen the Citizen's Charter is to strengthen citizenship' (Taylor 1999: 37). According to Taylor (1999: 37), ultimately 'the success of a strengthened Charter will depend upon how far citizens are not merely offered a service but have a say in the planning and delivery of that service'.

Enhancing public participation is part of the Blair government's democratic renewal programme for local government (see Department of the Environment, Transport and the Regions 1998). As Leach and Wingfield (1999: 47) point out, however, the main emphasis of Labour's agenda seems to be on improved responsiveness rather than the introduction of 'alternative structures of democracy'. They point to the danger of the participatory agenda being marginalized and local authorities concentrating 'their energies on customer-orientated methods which . . . do little to improve *political participation* in local government'. Such methods may actually distract from political participation because 'they enable individuals to interact with public bodies as customers rather than as citizens, thus avoiding the messy complexities of politics' (Leach and Wingfield 1999: 57–8, original emphasis).

Further reading

Approaches to customer orientation in the public sector are discussed by Flynn (1997). The web sites of individual local authorities provide information on the impact of the customer orientation on local government. On the decentralization of local services, see Burns et al. (1994). Readers requiring an understanding of the Blair government's approach to customer orientation should read *Service First* (Cabinet Office 1998b). This can be supplemented by *Modernising Government* (Cabinet Office 1999), which offers an overview of the Blair government's approach to public sector reform.

10

Conclusion: the new governance of welfare

For most of the post-war period, the welfare state in Britain was dominated by what we described in Chapter 1 as the public administration model of welfare delivery. The five core social services which formed the basis of the classic welfare state that emerged in the late 1940s were delivered by a combination of national and local governmental organizations – the central government departments concerned with the payment of social security benefits, elected local authorities, and the NHS – who, for the most part, were responsible for both the funding and provision of social services. On the periphery of the public face of welfare, a number of quasi-governmental bodies, such as the Housing Corporation, carried out a range of important managerial and promotional functions.

Looking at the, still evolving, organizational arrangements for the delivery of welfare at the beginning of the twenty-first century, there have been substantial changes. At the national level, the government department responsible for the delivery of social security benefits – what is now the DWP – has been transformed, with semi-autonomous executive agencies, headed by chief executives on short-term contracts, now directly responsible for the day-to-day delivery of benefits. At the local level, elected local authorities, for long the major front-line delivery agencies of the welfare state, have moved towards an enabling role, with a large number of quasi-governmental, voluntary and private sector bodies now having increasing responsibility for the delivery of welfare in the fields of education, housing and the personal social services. The organization and management of the NHS has also undergone radical reform, built around a split between those bodies commissioning health care services and those providing them. There is an emphasis on partnership between the public, private and voluntary sectors.

As we have seen throughout this book, since the early 1980s there has been an increasing questioning of the efficiency and effectiveness of traditional bureaucratic arrangements, in which professionals have played a key role, in the delivery of welfare, and a movement towards more 'business-like', performance-driven and customer-focused forms of delivery. Under the Thatcher and Major governments, the assumptions and practices of the traditional public administration model of welfare delivery were severely challenged, and there was the emergence of a new paradigm, sometimes described as the 'new public management', which emphasized a more managerialist and consumerist approach to the organization of the public sector. This approach has been continued by the Blair government, as part of its wider programme of 'modernizing government', although there have been important changes and shifts of emphasis. This concluding chapter reviews the impact of the Thatcher and Major governments on the arrangements for the delivery of the major social services, and considers how the public administration model of welfare delivery was affected by these developments. It then discusses the impact of the first Blair government.

The Thatcher and Major governments: the public administration model reassessed

In Chapter 1 of this book, we identified five key features of the traditional public administration model – its bureaucratic structure, the dominant role played by welfare professionals, the value of public accountability, the concern with equity, and the notion of self-sufficiency – which characterized the organization of the delivery of welfare for most of the post-war period. The status of these traditional characteristics was seriously challenged during the Thatcher and Major administrations.

As we saw in Chapter 1, bureaucratic structure, with its emphasis on hierarchy and uniformity, has been a key feature of the traditional organization of welfare delivery since 1945. A major consequence of concerns about inefficiency and waste under the Conservatives was the search for alternative forms of organizing the delivery of welfare. Thus, influenced by the proponents of the public choice school, with its preference for the dismantling of large centralized bureaucracies into smaller competing bodies, the Thatcher and Major governments attempted to break up traditional public bureaucratic structures through such policy initiatives as the right to buy and transfers of local authority housing stock, the opting out of many local education authority schools to the newly created grant-maintained sector, and the transformation of the majority of NHS hospitals and other health care units into self-governing trusts.

What Hoggett (1991: 247) has called 'the demise of bureaucratic control' and its replacement by forms of post-bureaucratic models of welfare delivery also included a movement away from the traditional top-down hierarchies associated with bureaucratic arrangements for delivering welfare. One manifestation of this particular trend was the devolution of managerial freedoms to smaller operational units within the organizations responsible for welfare delivery. Local management was introduced in schools; financial responsibility within the NHS was devolved to hospital doctors through the Resource Management Initiative; fund-holding GPs were established within the NHS; increased responsibility was delegated to care managers in local authority social services departments; managerial and financial responsibilities were devolved to chief executives in the Benefits Agency and other executive agencies.

In some areas of the welfare state, notably community care and the NHS, the Conservative years witnessed the abandonment of what has been referred to as 'control by hierarchy' and its replacement by 'control by contract' (Hoggett 1991: 250). One advantage of the use of contract as a means of delivering welfare is that by separating the purchaser and provider roles, it moves away from the traditional organization in which those responsible for a service have tended to identify with those providing it, rather than with those using it (Stewart 1993: 8). By setting out specific service targets, contracts are also a means of focusing attention on the quality of service delivery (see, for example, Longley 1993: 43).

The movement away from welfare delivery by hierarchical structures also included the development of the phenomenon of spatial decentralization within local authorities, the traditional bureaucratic approach to the delivery of local government welfare being challenged by the decentralization of the delivery of housing and the personal social services to neighbourhood and area offices. However, as we saw in Chapter 9, most local authorities have been cautious about the amount of freedom granted to decentralized offices, the values of bureaucratic forms of organization still being emphasized by senior managers.

The dominant role played by professionals in the delivery of welfare was also challenged by the new paradigms of efficiency and consumerism associated with the Thatcher and Major administrations. Perhaps the most significant development was the threat to the position of the medical profession, as manifested by the increased emphasis upon the role of managers in the NHS and by the replacement of consensus management with general management, what has been referred to as the 'shifting of the frontier' between doctors and NHS managers. The role of general management within the NHS was reinforced by the internal market reforms, with general managers being given a major role in a new contracting process and hospital consultants being made directly accountable to managers, as well as being given responsibility for clinical budgeting.

The position of welfare professionals was also affected by the increasing concern with consumerism and customers. The introduction of the Major government's Citizen's Charter together with the mini-charters published for the various social services, meant that the environment in which welfare professionals, and other welfare delivery personnel, were working changed. Detailed service standards and procedures whereby the consumers of social services could exert pressure on providers to improve the quality of services became important features of the delivery of welfare. Performance indicators monitored the progress, and compared the performance, of different delivery agencies. League tables enabled the users of services to compare the performance of competing delivery agencies.

The movement away from the professional mode of welfare delivery towards a more managerial mode also involved what one commentator has referred to as 'creating managers out of professionals' (Hoggett 1991: 254), requiring them to be more interested in the costs of services provided and the management of scarce resources. Thus the introduction of local management of schools, the devolution of financial control to hospital doctors and fund-holding GPs, and the devolution of responsibilities to care managers in local authority social services departments resulted in welfare professionals such as head teachers and their senior staff, doctors and social workers being required to manage the day-to-day operations of their particular operational units, including the handling of budgets and dealing with contractors.

A recurring theme in the debate about the delivery of welfare under the Thatcher and Major governments was the notion of accountability. The weaknesses in traditional approaches to accountability have been the subject of concern for many years, with the accountability of elected representatives (whether they be central government ministers or local government councillors) having long been recognized as an inadequate mechanism for securing the public accountability of delivery agencies and their personnel. As we saw in Chapter 4, the 1960s and 1970s witnessed attempts to increase 'accountability downwards' to the users of services through the introduction of new complaints mechanisms such as the various ombudsmen institutions. The same period saw moves towards the development of user participation in the social services. Such mechanisms were seen as ways of giving users 'voice' in the delivery of welfare (Bartlett and Le Grand 1993: 18). But it was the concern with the newer concept of consumer accountability that was such a significant feature of changes in the arrangements for the delivery of welfare in the late 1980s and early 1990s. Initiatives employed the concept of 'exit' (Hirschman 1970), whereby those consumers who were dissatisfied with the quality of public service provision could choose to leave those services. Thus, in the field of social housing council tenants were given the opportunity to 'exit' from local housing authorities through the 'right to buy' or by transferring to alternative landlords. In the field of education, the Education Reform Act

1988 allowed parents to ballot for state schools to opt out of local education authority control.

One important consequence of developments under the Conservatives was the disaggregation of the traditional organizational structures associated with the public administration model of welfare delivery. This disaggregation eroded accountability, as did the contract culture, as members of the public could not always be certain who was accountable for particular services. There was also the proliferation of non-elected bodies with responsibility for the delivery of large parts of the various social services formerly directly provided by elected local authorities and by health authorities which, although not elected, used to include local authority representation. What has been described as the 'new magistracy' (Stewart 1992: 7) could be found on the governing bodies of grant-maintained schools, CTCs and further education corporations. The boards of the new NHS trusts and the small number of HATs were also made up of appointed members. The creation of such bodies gave rise to a debate about a so-called 'accountability crisis'. These new arrangements for welfare delivery also resulted in confusion about the location of responsibility. Thus, it was argued that confusion was 'written into' the new structure of education, responsibility for the delivery of education being divided between the governing boards of grant-maintained schools, the governing boards of schools which remained in the local authority sector, local education authorities, the Funding Agency for Schools, and the Secretary of State for Education (Stewart 1992: 6–7).

The traditional imperative of equity was also undermined. A key theme in the restructuring of the delivery of welfare under the Conservatives was the introduction of quasi-markets, which were seen as enhancing consumer choice, a claim that was the subject of much dispute. For example, as we saw in Chapter 7, under the arrangements for community care and the NHS introduced in the early 1990s, choices about care were not made by the users of services, but by purchasers acting on their behalf – care managers, DHAs and fund-holding GPs. Furthermore, not all potential users of social services had the same capacity for making choices: people in lower socio-economic groups may have lower expectations about services and less information about alternatives than those in more affluent groups of society (Bailey 1993: 21). The providers of particular services may also restrict the choices available to certain groups of potential users. As we saw in Chapter 7, it was suggested that the new arrangements contained in the quasi-markets in health care and community care might tempt the providers of those services to engage in what has been described as 'adverse selection', with those people in most need of a service being excluded from its provision on the grounds of their cost. Clearly, these developments threatened the whole idea of social services underpinned by the notion of equity, as did the emergence within the new NHS after 1991 of what some observers viewed as a two-tier system of health care, with fund-holding GPs being able to secure preferential treatment for their patients.

The other major assumption that supported the organization of the welfare state for most of the post-war period, the concept of self-sufficiency, was also challenged by developments under the Conservatives. The idea that the delivery agencies responsible for the core services of the welfare state also normally provided those services was undermined by a number of developments. Local authority social services departments became increasingly engaged in relationships with private and voluntary sector organizations through contracts for the provision of community care. The notion of self-sufficiency was also challenged by the development of the enabling role in housing, education and the personal social services (Stewart and Walsh 1992: 509) – seen by some as presaging the end of local government. Yet, while some saw these developments as a threat to the traditional self-sufficiency of local authorities as front-line delivery agents of the welfare state, others saw them as a possible opportunity, opening up a broader enabling role than the one envisaged by the Conservative government and allowing local authorities to meet the needs of people in their areas (see, for example, Stewart 1989: 177; see also Clarke and Stewart 1988). Within the other major delivery agency of the welfare state, the NHS, the formerly self-sufficient DHAs operated as purchasers of health care, buying services from a range of health care providers, who included not only DHAs and NHS trusts, but also hospitals in the private sector.

The impact of the Blair government

The Labour government which took office in May 1997 inherited a system of welfare delivery that was very different from the one that had been bequeathed to the Conservatives in 1979. Under the Thatcher and Major administrations, there had been radical changes in the organization, management and culture of the delivery agencies of the welfare state. The traditional role of local authorities had been seriously challenged, and shifted towards an 'enabling' role. The large central government departments responsible for the delivery of social security benefits had been broken up into semi-autonomous agencies. There had been a management revolution in the other major delivery agency of the welfare state, the NHS, culminating in the introduction of the internal market and purchaser–provider split. Privatization, marketization and the search for efficiency had become important features of the system of welfare delivery. The Citizen's Charter and other initiatives reflected a growing concern with consumerism and customer sensitivity. The developments that had taken place under the Conservatives went way beyond the use of private sector management techniques – they involved 'a new way of thinking' about the state (Ridley 1995: 19).

The Labour Party was elected in 1997 on the basis of a promise to 'modernize' government – to deliver efficient, high quality and responsive public services. Tony Blair's speech at the Trades Union Congress annual conference a few months after the general election emphasized the challenge of fashioning a 'modern' welfare state in which the role of government would be 'not necessarily to provide all social provision, and fund all social provision, but to organize and regulate it most efficiently and fairly' (Blair 1997). As Newman (2001: 53) observes, under the Blair government, the vocabulary of 'modernization' – words such as 'modern', 'new', 'renewal' and 'innovation' – became part of the discourse of public sector reform. Indeed, 'modernization' was officially described as a 'hallmark' of the new administration (Cabinet Office 1999: 9).

There has been much debate about the concept of modernization and the extent to which it represents a new agenda (see, for example, Blackman and Palmer 1999; Newman 2001). As Flynn (1999: 586) observes, the Blair government's approach to the organization and management of the public sector cannot be 'analytically reduced to a set of ideological or polit- ical principles': it is a pragmatic approach. As other commentators have noted, the Blair government's modernization project is one of 'pragmatic reformism', emphasizing 'what works' (Blackman and Palmer 1999: 107). This approach has enabled it to reject parts of the Conservative legacy, 'not because it has a new ideology but because it is claimed that they did not work', and to retain other parts because it is argued that they do work (Blackman and Palmer 1999: 111). As Tony Blair has said continually, 'what matters is what works', a 'robust pragmatism' that has been described by Le Grand (1998: 27) as constituting the famous 'third way'. In this 'third way', there is 'no automatic commitment' to either the public sector or the private sector (Driver and Martell 2000: 152): public services should be provided through the sector that can provide them most effectively, whether it be the public, private or voluntary sector, or partnerships between these sectors (see, for example, Cabinet Office 1999: 35).

In attempting to 'modernize' the arrangements for the delivery of welfare, the Blair government has built upon the new public management reforms introduced by the Thatcher and Major governments, although, as we shall see, there have been important shifts of emphasis. There has been a continuing emphasis on efficiency, value for money and the customer orientation. Many of the initiatives associated with the Labour government had been important features of the previous Conservative administrations. In the words of one writer on public sector reform, there have been 'some striking continuities' (Painter 1999: 94).

Thus, like its Conservative predecessors, the Blair government is very concerned about efficiency and value for money. The Labour Party's 1997 election manifesto gave 'high priority to seeing how public money can be better used', saying that 'efficiency and value for money are central' (Labour Party 1997: 12). With this purpose in mind, following a comprehensive

spending review of government departments, the new government introduced a system of Public Service Agreements between departments and
the Treasury, which link the allocation of resources to value for money and
service improvements.

The new government also recognized the potential of competition
and private sector involvement in achieving efficiency and value for money
in service provision. Thus, although Labour abolished CCT in local
government, it replaced it with the Best Value regime, which emphasizes
continuous improvement in the quality of local authority services and
requires local authorities to demonstrate that the choice of supplier provides
best value in both price and quality. A similar type of regime has replaced
CCT in the NHS, with the private sector being brought in if NHS trusts
and PCTs can obtain value for money and better quality. Market testing in
central government departments has been replaced by BQS reviews, with
the focus on improving delivery, whether it is by the public sector, the
private sector or a partnership solution. As we saw in Chapter 7, the private
sector has continued to be closely involved in the delivery of such services
as education and health care, notably as a result of the relaunching of the
PFI and the development of public–private partnerships. The language of
competition might have been abandoned under the Blair government, but
the private sector is still to be used if it can provide a better service. As
Newman (2001: 50, original emphasis) has observed, there has been a 'move
away from competition as a politically imposed strategy to the presump-
tion that competition is now one of the *managerial* tools through which
performance can be improved'.

Another manifestation of what has been referred to as a 'more pragmatic approach to the use of the market' (Newman 2000: 50) has been the
Blair government's reform of the NHS. Although (as we saw in Chapter
7), this was, in part, facilitated by the Major government's retreat from the
marketization policy introduced by the Thatcher administration, Labour's
'new' NHS includes elements of the Conservative reforms (Ham 1999: 70).
Despite its abolition of the internal market, Labour retained the purchaser–
provider split (although this is now referred to as the commissioning–
provision distinction) in the delivery of health care, along with contracts,
although these are now labelled 'service agreements' and are longer term.
In the view of one informed observer of the NHS, the Labour reforms are
'an improved version of the internal market' (Glennerster 1999: 41). Indeed,
the new government referred to its NHS reforms as evolutionary change
rather than organizational upheaval (Department of Health 1997a: para. 1.3).

An important feature of the Blair government's approach to the
delivery of welfare, and closely linked to its concern with efficiency and value
for money, has been its emphasis on performance management. In fact, the
Labour government has been seen as advocating performance measurement
'even more zealously' than its Conservative predecessors (Horton and
Farnham 1999: 255). As we have seen in Chapters 6 and 8, it has subjected

the major social services to a wide range of peformance measurements – not only performance indicators and league tables, but also the star system for the rating of delivery agencies introduced in the NHS and local authorities, which has been extended to the personal social services. Labour, however, has 'a more rounded approach' to performance measurement than the Conservatives (Cutler and Waine 2000: 318), with a greater emphasis on quality rather than efficiency, as manifested in its NHS performance indicators.

The monitoring of the performance of welfare delivery agencies is one manifestation of the development of what has been described as an 'audit explosion' – the growth of various kinds of regulation, inspection and audit (Power 1994, 1997). Since the early 1990s Britain has been described as an 'audit society', characterized by the imposition of detailed accounting requirements and detailed performance indicators, underpinned by an audit and inspection system designed to ensure that public sector bodies meet these standards (Moran 2000: 7). Observers have talked about an 'age of inspection' in the social services (Day and Klein 1990). This emphasis upon inspection and audit was an important feature of the Thatcher and Major years, with the establishment of such bodies as the Audit Commission, Ofsted and the Social Services Inspectorate contributing to the growth of the developing 'audit society'. Such regulation appears to have grown as the Conservative governments sought to change the role of traditional front-line delivery agencies: there was what Hood and Scott (1996) have referred to as a 'mirror-image' growth in the regulation of such bodies.

The growth of such regulation has continued under the Blair government: there has been what has been described as a 'topsy-like growth' in inspection and oversight in the major social services (Travers 2001: 132; see also Hood et al. 2000). As we saw in Chapter 8, additional powers were given to Ofsted, whose powers were extended from schools to local education authorities. The Blair government also created a Housing Inspectorate (within the Best Value Inspectorate). In the NHS, it established a Commission for Health Improvement to regulate clinical standards, with the power to conduct spot checks and recommend corrective action, together with a National Institute for Clinical Excellence to promote clinical audit and cost-effectiveness. In the field of higher education, a Quality Assurance Agency for Higher Education emerged from the amalgamation of the Higher Education Quality Council and the assessment functions of the HEFCE.

These developments have been accompanied by a change of style in regulation involving the idea of what Hood and his colleagues (2000: 292–4) refer to as 'enforced self-regulation'. This involves striking 'the right balance between intervening where services are failing and giving successful organizations the freedom to manage' (Cabinet Office 1999: 7). As Flynn (1999: 589) points out, whereas traditional methods of audit and inspection were mainly concerned with the establishment of 'minimum levels of compliance with financial and professional procedures', this new regime 'requires the exercise of judgement not just of conformity but also of failure and excellence'. Ministers have been given reserve powers of intervention, culminating in the transfer of functions to third parties in the case of serious service failures. As we saw in Chapter 6, certain local education authorities and local authority social services departments have been named and blamed by the Blair government, with some LEA services being transferred to the private sector. On the other hand, excellent performing local authorities have been given beacon council status, and can be rewarded with new powers. The government has similar powers for dealing with failing NHS bodies, with very high performing organizations being rewarded with greater autonomy.

The Blair government also shares its predecessor's enthusiasm for the customer orientation. One of the key themes of the *Modernising Government* White Paper was 'responsive public services', with the commitment to 'deliver public services to meet the needs of citizens, not the convenience of service providers' (Cabinet Office 1999: 7). John Major's Citizen's Charter was relaunched in 1998 as *Service First*, with a more bottom-up approach involving greater consultation with the users of services (Cabinet Office 1998b). As we saw in Chapter 9, another important aspect of consumerist approaches in the 1980s and early 1990s was the increasing use of user surveys and other consumer-based initiatives by local authorities and health authorities. Such developments have been encouraged by the Blair government, which has stated that it is vital that local authorities give service users the maximum opportunity to shape local services, through the use of such mechanisms as citizens' juries, focus groups and citizens' panels (Department of the Environment, Transport and the Regions 1998: paras 4.2, 4.12).

Closely linked to the notion of responsive public services is the theme of information-age government, using new technology to deliver public services more effectively, which is given a high value in the Blair government's modernization agenda. Information technology has great potential in enabling services such as social security and the NHS to become more customer friendly. Following heavy investment in information technology systems in its previous guise as the DSS, the DWP's extension of internet information and services will be central to the provision of a more integrated service for the delivery of social security benefits in the early twenty-first century. Jobseekers can use the internet to look for, and apply for jobs, through Jobcentre Plus anywhere in the UK. The NHS is also using information technology to achieve national coverage of its NHS Direct initiative. Again, these initiatives are extensions of developments that took place under the previous Conservative administration. An important, but little-noticed, element in the Major government's attempts to provide more efficient and user-friendly services was its vision of 'electronic government', whereby consumers would be able to link with government offices from their home television sets or from public kiosks (Office of Public Service 1996). By the time of the election of the Blair government, information technology was already playing a major role in the reinvention of the delivery of public services.

Although there is much continuity with the approach of Conservative administrations – an emphasis on efficiency and value for money, private sector involvement, performance measurement and inspection, and consumer-orientated services – there have also been important changes in the organization and management of welfare delivery under the Blair government. Labour's modernization programme includes a number of significant new features, notably joined-up government and partnerships, that are of particular relevance to the arrangements for the delivery of welfare.

One very important product of modernization has been the emphasis on joined-up government. As we saw in Chapter 4, the need to combat the effects of departmentalism and the fragmentation of central government has been an ongoing feature of governments since the early 1960s, and was manifested in such initiatives as the creation of the giant DHSS, JASP, and joint planning between the NHS and local authority social services departments. The emphasis on coordination and collaboration (what is officially described as joined-up government) has been a central theme of the Blair government. The *Modernising Government* White Paper (Cabinet Office 1999: 15) stated that management reforms under the Thatcher and Major governments had given too little attention into 'making sure that policies are devised and delivered in a consistent and effective way across institutional boundaries'. As we saw in Chapter 5, under the Labour government, joined-up government has been manifested in such organizational changes as the creation of the Social Exclusion Unit, the transfer of the Contributions Agency to the Inland Revenue, and the establishment of the DWP. The Treasury's Comprehensive Spending Review encourages greater interdepartmental working by allocating money to policies that cut across departments. Other manifestations of this emphasis on joined-up government include the establishment of such cross-cutting initiatives as education and health action zones and the *Sure Start* programme.

The Blair government has attempted to take its drive for joined-up government even further by 'actively encouraging initiatives to encourage partnership delivery by all parts of government' (Cabinet Office 1999: 32). Partnership is seen as one of the essential features of the 'third way' (Hudson 1999: 203). As one commentary on the Blair government's public service reforms has put it: 'If the Conservative's mantra was competition, New Labour's is partnership . . . Partnership is the preferred model of government, not bureaucracy or the market' (Horton and Farnham 1999: 255).

The Blair government's 1997 White Paper on the new NHS presented partnership as part a 'third way' of running the NHS, stating that:

> There will be no return to the old centralised command and control systems of the 1970s. That approach stifled innovation and put the

needs of institutions ahead of the needs of patients. But nor will there be a continuation of the divisive internal market system of the 1990s . . . Instead there will be a 'third way' of running the NHS – a system based on partnership and driven by performance . . . It will neither be the model from the late 1970s nor the model from the early 1990s. It will be a new model for a new century.

(Department of Health 1997a: paras 2.1–2.3)

Partnership is also central to the Blair government's approach to the personal social services, the Government referring to a 'third way for social care', with better and clearer relationships between local authority social services departments and other agencies (Department of Health 1998: paras 1.8, 1.11). The *Modernising the Social Services* White Paper (Department of Health 1998: para. 2.52) argues that it is for 'agencies to collaborate to ensure that an approach to one will automatically trigger contributions from partner agencies as required'. As Hudson (1999: 194) observes, the collaborative imperative is 'at the heart' of the framework for change.

As we discussed in Chapter 6, partnerships are also at 'the cutting edge' of the Labour government's vision for local government (Greenwood et al. 2001: 136). The Blair government's pronouncements on local government have emphasized an approach based on partnership (see, for example, Department of the Environment, Transport and the Regions 1998: para. 7.23). In the words of Tony Blair's own vision for local government:

> It is in partnership with others – public agencies, private companies, community groups and voluntary organisations – that local government's future lies. Local authorities will still deliver some services but their distinctive leadership role will be to weave and knit together the contribution of the various local stakeholders.
>
> (Blair 1998a: 13)

Another important component of this partnership agenda is public–private partnerships. As we saw in Chapter 7, a key element in Labour's strategy for modernizing public services is partnerships between the public and private sectors. The Blair government's commitment to such partnerships was clearly expressed by the then Chancellor of the Duchy of Lancaster in 1998:

> What matters to the citizen, and therefore to the Government, is quality for the customer at the most reasonable cost to the taxpayer. If these are right, the distinctions between public and private are not so important. We want to encourage business to play a fuller role in providing public services. That is why we stress Public–Private Partnerships.
>
> (Cabinet Office 1998a: 3)

In the words of another Cabinet minister, these kinds of 'partnerships are here and they are here to stay' (Commission on Public Private Partnerships 2001: 33).

Developments such as these make it clear that, under the Blair government, the clock will not be put back to the old public administration model of welfare delivery. The Blair government rejects the 'command bureaucracy model' – with its emphasis on hierarchy and rules – associated with 'old' Labour (Rhodes 2001: 113). The Blair government has also continued the challenge to the role of the welfare professions launched by the Thatcher government. There is tighter regulation of the activities of welfare professionals and the imposition of detailed performance standards. Indeed, the changes to the organization and management of the NHS introduced by the Blair government have been described as constituting 'a bigger challenge' to the NHS professions than anything that the previous Conservative governments had done (Glennerster 2001: 401). Another feature of the traditional public administration model, the notion of self-sufficient service providers like local authorities has also been further challenged, with the development of Labour's wider concept of enabling and the introduction of such initiatives as the Best Value regime and public–private partnerships. 'Hit squads' and similar initiatives have presaged the transfer of local education provision to the private sector and other agencies. The development of new modes of accountability has also continued under the Blair government. There is a continuing emphasis on what has been described as 'grass-roots accountability' to customers and consumers, as epitomized by the relaunching of the Major government's Citizen's Charter as *Service First* (Greenwood et al. 2001: 247). The continuing use of performance indicators, and their role in providing customers and others with a basis for judging performance, is a further manifestation of new approaches to accountability. The development of public–private partnerships under the Labour administration also has implications for traditional political accountability. Echoing earlier criticisms about the impact of the contract culture under the Conservatives, the debate about such partnerships include the concern about the transfer of public services to private bodies 'which are not publicly accountable in the traditional sense' (Commission on Public Private Partnerships 2001: 235). The one key feature of the traditional public administration model that does feature prominently in the Blair government's modernization agenda is the value of equity. This particular value is central to Labour's plans for the NHS, with the government committed to ending what it described as the unfairness for patients created by the Conservatives' internal market in health care, in which the family doctor community had been split between GP fund-holders and non-fund-holders (Department of Health 1997a: para. 2.12).

Conclusions

Developments since the early 1980s have produced a system of welfare delivery that is very different from the system that emerged in the late 1940s, was consolidated in the 1950s and 1960s, and still operated in the 1970s and early 1980s. A system dominated by central government departments, local authorities and the NHS – the 'public face' of welfare – and based upon the practices and values of the public administration model, is being replaced by a new set of practices and values, based upon a new language of welfare delivery which emphasizes efficiency and value for money, performance measurement, private sector involvement, partnerships, joined-up government, and consumerism and customer care.

What was once described as the government of welfare has given way to the governance of welfare, a new process of delivering the major social services. One major feature of this new governance of welfare has been the introduction, under successive governments, of a series of initiatives that help to make up what is referred to as the new public management. Its characteristics have included the adoption of management procedures and techniques from the private sector; the disaggregation of large-scale bureaucracies; the emphasis on cost-cutting and value for money; the contracting out of functions; and the customer orientation. Another feature of this new governance of welfare is the fact that the delivery of welfare now takes place not just through the 'public face' of welfare, but through an increasingly fragmented structure of networks and partnerships of organizations drawn from the public, private and voluntary sectors. As Rhodes (2000: 270) observes, the Blair government uses networks to 'institutionalise its ideals of partnership and an enabling state'.

Although launched by the Conservative governments of the 1980s and 1990s, the new governance of welfare has been developed by the Blair government. As we have seen, the changes associated with the Labour government since 1997 are, in many ways, a progression of the restructuring of the arrangements for the delivery of welfare under the Thatcher and Major governments. The need to improve the efficiency and consumer sensitivity of the delivery of welfare have been key features of Labour's approach to public sector reform. Despite some new initiatives and changes of emphasis, there has been much continuity with developments under the previous administrations. Labour has continued the transformation of the old public administration model of welfare delivery – it 'has no wish to return to former systems of traditional public administration' (Horton and Farnham 1999: 252).

Further changes to the arrangements for the delivery of welfare, and the developing governance of welfare, were promised for Labour's second term. Talking about a 10-year goal, Labour's 2001 election manifesto asked for a mandate for more radical change in the key social services of the NHS, social security and education, stating that the renewal of public services was at the heart of its programme. It made it clear that where service quality was not improving quickly enough, alternative providers should be used, and that the private sector should be involved (Labour Party 2001: 6, 17). In a clear repudiation of the old public administration model, Tony Blair called for a decisive break with what he described as 'the tradition of monolithic, centrally driven public services'. He wanted local managers and professionals to be 'entrepreneurs'. Partnership between the public, private and voluntary sectors was of critical importance – what mattered was 'the quality and value of the service on offer' (*Guardian* 21 May 2000). These promises were reiterated in another speech just weeks after Labour's re-election, when the prime minister declared that there was a need to accelerate the pace of change in the public services (Blair 2001). Radical change was on the agenda – public services needed further reform if they were to 'deliver the uniformly high standards and consumer focus that people expect in the 21st century'. When it came into office in May 1997, the Blair government was faced with a very different set of arrangements for the delivery of welfare than that inherited by the Thatcher government 18 years earlier. Given the developments and pace of change under the first Blair administration, the arrangements for the delivery of welfare could look even more different by 2010.

References

Adam Smith Institute (1984) *The Omega File: Education Policy*. London: Adam Smith Institute.

Adams, C., Bennett, R. and Timmins, N. (2001) Milburn tries to quell fears over public services, *Financial Times*, 2 October.

Albrow, M. (1970) *Bureaucracy*. London: Pall Mall Press.

Alcock, P. (1987) *Poverty and State Support*. London: Longman.

Alexander, A. (1982a) *Local Government in Britain since Reorganisation*. London: Allen & Unwin.

Alexander, A. (1982b) *The Politics of Local Government in the United Kingdom*. London: Longman.

Allsop, J. (1984) *Health Policy and the National Health Service*. London: Longman.

Armstrong, Sir W. (1970) The Civil Service Department and its tasks, *O and M Bulletin*, 25(2): 63–79.

Arnstein, S.R. (1971) A ladder of citizen participation in the USA, *Journal of the Town Planning Institute*, 57(4): 176–82.

Ascher, K. (1987) *The Politics of Privatisation: Contracting Out Public Services*. London: Macmillan.

Ashburner, L. and Cairncross, L. (1993) Membership of the 'new style' health authorities: continuity or change?, *Public Administration*, 71(3): 357–75.

Association of Metropolitan Authorities (1987) *Press Notice 181/87*, 29 October.

Audit Commission (1983) *Handbook on Economy, Efficiency and Effectiveness*. London: HMSO.

Audit Commission (1985) *Managing Social Services for the Elderly*. London: HMSO.

Audit Commission (1986) *Managing the Crisis in Council Housing*. London: HMSO.

Audit Commission (1988a) *The Competitive Council*, Management Paper 1. London: HMSO.

Audit Commission (1988b) *Performance Review in Local Government: A Handbook for Auditors and Local Authorities: Action Guide.* London: HMSO.

Audit Commission (1989) *Losing an Empire: Finding a Role: The ILEA of the Future*, Occasional Paper 10. London: HMSO.

Audit Commission (1992) *Community Care: Managing the Cascade of Change.* London: HMSO.

Audit Commission (1998) *Home Alone: The Role of Housing in Community Care.* London: Audit Commission.

Audit Commission (1999) *Held in Trust: The LEA of the Future.* London: Audit Commission.

Audit Commission (2000a) *Forget Me Not: Mental Health Services for Older People.* London: Audit Commission.

Audit Commission (2000b) *On Target: The Practice of Performance Indicators.* London: Audit Commission.

Audit Commission (2001) *Changing Gear: Best Value Annual Statement 2001.* London: Audit Commission.

Baggott, R. (1994) *Health and Health Care in Britain.* London: Macmillan.

Baggott, R. (1998) *Health and Health Care in Britain*, 2nd edn. London: Macmillan.

Bailey, S.J. (1993) Public choice theory and the reform of local government in Britain, *Public Policy and Administration*, 8(2): 7–24.

Bains, M. (1972) *The New Local Authorities: Management and Structure.* London: HMSO.

Baker, L. (1993) HATs brim with success, *Housing*, 29(5): 4.

Barclay, P.M. (1982) *Social Workers: Their Role and Tasks.* London: Bedford Square Press.

Barker, T. with Byrne, I. and Veall, A. (2000) *Ruling by Task Force: Politico's Guide to Labour's New Elite.* London: Politico's.

Barnes, M., Harrison, S., Mort, M. and Shardlow, P. (1999a) *Unequal Partners: User Groups and Community Care.* Bristol: Policy Press.

Barnes, M., Harrison, S., Mort, M., Shardlow, P. and Wistow, G. (1999b) The new management of community care: user groups, citizenship and co-production, in G. Stoker (ed.) *The New Management of British Local Governance.* London: Macmillan.

Barnett, J. (1982) *Inside the Treasury.* London: André Deutsch.

Barron, A. and Scott, C. (1992) The Citizen's Charter Programme, *Modern Law Review*, 55(4): 526–46.

Bartlett, W. and Le Grand, J. (1993) The theory of quasi-markets, in J. Le Grand and W. Bartlett (eds) *Quasi-Markets and Social Policy.* London: Macmillan.

Bassett, K. (1980) The sale of council houses as a political issue, *Policy and Politics*, 8(3): 290–307.

Batty, D. (2001) Government unveils hospital league tables, *The Guardian*, 25 September.

Bellamy, C. and Taylor, J.A. (1998) *Governing in the Information Age.* Buckingham: Open University Press.

Beresford, P. and Croft, S. (1990) Opportunity knocks, *Insight*, 18 July.

Best, G. (1987) *The Future of NHS General Management: Where Next?* London: King's Fund.

Beveridge, W. (1942) *Report of the Committee on Social Insurance and Allied Services*, Cmd 6404. London: HMSO.

Bexley, London Borough of (1984) *Annual Review of Service Performance, 1983/84*. London: London Borough of Bexley.

Birkinshaw, P. (1985) *Grievances, Remedies and the State*. London: Sweet and Maxwell.

Blackman, T. and Palmer, A. (1999) Continuity or modernisation? The emergence of New Labour's welfare state, in H. Dean and R. Woods (eds) *Social Policy Review 11*. Luton: Social Policy Association.

Blackstone, T. and Plowden, W. (1988) *Inside the Think Tank: Advising the Cabinet 1971–83*. London: Heinemann.

Blair, T. (1997) Address to Trades Union Congress, 9 September, www.tuc.org.uk/congress.tuc

Blair, T. (1998a) *Leading the Way: A New Vision for Local Government*. London: Institute for Public Policy Research.

Blair, T. (1998b) In Britain today, millions are still trapped in a cash economy: vulnerable, extorted, prey to loan sharks. In Britain today, that is not acceptable, *Observer*, 31 May.

Blair, T. (2001) Reform of public services, 16 July, www.source.net/articles

Boaden, N. (1971) *Urban Policy-Making*. Cambridge: Cambridge University Press.

Boaden, N., Goldsmith, M., Hampton, W. and Stringer, P. (1982) *Public Participation in Local Services*. London: Longman.

Bowie, C., Richardson, A. and Sykes, W. (1995) Consulting the public about health service priorities, *British Medical Journal*, 311: 1155–8.

Boyne, G., Gould-Williams, J., Law, K. and Walker, R. (2001) The impact of best value on local authority performance: evidence from the Welsh pilots, *Local Government Studies*, 27(2): 44–68.

Bradshaw, J. (1992) Social security, in D. Marsh and R.A.W. Rhodes (eds) *Implementing Thatcherite Policies: Audit of an Era*. Buckingham: Open University Press.

Bramley, G. (1993) Quasi-markets and social housing, in J. Le Grand and W. Bartlett (eds) *Quasi-Markets and Social Policy*. London: Macmillan.

Brenton, M. (1985a) *The Voluntary Sector in British Social Services*. London: Longman.

Brenton, M. (1985b) Privatisation and voluntary social services, in M. Brenton and C. Jones (eds) *The Year Book of Social Policy in Britain 1984–5*. London: Routledge and Kegan Paul.

Brown, R.G.S. (1973) *The Changing National Health Service*. London: Routledge and Kegan Paul.

Brown, R.G.S. (1975) *The Management of Welfare*. London: Fontana.

Brown, R.G.S. (1979) *Reorganising the National Health Service: A Case Study of Administrative Change*. Oxford: Basil Blackwell/Martin Robertson.

Brown, R.G.S. and Steel, D.R. (1979) *The Administrative Process in Britain*, 2nd edn. London: Methuen.

Bulpitt, J. (1983) *Territory and Power in the United Kingdom*. Manchester: Manchester University Press.

Bulpitt, J. (1989) Walking back to happiness? Conservative Party governments and elected local authorities in the 1980s, in C. Crouch and D. Marquand (eds) *The New Centralism: Britain Out of Step in Europe?* Oxford: Blackwell.

Burchardt, J. and Hills, J. (1999) Public expenditure and the public/private mix, in M. Powell (ed.) *New Labour, New Welfare State? The 'Third Way' in British Social Policy*. Bristol: Policy Press.

Burningham, D. (1992) An overview of the use of performance indicators in local government, in S. Harrison and C. Pollitt (eds) *Handbook of Public Services Management*. Oxford: Blackwell.

Burns, D., Hambleton, R. and Hoggett, P. (1994) *The Politics of Decentralisation: Revitalising Local Democracy*. London: Macmillan.

Butcher, T. (2000) The civil service: structure and management, in R. Pyper and L. Robins (eds) *United Kingdom Governance*. London: Macmillan.

Butler, E. (1988) Cure for health service ills, *The Guardian*, 5 May.

Byrne, T. (1990) *Local Government in Britain*, 5th edn. Harmondsworth: Penguin.

Byrne, T. (2000) *Local Government in Britain*, 7th edn. Harmondsworth: Penguin.

Cabinet Office (1998a) *Better Quality Services: A Handbook on Creating Public–Private Partnerships through Market-Testing and Contracting Out*. London: HMSO.

Cabinet Office (1998b) *Service First: The New Charter Programme*. London: Cabinet Office.

Cabinet Office (1999) *Modernising Government*, Cm 4310. London: The Stationery Office.

Cabinet Office (2000) *Review of the Public Sector Ombudsmen in England: A Report by the Cabinet Office*. London: The Stationery Office.

Cairncross, L., Clapham, D. and Goodlad, R. (1994) Tenant participation and tenant power in British council housing, *Public Administration*, 72(2): 177–200.

Cairncross, L., Clapham, D. and Goodlad, R. (1997) *Housing Management, Consumers and Customers*. London: Routledge.

Callaghan, J. (1987) *Time and Chance*. London: Collins.

Carr-Hill, R., McIver, S. and Dixon, P. (1989) *The NHS and its Customers: Executive Summary*. York: Centre for Health Economics, University of York.

Carter, N. (1989) Performance indicators: 'backseat driving' or 'hands-off' control?, *Policy and Politics*, 17(2): 131–8.

Carter, N. and Greer, P. (1993) Evaluating agencies: Next Steps and performance indicators, *Public Administration*, 71(3): 407–16.

Carter, N., Klein, R. and Day, P. (eds) (1992) *How Organisations Measure Success: The Use of Performance Indicators in Government*. London: Routledge.

Castle, B. (1980) *The Castle Diaries 1974–76*. London: Weidenfeld and Nicolson.

Central Advisory Council for Education (England) (1967) *Children and their Primary Schools* (Plowden Report). London: HMSO.

Central Policy Review Staff (1975) *A Joint Framework for Social Policies*. London: HMSO.

Central Policy Review Staff (1977) *Relations between Central Government and Local Authorities*. London: HMSO.

Central Statistical Office (1979) *Annual Abstract of Statistics 1979 Edition*. London: HMSO.

Challis, L., Day, P. and Klein, R. (1984) Residential care on demand, *New Society*, 68(1115): 32.

Challis, L., Fuller, S., Henwood, M. et al. (1988) *Joint Approaches to Social Policy: Rationality and Practice*. Cambridge: Cambridge University Press.

Chandler, J.A. (1991) *Local Government Today*. Manchester: Manchester University Press.

Chandler, J. (1996) *Local Government Today*, 2nd edn. Manchester: Manchester University Press.

Chester, D.N. and Willson, F.M.G. (1957) *The Organisation of British Central Government 1914–56*. London: Allen & Unwin.

Chester, D.N. and Willson, F.M.G. (1968) *The Organisation of British Central Government 1914–64*, 2nd edn. London: Allen & Unwin.

Clapham, D., Kemp, P. and Smith, S.J. (1990) *Housing and Social Policy*. London: Macmillan.

Clarke, J., Gewirtz, S. and McLaughlin, E. (2000) Reinventing the welfare state, in J. Clarke, S. Gewirtz and E. McLaughlin (eds) *New Managerialism: New Welfare?* London: Sage.

Clarke, M. and Stewart, J. (1985) *Local Government and the Public Service Orientation: Or does a Public Service Provide for the Public?* Luton: Local Government Training Board.

Clarke, M. and Stewart, J. (1988) *The Enabling Council: Developing and Managing a New Style of Local Government*. Luton: Local Government Training Board.

Clothier, Sir C. (1986) The value of an Ombudsman, *Public Law*, summer: 204–11.

Cochrane, A. (1993) *Whatever Happened to Local Government?* Buckingham: Open University Press.

Cohen, N. (1999) How Britain mortgaged the future, *New Statesman*, 18 October.

Cole, I. (1993) The decentralization of housing services, in P. Malpass and R. Means (eds) *Implementing Housing Policy*. Buckingham: Open University Press.

Cole, I. and Furbey, R. (1994) *The Eclipse of Council Housing*. London: Routledge.

Coleman, V. (1989) *The Health Scandal: Your Health in Crisis*. London: Mandarin.

Commission for Local Administration in England (2001) *Local Government Ombudsman Annual Report 2000/2001*. London: Commission for Local Administration in England.

Commission on Public Private Partnerships (2001) *Building Better Partnerships*. London: Institute for Public Policy Research.

Common, R. and Flynn, N. (1992) *Contracting for Care*. York: Joseph Rowntree Foundation.

Compton, Sir Edmund (1970) The administrative performance of government, *Public Administration*, 48(1): 3–14.

Connelly, J. (1992) All customers now? Some notes on consumerism in the public services, *Teaching Public Administration*, 12(2): 29–32.

Connolly, M., McKeown, P. and Milligan-Byrne, G. (1994) Making the public sector more user friendly? A critical examination of the Citizen's Charter, *Parliamentary Affairs*, 47(1): 23–37.

Conservative Party (1983) *The Challenge of Our Times*. London: Conservative Party.

Coote, A. and Mattinson, D. (1997) *Twelve Good Neighbours: The Citizen as Juror*, Discussion Paper 31. London: Fabian Society.

Corby, S. (1999) The National Health Service, in S. Horton and D. Farnham (eds) *Public Management in Britain*. London: Macmillan.

Corrigan, P., Jones, T., Lloyd, J. and Young, J. (1988) *Socialism, Merit and Efficiency*, Fabian Tract 530. London: Fabian Society.

Council of Europe (1993) *The Role of Competitive Tendering in the Efficient Provision of Local Services*. Strasbourg: Council of Europe Press.

Council on Tribunals (1985) *Annual Report 1984–85*, HC 54. London: HMSO.

Council on Tribunals (1986) *Social Security – Abolition of Independent Appeals under the Proposed Social Fund*, Cmnd 9722. London: HMSO.

Council on Tribunals (2001) *Annual Report 2000–2001*, HC 343. London: The Stationery Office.

Crosland, S. (1982) *Tony Crosland*. London: Jonathan Cape.

Crossman, R.H.S. (1976) The role of the volunteer in the modern social services, Sydney Ball Memorial Lecture 1973, in A.H. Halsey (ed.) *Traditions in Social Policy*. Oxford: Blackwell.

Crossman, R.H.S. (1977) *The Diaries of a Cabinet Minister, Volume Three*. London: Hamish Hamilton and Jonathan Cape.

Curwen, P. (2000) The Private Finance Initiative: a cure for the ills of the health service?, *Teaching Public Administration*, 20(1): 6–25.

Cutler, T. and Waine, B. (2000) Managerialism reformed? New Labour and public sector management, *Social Policy and Administration*, 34(3): 318–32.

Davidson, N. (1987) *A Question of Care: The Changing Face of the National Health Service*. London: Michael Joseph.

Davies, B.P. (1968) *Social Needs and Resources in Local Services*. London: Michael Joseph.

Davies, B.P. (1972) *Variations in Children's Services among British Urban Authorities*. London: Bell.

Davis, G. and Wikeley, N. (1998) *Child Support in Action*. Oxford: Hart.

Day, P. and Klein, R. (1983) The mobilisation of consent versus the management of conflict: decoding the Griffiths Report, *British Medical Journal*, 287: 1813–16.

Day, P. and Klein, R. (1987) *Accountabilities: Five Public Services*. London: Tavistock.

Day, P. and Klein, R. (1990) *Inspecting the Inspectorates: Services for the Elderly*. York: Joseph Rowntree Memorial Trust.

Deakin, N. (1987) *The Politics of Welfare*. London: Methuen.

Deakin, N. (1994) *The Politics of Welfare: Continuities and Change*, 2nd edn. London: Harvester Wheatsheaf.

Deakin, N. and Parry, R. (1999) *The Treasury and Social Policy*. London: Macmillan.

Deakin, N. and Wright, A. (1990) Conclusions, in N. Deakin and A. Wright (eds) *Consuming Public Services*. London: Routledge.

Department for Education and Skills (DfES) (2001) *Schools: Achieving Success*, Cm 5230. London: The Stationery Office.

Department of Health (DoH) (1989a) *Working for Patients*, Cm 555. London: HMSO.

Department of Health (DoH) (1989b) *Caring for People: Community Care in the Next Decade and Beyond*, Cm 849. London: HMSO.

Department of Health (DoH) (1990) *Community Care in the Next Decade and Beyond: Policy Guidance*. London: HMSO.

Department of Health (DoH) (1991a) *Purchase of Service*. London: HMSO.

Department of Health (DoH) (1991b) *The Patient's Charter*. London: DoH.

Department of Health (DoH) (1994) *Being Heard: The Report of a Review Committee on NHS Complaints Procedures* (Wilson Report). London: DoH.

Department of Health (1996) *Statistical Bulletin: Community Care Statistics, 1995*. London: Government Statistical Office.

Department of Health (DoH) (1997a) *The New NHS: Modern, Dependable*, Cm 3807. London: The Stationery Office.

Department of Health (DoH) (1997b) Minister warns council: Government ready to intervene, Press Release, 97/277, 15 October.

Department of Health (DoH) (1998) *Modernising the Social Services: Promoting Independence, Improving Protection, Raising Standards*, Cm 4169. London: The Stationery Office.

Department of Health (DoH) (2000a) *The NHS Plan: A Plan for Investment, A Plan for Reform*, Cm 4818. London: The Stationery Office.

Department of Health (DoH) (2000b) New contracting out policy puts value ahead of cost-cutting. Compulsory market testing for NHS support services to be dropped. Press Release 2000/0536, 27 September.

Department of Health (DoH) (2001a) *Involving Patients and the Public in Healthcare: A Discussion Document*. London: DoH.

Department of Health (DoH) (2001b) *Shifting the Balance of Power within the NHS: Securing Delivery*. London: DoH.

Department of Health (DoH) (2001c) *Reforming the NHS Complaints Procedure: A Listening Document*. London: DoH.

Department of Health (DoH) (2001d) *Statistical Bulletin: Community Care Statistics 2001: Residential Personal Social Services for Adults: England*. London: DoH.

Department of Health (DoH) (2001e) Fresh moves to put patients at centre of NHS, Press Release, 3 September.

Department of Health (DoH) (2002) *Delivering the NHS Plan: Next Steps on Investment, Next Steps on Reform*, Cm 5503. London: The Stationery Office.

Department of Health and Social Security (DHSS) (1972a) *National Health Service Reorganisation*, Cmnd 5055. London: HMSO.

Department of Health and Social Security (DHSS) (1972b) *Management Arrangements for the Reorganised National Health Service*. London: HMSO.

Department of Health and Social Security (DHSS) (1976) *Priorities for Health and Personal Social Services in England*. London: HMSO.

Department of Health and Social Security (DHSS) (1981) *Care in Action*. London: HMSO.

Department of Health and Social Security (DHSS) (1982) *Social Security Operational Strategy: A Framework for the Future*. London: HMSO.

Department of Social Security (DSS) (1989) *Our Business is Service*. London: DSS.

Department of Social Security (DSS) (2001) *Departmental Report: The Government's Expenditure Plans 2001–02 to 2003–04 and Main Estimate 2001–02*, Cm 5115. London: The Stationery Office.

Department of Transport, Local Government and the Regions (DTLR) (2001) *Strong Local Leadership – Quality Public Services*, Cm 5327. London: The Stationery Office.

Department for Work and Pensions (DWP) (2002) *Departmental Framework*. London: DWP.

Department of the Environment (DoE) (1971) *Local Government in England: Government Proposals for Reorganisation*, Cmnd 4584. London: HMSO.

Department of the Environment (DoE) (1977) *Local Government Finance*, Cmnd 6813. London: HMSO.

Department of the Environment (DoE) (1986) *Paying for Local Government*, Cmnd 9721. London: HMSO.

Department of the Environment (DoE) (1987) *Housing: The Government's Proposals*, Cm 214. London: HMSO.

Department of the Environment (DoE) (1989) *Local Authorities Housing Role: 1989 HIP Round. Appendix to Letter from DOE to Local Authorities Inviting Annual Submission of Housing Strategy and Investment Programme*. London: Department of the Environment.

Department of the Environment (DoE) (1991a) *The Structure of Local Government in England: A Consultation Paper*. London: Department of the Environment.

Department of the Environment (DoE) (1991b) *The Internal Management of Local Authorities in England: A Consultation Paper*. London: Department of the Environment.

Department of the Environment, Transport and the Regions (DETR) (1998) *Modern Local Government: In Touch with the People*, Cm 4014. London: The Stationery Office.

Department of the Environment, Transport and the Regions (DETR) (2000a) *Quality and Choice: A Decent Home for All: The Housing Green Paper*. London: Department of the Environment, Transport and the Regions.

Department of the Environment, Transport and the Regions (DETR) (2000b) *National Framework for Tenant Participation Compacts*. London: Department of the Environment, Transport and the Regions.

Department of the Environment, Transport and the Regions (DETR) (2000c) *Local Government Financial Statistics England: No. 11 2000*. London: Department of the Environment, Transport and the Regions.

Department of the Environment, Transport and the Regions (DETR) (2001a) *Best Value and Audit Commission Performance Indicators for 2001–2002*. London: Department of the Environment, Transport and the Regions.

Department of the Environment, Transport and the Regions (DETR) (2001b) *Quality and Choice: A Decent Home for All: The Way Forward for Housing*. London: Department of the Environment, Transport and the Regions.

Doern, G.B. (1993) The UK Citizen's Charter: origins and implications in three agencies, *Policy and Politics*, 2(1): 17–29.

Donnison, D. (1982) *The Politics of Poverty*. Oxford: Martin Robertson.

Donnison, D. (1984) The progressive potential of privatisation, in J. Le Grand and R. Robinson (eds) *Privatisation and the Welfare State*. London: Allen & Unwin.

Drakeford, M. (2000) *Privatisation and Social Policy*. London: Longman.

Drewry, G. (1988) Rubbing noses in the future: social policy and the demise of CPRS, in M. Bury and J. Macnicol (eds) *Aspects of Ageing: Essays in Social Policy and Old Age*, Social Policy Paper 3. Egham: Royal Holloway and Bedford New College.

Drewry, G. (1993) Mr Major's charter: empowering the consumer, *Public Law*, summer: 248–56.

Drewry, G. and Butcher, T. (1991) *The Civil Service Today*, 2nd edn. Oxford: Blackwell.

Driver, S. and Martell, L. (2000) Left, right and the third way, *Policy and Politics*, 28(2): 147–61.

Dunleavy, P. (1989) The architecture of the British central state, Part I: framework for analysis, *Public Administration*, 67(3): 249–75.

Dunleavy, P. and Rhodes, R.A.W. (1983) Beyond Whitehall, in H. Drucker, P. Dunleavy, A. Gamble and G. Peele (eds) *Developments in British Politics*. London: Macmillan.

Dunleavy, P. and Rhodes, R.A.W. (1986) Government beyond Whitehall, in H. Drucker, P. Dunleavy, A. Gamble and G. Peele (eds) *Developments in British Politics 2*. London: Macmillan.

Dunsire, A. (1981) Central control over local authorities: a cybernetic approach, *Public Administration*, 59(2): 173–88.

Dunsire, A. (1982) Challenges to public administration in the 1980s, *Public Administration Bulletin*, 39: 8–21.

Dunsire, A. and Hood, C. (1989) *Cutback Management in Public Bureaucracies: Popular Theories and Observed Outcomes in Whitehall*. Cambridge: Cambridge University Press.

Education and Employment Committee (1999a) *Fifth Report 1998–99, The Role of School Governors*, HC 509-I. London: The Stationery Office.

Education and Employment Committee (1999b) *Sixth Report 1998–99, The One Service Pilots*, HC 412. London: The Stationery Office.

Education and Employment Committee (2000) *Seventh Report 1999–2000, The Role of Private Sector Organisations in Public Education*, HC 118. London: The Stationery Office.

Elcock, H. (1983) Disabling professionalism: the real threat to local democracy, *Public Money*, 3(1): 23–7.

Elcock, H. (1986a) *Local Government: Politicians, Professionals and the Public in Local Authorities*, 2nd edn. London: Methuen.

Elcock, H. (1986b) Going local in Humberside: decentralisation as a tool for social services management, *Local Government Studies*, 12(4): 35–49.

Elcock, H. (1988) Alternatives to representative government in Britain: going local, *Public Policy and Administration*, 3(2): 38–50.

Elcock, H. (1990) Administrative justice and the citizen, *Teaching Public Administration*, 10(1): 33–46.

Elcock, H. (1991) *Change and Decay? Public Administration in the 1990s*. London: Longman.

Elcock, H. (1996) Local government, in D. Farnham and S. Horton (eds) *Managing the New Public Services*, 2nd edn. London: Macmillan.

Elcock, H., Jordan, A.G. and Midwinter, A.F. (eds) (1989) *Budgeting in Local Government: Managing the Margins*. London: Longman.

Else, P. and Marshall, G.P. (1979) *The Management of Public Expenditure*. London: Policy Studies Institute.

Elston, M.A. (1991) The politics of professional power: medicine in a changing health service, in J. Gabe, M. Calnan and M. Bury (eds) *The Sociology of Health*. London: Routledge.

Enthoven, A. (1985) *Reflections on the Management of the National Health Service*. London: Nuffield Provincial Hospitals Trust.

Enthoven, A. (1991) Internal market reform of the British NHS, *Health Affairs*, 10(1): 60–70.

Environment, Transport and Regional Affairs Committee (2000) *Tenth Report 1999–2000: Audit Commission*, HC 174. London: The Stationery Office.

Environment, Transport and Regional Affairs Committee (2001) *1999–2000: Local Authority Governance*, Memoranda. LAG 17, Memorandum by the Improvement and Development Agency, HC 225. London: The Stationery Office.

Expenditure Committee (1977) *Eleventh Report 1976–77: The Civil Service*, HC 535. London: HMSO.

Farnham, D. (1992) The Citizen's Charter: improving the quality of the public services or furthering market values?, *Talking Politics*, 4(2): 75–80.

Fenwick, J. (1989) Consumerism and local government, *Local Government Policy Making*, 16(1): 45–52.

Fenwick, J. and Bailey, M. (1998) Decentralisation and reorganisation in local government, *Public Policy and Administration*, 13(2): 26–39.

Fenwick, J. and Snape, S. (1996) Closer to the customer? Local government and international experience, *Public Policy and Administration*, 11(4): 45–55.

Flynn, N. (1997) *Public Sector Management*, 3rd edn. Hemel Hempstead: Prentice Hall/Harvester Wheatsheaf.

Flynn, N. (1999) Modernising British government, *Parliamentary Affairs*, 52(4): 582–97.

Flynn, R. (1992) *Structures of Control in Health Management*. London: Routledge.

Forrest, R. (1993) Contracting housing provision: competition and privatization in the housing sector, in P. Taylor-Gooby and R. Lawson (eds) *Markets and Managers: New Issues in the Delivery of Welfare*. Buckingham: Open University Press.

Forrest, R. and Murie, A. (1991) *Selling the Welfare State: The Privatisation of Public Housing*, revised edn. London: Routledge.

Fowler, N. (1967) The Home Office: ragbag of Whitehall, *New Society*, 10(256): 251–3.

Fowler, N. (1991) *Ministers Decide*. London: Chapmans.

Franks, Sir O. (1957) *Report of the Committee on Administrative Tribunals and Inquiries*, Cmnd 218. London: HMSO.

Fudge, C. (1984) Decentralisation: socialism goes local?, in M. Boddy and C. Fudge (eds) *Local Socialism*. London: Macmillan.

Fulbrook, J., Brooke, R. and Archer, P. (1973) *Tribunals: A Social Court?* Fabian Tract 427. London: Fabian Society.

Gaffney, D. and Pollock, A.M. (1999) Pump-priming the PFI: why are privately financed hospitals schemes being subsidised?, *Public Money and Management*, 19(1): 55–62.

Garrett, J. (1980) *Managing the Civil Service*. London: Heinemann.

Gewirtz, S. (1999) Education action zones: emblems of the third way?, in H. Dean and R. Woods (eds) *Social Policy Review 11*. Luton: Social Policy Association.

Giddings, P. (1993) Complaints, remedies and the Health Service Commissioner, *Public Administration*, 71(3): 377–94.

Giddings, P. (1999) The Health Service Ombudsman after twenty-five years, *Public Law*, summer: 200–10.

Giddings, P. (2001) Whither the ombudsman?, *Public Policy and Administration*, 16(2): 1–16.

Giddings, P. and Gregory, R. (1996) Landlords, tenants and complaints: the Housing Association Tenants Ombudsman, *Public Policy and Administration*, 11(2): 79–91.

Gladstone, F.J. (1979) *Voluntary Action in a Changing World*. London: Bedford Square Press.

Glennerster, H. (1992a) *Paying for Welfare: The 1990s*, 2nd edn. Hemel Hempstead: Harvester Wheatsheaf.

Glennerster, H. (1992b) *Paying for Welfare: Issues for the Nineties*, Welfare State Programme Paper 82. London: London School of Economics.

Glennerster, H. (1999) A third way?, in H. Dean and R. Woods (eds) *Social Policy Review 11*. Luton: Social Policy Association.

Glennerster, H. (2001) Social policy, in A. Seldon (ed.) *The Blair Effect: The Blair Government 1997–2001*. London: Little, Brown.

Glennerster, H., with Korman, N. and Marslen-Wilson, F. (1983) *Planning for Priority Groups*. Oxford: Martin Robertson.

Glennerster, H., Power, A. and Travers, T. (1991) A new era for social policy: a new enlightenment or a new leviathan?, *Journal of Social Policy*, 20(3): 389–414.

Godber, Sir G. (1975) Regional devolution and the National Health Service, in E. Craven (ed.) *Regional Devolution and Social Policy*. London: Macmillan.

Goldsworthy, D. (1993) Efficiency and effectiveness in public management: a UK perspective, *Administration*, 41(2): 137–48.

Goodwin, M. and Duncan, S. (1989) The crisis of local government: uneven development and the Thatcher administrations, in J. Mohan (ed.) *The Political Geography of Modern Britain*. London: Macmillan.

Gould, F. and Roweth, B. (1980) Public spending and social policy: the United Kingdom 1950–1977, *Journal of Social Policy*, 9(3): 337–57.

Gray, A. and Jenkins, W.I. (1982) Efficiency and the self-evaluating organisation – the central government experience, *Local Government Studies*, 8(2): 47–54.

Gray, A. and Jenkins, W.I. (1985) *Administrative Politics in British Government*. Brighton: Wheatsheaf.

Gray, A. and Jenkins, W.I. (1986) Accountable management in British government: some reflections on the financial management initiative, *Financial Accountability and Management*, 2(3): 171–87.

Greenwood, J. and Wilson, D. (1989) *Public Administration in Britain Today*, 2nd edn. London: Unwin Hyman.

Greenwood, J., Pyper, R. and Wilson, D. (2001) *New Public Administration in Britain*, 3rd edn. London: Routledge.

Greenwood, R., Walsh, K., Hinings, C.R. and Ranson, S. (1980) *Patterns of Management in Local Government*. Oxford: Martin Robertson.

Greer, P. (1994) *Transforming Central Government: The Next Steps Initiative*. Buckingham: Open University Press.

Grice, A. (1994) Ministers feud over jobseeker scheme, *Sunday Times*, 2 January.

Griffith, J.A.G. (1966) *Central Departments and Local Authorities*. London: Allen & Unwin.

Griffiths, R. (1983) *National Health Service Management Enquiry*. London: DHSS.

Griffiths, R. (1988a) *Community Care: Agenda for Action*. London: HMSO.

Griffiths, R. (1988b) Does the public service serve? The consumer dimension, *Public Administration*, 66(2): 195–204.

Gunn, L.A. (1988) Public management: a third approach, *Public Money and Management*, 8(1/2): 21–6.

Gyford, J. (1985) *The Politics of Local Socialism*. London: Allen & Unwin.

Gyford, J. (1991) *Citizens, Consumers and Councils*. London: Macmillan.

Gyford, J., Leach, S. and Game, C. (1989) *The Changing Politics of Local Government*. London: Unwin Hyman.

Hadley, R. and Hatch, S. (1981) *Social Welfare and the Future of the State*. London: Allen & Unwin.

Hadley, R. and Young, K. (1990) *Creating a Responsive Public Service*. Brighton: Harvester Wheatsheaf.

Hague, D.C. (1971) The Ditchley Conference: a British view, in B.C.R. Smith and D.C. Hague (eds) *The Dilemma of Accountability in Modern British Government: Independence Versus Control*. London: Macmillan.

Haldane, Lord (1918) *Report of the Machinery of Government Committee*, Cd 9230. London: HMSO.

Hall, D. and Stewart, J. (1997) *Citizen's Juries: An Evaluation*. Luton: Local Government Management Board.

Ham, C. (1977) Power, patients and pluralism, in K. Barnard and K. Lee (eds) *Conflicts in the National Health Service*. London: Croom Helm.

Ham, C. (1992) *Health Policy in Britain*, 3rd edn. London: Macmillan.

Ham, C. (1999) *Health Policy in Britain*, 4th edn. Basingstoke: Palgrave.

Hambleton, R. and Hoggett, P. (1988) Beyond bureaucratic paternalism, in P. Hoggett and R. Hambleton (eds) *Decentralisation and Democracy: Localising Public Services*, Occasional Paper 28. Bristol: School of Advanced Urban Studies, University of Bristol.

Hamnett, C. (1993) Running housing policy and the British housing system, in R. Maidment and G. Thompson (eds) *Managing the United Kingdom: An Introduction to its Political Economy and Public Policy*. London: Sage.

Hampton, W. (1991) *Local Government and Urban Politics*, 2nd edn. London: Longman.

Hansard (1971) Vol. 820, col. 599. London: HMSO.

Hansard (1985) Vol. 71, col. 413. London: HMSO.

Hansard (1987) Vol. 123, col. 620. London: HMSO.

Hansard (1991) Vol. 198, col. 1365. London: HMSO.

Hansard (2000) Vol. 346, col. 258W. London: The Stationery Office.

Hansard (2002) Vol. 382, cols 315–16. London: The Stationery Office.

Hanson, H. and Walles, M. (1984) *Governing Britain*, 4th edn. London: Fontana.

Harden, I. and Lewis, N. (1986) *The Noble Lie: The British Constitution and the Rule of Law*. London: Hutchinson.

Harlow, C. (1999) Accountability, new public management and the problems of the Child Support Agency, *Journal of Law and Society*, 26(2): 150–74.

Harries, A. and Vincent-Jones, P. (2001) Housing management in three metropolitan local authorities: the impact of CCT and implications for best value, *Local Government Studies*, 27(2): 69–92.

Harris, M. (1986) Looking at voluntary agencies, *RIPA Report*, 7(1): 11–12.

Harrison, S. (1988) *Managing the National Health Service: Shifting the Frontier?* London: Chapman and Hall.

Harrison, S. and Pollitt, C. (1994) *Controlling Health Professionals: The Future of Work and Organization in the National Health Service*. Buckingham: Open University Press.

Harrison, S., Hunter, D.J. and Pollitt, C. (1990) *The Dynamics of British Health Policy*. London: Unwin Hyman.

Harrop, K.J., Mason, C., Vielba, C.A. and Webster, B.A. (1978) *The Implementation and Development of Area Management*. Birmingham: Institute of Local Government Studies, University of Birmingham.

Harrow, J. and Willcocks, L. (1990) Public services management: activities, initiatives and limits to learning, *Journal of Management Studies*, 27(3): 281–304.

Hartas, W. and Harrop, K. (1991) Patterns of change in local government since 1945, *Teaching Public Administration*, 11(1): 25–36.

Hatch, S. (1980) *Outside the State*. London: Croom Helm.

Hatch, S. (1986) Review of M. Brenton, *The Voluntary Sector in British Social Services*, *Journal of Social Policy*, 15(3): 389–90.

Haynes, R.J. (1980) *Organisation Theory and Local Government.* London: Allen & Unwin.

Haywood, S.C. and Elcock, H.J. (1982) Regional Health Authorities: regional government or central agencies?, in B.W. Hogwood and M. Keating (eds) *Regional Government in England.* Oxford: Clarendon Press.

Health Service Commissioner (2001) *First Report 2001–2002: Annual Report 2000–2001,* HC 3. London: The Stationery Office.

Heclo, H. and Wildavsky, A. (1981) *The Private Government of Public Money,* 2nd edn. London: Macmillan.

Henkel, M. (1992) The Audit Commission, in S. Harrison and C. Pollitt (eds) *Handbook of Public Services Management.* Oxford: Blackwell.

Hennessy, P. (1990) *Whitehall.* London: Fontana.

Henney, A. (1984) *Inside Local Government: A Case for Radical Reform.* London: Sinclair Browne.

Heseltine, M. (1980) Ministers and management in Whitehall, *Management Services in Government,* 35(2): 61–8.

Hetherington, P. (1991) Major pledges public service 'revolution', *The Guardian,* 11 May.

Higgins, J. (1988) *The Business of Medicine.* London: Macmillan.

Hill, M. (1993) *The Welfare State in Britain.* Aldershot: Edward Elgar.

Hill, M. (1994) Social security policy under the Conservatives, in S.P. Savage, R. Atkinson and L. Robins (eds) *Public Policy in Britain.* London: Macmillan.

Hillgate Group (1986) *Whose Schools? A Radical Manifesto.* London: Hillgate Group.

Hills, J. (1987) *The Voluntary Sector in Housing: The Role of British Housing Associations,* Welfare State Programme Paper 20. London: London School of Economics.

Hills, J. and Mullings, B. (1991) Housing: a decent home for all at a price within their means?, in J. Hills (ed.) *The State of Welfare: The Welfare State in Britain since 1974.* Oxford: Clarendon Press.

Hirschman, A. (1970) *Exit, Voice and Loyalty.* Cambridge, MA: Harvard University Press.

HM Treasury (1991) *Competing for Quality: Buying Public Services,* Cm 1730. London: HMSO.

HM Treasury (1993) *Economic Briefing,* 5, August.

Hogg, C. (1990) Health, in N. Deakin and A. Wright (eds) *Consuming Public Services.* London: Routledge.

Hoggett, P. (1991) A new management in the public sector?, *Policy and Politics,* 19(4): 243–56.

Hogwood, B.W. and Gunn, L.A. (1984) *Policy Analysis for the Real World.* Oxford: Oxford University Press.

Hollis, G., Ham, G. and Ambler, M. (eds) (1992) *The Future Role and Structure of Local Government.* London: Longman.

Home Office (1998) *Getting it Right Together: Compact on Relations between Government and the Voluntary and Community Sectors in England,* Cm 4100. London: The Stationery Office.

Hood, C. (1982) Governmental bodies and government growth, in A. Barker (ed.) *Quangos in Britain: Government and the Networks of Public Policy-Making.* London: Macmillan.

Hood, C. and Scott, C. (1996) Bureaucratic regulation and new public management in the United Kingdom: mirror-image developments, *Journal of Law and Society*, 23(3): 321–45.

Hood, C., James, O. and Scott, C. (2000) Regulation of government: has it increased, is it increasing, should it be diminished?, *Public Administration*, 78(2): 283–304.

Horton, S. and Farnham, D. (1999) New Labour and the management of public services: legacies, impact and prospects, in S. Horton and D. Farnham (eds) *Public Management in Britain*. London: Macmillan.

Hudson, B. (1986) In pursuit of coordination: housing and the personal social services, *Local Government Studies*, 12(2): 53–66.

Hudson, B. (1992) Quasi-markets in health and social care in Britain: can the public sector respond?, *Policy and Politics*, 20(2): 131–42.

Hudson, B. (1999) Dismantling the Berlin Wall: developments at the health-social care interface, in H. Dean and R. Woods (eds) *Social Policy Review 11*. Luton: Social Policy Association.

Hunter, D.J. (1984) Managing health care, *Social Policy and Administration*, 18(1): 41–67.

Hunter, D.J. and Wistow, G. (1987) *Community Care in Britain: Variations on a Theme*. London: King's Fund.

Jackman, R. (1982) Does central government need to control the total of local government spending?, *Local Government Studies*, 8(3): 75–90.

Jackman, R. (1985) Local government finance, in M. Loughlin, M.D. Gelfand and K. Young (eds) *Half a Century of Municipal Decline 1935–1985*. London: Allen & Unwin.

James, O. (2001) Evaluating executive agencies in UK Government, *Public Policy and Administration*, 16(3): 24–52.

James, S. (1999) *British Cabinet Government*, 2nd edn. London: Routledge.

Jeffrey, B. (1997) Creating participatory structures in local government, *Local Government Policy Making*, 23(4): 25–31.

Jenkins, P. (1987) *Mrs Thatcher's Revolution: The Ending of the Socialist Era*. London: Jonathan Cape.

Jennings, R.E. (1977) *Education and Politics: Policy-Making in Local Education Authorities*. London: Batsford.

John, P. (1990) *Recent Trends in Central–Local Government Relations*. London: Joseph Rowntree Foundation/Policy Studies Institute.

Johnson, N. (1974) Defining accountability, *Public Administration Bulletin*, 17: 3–13.

Johnson, N. (1987) *The Welfare State in Transition*. Brighton: Wheatsheaf.

Johnson, N. (1999) The personal social services and community care, in M. Powell (ed.) *New Labour, New Welfare State? The 'Third Way' in British Social Policy*. Bristol: Policy Press.

Jones, G. and Stewart, J. (1983) *The Case for Local Government*. London: Allen & Unwin.

Jordan, A.G. and Richardson, J.J. (1987) *British Politics and the Policy Process*. London: Allen & Unwin.

Judge, K. (1982) The public purchase of social care: British confirmation of the American experience, *Policy and Politics*, 10(4): 397–416.

Justice-All Souls (1988) *Administrative Justice: Some Necessary Reforms: Report of the Committee of the Justice-All Souls Review of Administrative Law in the United Kingdom*. Oxford: Clarendon Press.

Karn, V. (1985) Housing, in S. Ranson, G. Jones and K. Walsh (eds) *Between Centre and Locality*. London: Allen & Unwin.

Karn, V. (1993) Remodelling a HAT: the implementation of the Housing Action Trust legislation 1987–92, in P. Malpass and R. Means (eds) *Implementing Housing Policy*. Buckingham: Open University Press.

Kavanagh, D. and Richards, D. (2001) Departmentalism and joined-up government: back to the future?, *Parliamentary Affairs*, 54(1): 1–18.

Keith-Lucas, B. and Richards, P.G. (1978) *A History of Local Government in the Twentieth Century*. London: Allen & Unwin.

Kelly, A. (1991) The new managerialism in the social services, in P. Carter, T. Jeffs and M.K. Smith (eds) *Social Work and Social Welfare Yearbook 3*. Buckingham: Open University Press.

Kemp, P.A. (1999a) Housing policy under New Labour, in M. Powell (ed.) *New Labour, New Social Policy? The 'Third Way' in British Social Policy*. Bristol: Policy Press.

Kemp, P.A. (1999b) Making the market work? New Labour and the housing question, in H. Dean and R. Woods (eds) *Social Policy Review 11*. Luton: Social Policy Association.

Kendall, I. and Holloway, D. (2001) Education policy, in S.P. Savage and R. Atkinson (eds) *Public Policy Under Blair*. London: Palgrave.

Key, T. (1988) Contracting out ancillary services, in R. Maxwell (ed.) *Reshaping the National Health Service*. Hermitage: Policy Journals.

Kingdom, J. (1991) *Local Government and Politics in Britain*. London: Philip Allan.

King's Fund Institute (1989) *Managed Competition: A New Approach to Health Care in Britain*. London: King's Fund Institute.

Klein, R. (1973) *Complaints against Doctors: A Study in Professional Accountability*. London: Charles Knight.

Klein, R. (1989) *The Politics of the National Health Service*, 2nd edn. London: Longman.

Klein, R. (1990) What future for the Department of Health?, *British Medical Journal*, 301: 481–4.

Kogan, M. (ed.) (1971) *The Politics of Education*. Harmondsworth: Penguin.

Kogan, M. (1978) *The Politics of Educational Change*. London: Fontana/Collins.

Kogan, M. (1987) Education, in M. Parkinson (ed.) *Reshaping Local Government*. Hermitage: Policy Journals.

Labour Party (1991) *Citizen's Charter: Labour's Better Deal for Consumers and Citizens*, London: Labour Party.

Labour Party (1997) *New Labour: Because Britain Deserves Better*. London: Labour Party.

Labour Party (2001) *Ambitions for Britain: Labour's Manifesto 2001*. London: Labour Party.

Laffin, M. (1986) *Professionalism and Policy: The Role of the Professions in the Central–Local Government Relationship*. Aldershot: Gower.

Laffin, M. and Young, K. (1990) *Professionalism in Local Government*. London: Longman.

Lansley, S., Goss, S. and Woolmar, C. (1989) *Councils in Conflict: The Rise and Fall of the Municipal Left*. London: Macmillan.

Lapping, A. (1968) A Ministry of Social Welfare? *New Society*, 11(295): 748–9.

Lawson, N. (1980) *The New Conservatism*. London: Centre for Policy Studies.

Layfield, F. (1976) *Local Government Finance: Report of the Committee of Enquiry*, Cmnd 6453. London: HMSO.

Leach, R. and Percy-Smith, J. (2001) *Local Governance in Britain*. London: Macmillan.

Leach, S. (1992) The disintegration of an initiative, in S. Leach, J. Stewart, K. Spencer, K. Walsh and J. Gibson, *The Heseltine Review of Local Government: A New Vision or Opportunities Missed?* Birmingham: Institute of Local Government Studies, University of Birmingham.

Leach, S. and Wingfield, M. (1999) Public participation and the democratic renewal agenda: prioritisation or marginalisation?, *Local Government Studies*, 25(4): 46–59.

Leggatt, A. (2001) *Tribunals for Users – One System, One Service: Report of the Review of Tribunals by Sir Andrew Leggatt*. London: The Stationery Office.

Le Grand, J. (1990) The state of welfare, in J. Hills (ed.) *The State of Welfare: The Welfare State in Britain Since 1945*. Oxford: Clarendon Press.

Le Grand, J. (1991) Quasi-markets and social policy, *Economic Journal*, 101(408): 1256–67.

Le Grand, J. (1998) The third way begins with Cora, *New Statesman*, 6 March.

Levitt, R. and Wall, A. (1992) *The Reorganized National Health Service*. London: Chapman and Hall.

Lewis, J. (1999) Reviewing the relationship between the voluntary sector and the state in Britain in the 1990s, *Voluntas: International Journal of Voluntary and Nonprofit Organizations*, 10(3): 255–70.

Lewis, N. (1985) Who controls quangos and the nationalized industries?, in J. Jowell and D. Oliver (eds) *The Changing Constitution*. Oxford: Clarendon Press.

Lewis, N. and Birkinshaw, P. (1993) *When Citizens Complain: Reforming Justice and Administration*. Buckingham: Open University Press.

Liberal Democrats (1991) *Citizens' Britain: Liberal Democrat Policies for a People's Charter*. London: Liberal Democrats.

Lightfoot, L. (1998a) Government seeks firms to take over poor schools, *Daily Telegraph*, 7 January.

Lightfoot, L. (1998b) Education action zones: minister gives stern warning to councillors, *Daily Telegraph*, 8 January.

Ling, T. (2000) Unpacking partnership: the case of health care, in J. Clarke, S. Gewirtz and E. McLaughlin (eds) *New Managerialism: New Welfare?* Sage: London.

Lipsky, M. (1979) The assault on human services: street-level bureaucrats, accountability and the fiscal crisis, in S. Greer, R.D. Hedlund and J.L. Gibson (eds) *Accountability in Urban Society: Public Agencies under Fire*, Vol. 15, *Urban Affairs Annual Review*. Beverly Hills, CA: Sage.

Local Government Information Unit (1991) *The Citizen's Charter*, special briefing no. 36.

Long, A.F. (1992) Evaluating health services: from value for money to the valuing of health services, in C. Pollitt and S. Harrison (eds) *Handbook of Public Services Management*. Oxford: Blackwell.

Longley, D. (1993) *Public Law and Health Service Accountability*. Buckingham: Open University Press.

Loughlin, M. (1985) Administrative law, government and the courts, in M. Loughlin, M.D. Gelfand and K. Young (eds) *Half a Century of Municipal Decline 1935–1985*. London: Allen & Unwin.

Loughlin, M. (1986) *Local Government in the Modern State*. London: Sweet & Maxwell.

Lowe, R. (1993) *The Welfare State in Britain since 1945*. London: Macmillan.

Lowndes, V. (1992) Decentralisation: the potential and pitfalls, *Local Government Policy Making*, 18(4): 53–63.

Lowndes, V. and Stoker, G. (1992) An evaluation of neighbourhood decentralisation – Part 1: customer and citizen participation, *Policy and Politics*, 20(1): 47–61.

Lowndes, V. and Wilson, D. (2001) Social capital and local governance: exploring the institutional design variable, *Political Studies*, 49(4): 629–47.

Lowndes, V., Stoker, G., Pratchett, L. et al. (1998) *Enhancing Public Participation in Local Government*. London: Department of the Environment, Transport and the Regions.

Lowndes, V., Stoker, G. and Pratchett, L. (2001) Trends in public participation: Part 1 – local government perspectives, *Public Administration*, 79(1): 205–22.

McAuslan, P. (1983) Administrative law, collective consumption and judicial policy, *Modern Law Review*, 46(1): 1–20.

McCarthy, M. (1989) Personal social services, in M. McCarthy (ed.) *The New Politics of Welfare: An Agenda for the 1990s?* London: Macmillan.

McEldowney, J. (2000) The control of public expenditure, in J. Jowell and D. Oliver (eds) *The Changing Constitution*, 4th edn. Oxford: Oxford University Press.

McGregor, G. (1990) Privatisation on parade, *Health Service Journal*, 3 May.

McHugh, J. (2001) PPPs could be 'Blair's Railtrack', *Public Finance*, 29 June–4 July.

McKnight, J. (1985) Pressure points: the crisis in management, in S. Ward (ed.) *DHSS in Crisis: Social Security under Pressure and under Review*. London: Child Poverty Action Group.

McLachlan, G. (1979) Foreword, in W.J.M. Mackenzie, *Power and Responsibility in Health: The National Health Service as a Political Institution*. Oxford: Oxford University Press.

MacPherson, S. (1987) Department of Health and Social Security, in A. Harrison and A. Gretton (eds) *Reshaping Central Government*. Hermitage: Policy Journals.

McSweeney, B. (1988) Accounting for the Audit Commission, *Political Quarterly*, 59(1): 28–43.

McVicar, M. (1993) Education, in D. Farnham and S. Horton (eds) *Managing the New Public Services*. London: Macmillan.

Malpass, P. (1992) Housing policy and the disabling of local authorities, in J. Birchall (ed.) *Housing Policy in the 1990s*. London: Routledge.

Malpass, P. and Murie, A. (1990) *Housing Policy and Practice*, 3rd edn. London: Macmillan.

Mandelson, P. and Liddle, R. (1996) *The Blair Revolution: Can New Labour Deliver?* London: Faber & Faber.

Margetts, H. (1991) The computerization of social security: a way forward or a step backwards?, *Public Administration*, 69(3): 325–43.

Marshall, T. (1963) *Sociology at the Crossroads*. London: Heinemann.

Martin, S. (2000) Implementing 'Best Value': local public services in transition, *Public Administration*, 78(1): 209–27.

Marwick, A. (1982) *British Society since 1945*. London: Allen Lane.

Mason, P. (1993) Market mayhem, *Nursing Times*, 15 September.

Mather, G. (1989) Thatcherism and local government, in J. Stewart and G. Stoker (eds) *The Future of Local Government*. London: Macmillan.

Maud, Sir J. (1967) *Committee on the Management of Local Government, Vol. I: Report.* London: HMSO.

Means, R. (1993) Perspectives on implementation, in P. Malpass and R. Means (eds) *Implementing Housing Policy.* Buckingham: Open University Press.

Merrison, Sir A. (1979) *Royal Commission on the National Health Service*, Cmnd 7615. London: HMSO.

Metcalfe, L. and Richards, S. (1990) *Improving Public Management*, 2nd edn. London: Sage.

Midwinter, A. and Monaghan, C. (1993) *From Rates to the Poll Tax.* Edinburgh: Edinburgh University Press.

Minister of Reconstruction (1944) *Social Insurance: Part I*, Cmnd 6550. London: HMSO.

Moodie, M., Mizen, H., Heron, R. and Mackay, B. (1988) *The Business of Service: The Report of the Regional Organization Scrutiny.* London: DHSS.

Moon, G. and Kendall, I. (1993) The National Health Service, in D. Farnham and S. Horton (eds) *Managing the New Public Services.* London: Macmillan.

Moran, M. (2000) From command state to regulatory state, *Public Policy and Administration*, 15(4): 1–13.

Morris, N. and Grice, A. (2001) Investment for public services 'linked to reforms', *The Independent*, 17 May.

Mullins, D., Niner, P. and Riseborough, M. (1993) Large-scale voluntary transfers, in P. Malpass and R. Means (eds) *Implementing Housing Policy.* Buckingham: Open University Press.

Nairne, Sir P. (1983) Managing the DHSS elephant: reflections on a giant department, *Political Quarterly*, 54(3): 243–56.

National Audit Office (1986) *The Rayner Scrutiny Programme: 1979–83*, HC 322. London: HMSO.

National Audit Office (1987) *Community Care Developments*, HC 108. London: HMSO.

National Audit Office (1988) *Department of Health and Social Security: Quality of Service to the Public*, HC 451. London: HMSO.

National Audit Office (1998) *Benefits Agency: Performance Measurement*, HC 952. London: The Stationery Office.

National Audit Office (2001) *Inappropriate Adjustments to NHS Waiting Lists*, HC 452. London: The Stationery Office.

National Consumer Council (1986) *Measuring Up: Consumer Assessment of Local Authority Services: A Guideline Study.* London: National Consumer Council.

Newman, J. (2000) Beyond the new public management? Modernizing public services, in J. Clarke, S. Gewirtz and E. McLaughlin (eds) *New Managerialism, New Welfare?* London: Sage.

Newman, J. (2001) *Modernising Government: New Labour, Policy and Society.* London: Sage.

Newton, K. and Karran, T.J. (1985) *The Politics of Local Expenditure.* London: Macmillan.

NHS Executive (1998) *The New NHS: A National Framework for Assessing Performance.* Leeds: NHS Executive.

NHS Management Executive (1991) *NHS Reforms: The First Six Months.* London: Department of Health.

Niskanen, W. (1971) *Bureaucracy and Representative Government.* Chicago: Aldine.

Norton, P. (1982) 'Dear Minister . . .' – the importance of MP-to-minister correspondence, *Parliamentary Affairs*, 35(1): 59–72.

Office for National Statistics (2001) *Annual Abstract of Statistics 2001 Edition*. London: The Stationery Office.

Office of Public Service (1996) *government.direct. A Prospectus for the Electronic Delivery of Government Services*, Cm 3438. London: HMSO.

Oliver, D. (1991) *Government in the United Kingdom: The Search for Accountability, Effectiveness and Citizenship*. Buckingham: Open University Press.

Osborne, D. and Gaebler, T. (1992) *Reinventing Government: How the Entrepreneurial Spirit is Transforming the Public Sector*. Reading, MA: Addison-Wesley.

Packwood, T., Buxton, H. and Keen, J. (1990) Resource management in the National Health Service: a first case history, *Policy and Politics*, 18(4): 245–55.

Painter, C. (1999) Public service reform from Thatcher to Blair: a third way, *Parliamentary Affairs*, 51(1): 94–112.

Painter, C. and Isaac Henry, K. (1999) Managing local public services, in S. Horton and D. Farnham (eds) *Public Management in Britain*. London: Macmillan.

Paris, C. and Blackaby, B. (1979) *Not Much Improvement*. London: Heinemann.

Parliamentary Commissioner for Administration Select Committee (1992) *Second Report 1991–92: The Implications of the Citizen's Charter for the Work of the Parliamentary Commissioner for Administration*, HC 158. London: HMSO.

Parliamentary Ombudsman (2001) *First Report 2001–2002. Annual Report 2000–01*, HC 5. London: The Stationery Office.

Pater, J.E. (1981) *The Making of the National Health Service*. London: King's Fund.

Performance and Innovation Unit (2000) *Wiring it Up: Whitehall's Management of Cross-Cutting Policies and Services*. London: The Stationery Office.

Perrin, J. (1992) Administrative and financial management of local health services, in E. Beck, S. Lonsdale, S. Newman and D. Patterson (eds) *In the Best of Health? The Status and Future of Health Care in Britain*. London: Chapman and Hall.

Peters, T.J. and Waterman, R.H. (1982) *In Search of Excellence: Lessons from America's Best-Run Companies*. New York: Warner.

Pickvance, C. (1991) The difficulty of control and the case of structural reform: British local government in the 1980s, in C. Pickvance and E. Preteceille (eds) *State Restructuring and Local Power*. London: Gower.

Pinker, R. (1992) Making sense of the mixed economy of welfare, *Social Policy and Administration*, 26(4): 273–84.

Pitt, D. and Smith, B. (1981) *Government Departments: An Organizational Perspective*. London: Routledge and Kegan Paul.

Plowden, Sir E. (1961) *The Control of Public Expenditure*, Cm 1432. London: HMSO.

Pollitt, C. (1980) Rationalising the machinery of government: the Conservatives 1970–74, *Political Studies*, 28(1): 84–98.

Pollitt, C. (1984a) *Manipulating the Machine: Changing the Pattern of Ministerial Departments 1960–83*. London: Allen & Unwin.

Pollitt, C. (1984b) Professionals and public policy, *Public Administration Bulletin*, 44: 29–46.

Pollitt, C. (1985) Measuring performance: a new system for the National Health Service, *Policy and Politics*, 13(1): 1–15.

Pollitt, C. (1986) Beyond the managerial model: the case for broadening performance assessment in government and the public services, *Financial Accountability and Management*, 2(3): 155–70.

Pollitt, C. (1987) Performance measurement and the consumer: hijacking a bandwagon?, in National Consumer Council, *Performance Measurement and the Consumer*. London: National Consumer Council.

Pollitt, C. (1991) *The Politics of Quality: Managers, Professionals and Consumers in the Public Services*. Egham: Royal Holloway and Bedford New College.

Pollitt, C. (1993) *Managerialism and the Public Services*, 2nd edn. Oxford: Blackwell.

Pollitt, C. and Harrison, S. (eds) (1992) *Handbook of Public Services Management*. Oxford: Blackwell.

Ponting, C. (1986) *Whitehall: Tragedy and Farce*. London: Hamish Hamiliton.

Poole, K.P. (1978) *The Local Government Service in England and Wales*. London: Allen & Unwin.

Potter, J. (1988) Consumerism and the public sector: how well does the coat fit?, *Public Administration*, 66(2): 149–64.

Powell, J.E. (1966) *A New Look at Medicine and Politics*. London: Pitman.

Power, A. (1987) *The Crisis in Council Housing: Is Public Housing Manageable?*, Welfare State Programme Paper 21. London: London School of Economics.

Power, A. (1988) *Under New Management: The Experience of Thirteen Islington Cooperatives*. London: Priority Estates Project.

Power, M. (1994) *The Audit Explosion*. London: Demos.

Power, M. (1997) *The Audit Society*. Oxford: Oxford University Press.

Priestley, C. (1986) Promoting the efficiency of central government, in A. Shenfield et al. *Managing the Bureaucracy*. London: Adam Smith Institute.

Prime Minister (1988) *Implementing Management in Government: The Next Steps*. London: HMSO.

Prime Minister (1991) *The Citizen's Charter: Raising the Standard*, Cm 1599. London: HMSO.

Prime Minister (1992) *The Citizen's Charter: First Report 1992*, Cm 2101. London: HMSO.

Public Accounts Committee (PAC) (1971) *Third Report 1970–71*, HC 537. London: HMSO.

Public Accounts Committee (PAC) (1976) *Sixth Report 1975–76*, HC 584. London: HMSO.

Public Accounts Committee (PAC) (1977) *Ninth Report 1976–77*, HC 532. London: HMSO.

Public Accounts Committee (PAC) (1978) *Ninth Report 1977–78*, HC 622. London: HMSO.

Public Accounts Committee (PAC) (1981) *Seventeenth Report 1980–81: Financial Control and Accountability in the National Health Service*, HC 255. London: HMSO.

Public Accounts Committee (PAC) (1988) *Forty-Fourth Report 1987–88: Quality of Service to the Public at DHSS Local Offices*, HC 491. London: HMSO.

Public Accounts Committee (PAC) (2000) *Fourth Report 1999–2000: Appropriation Accounts 1997–98 Class XII, Vote 1 (Central Government Administered Social Security Benefits and Other Payments)*, HC 103. London: The Stationery Office.

Public Administration Committee (2000) *Sixth Report 2000–2001: Innovations in Citizen Participation in Government*, HC 373. London: The Stationery Office.

Radford, M. (1991) Auditing for change: local government and the Audit Commission, *Modern Law Review*, 54(6): 912–32.

Ranade, W. (1994) *A Future for the NHS? Health Care in the 1990s*. London: Longman.

Ranson, S. (1985) Education, in S. Ranson, G. Jones and K. Walsh (eds) *Between Centre and Locality*. London: Allen & Unwin.

Ranson, S. (1990) Education, in N. Deakin and A. Wright (eds) *Consuming Public Services*. London: Routledge.

Ranson, S. (1992a) *The Role of Local Government in Education: Assuring Quality and Accountability*. London: Longman.

Ranson, S. (1992b) Education, in F. Terry and P. Jackson (eds) *Public Domain Yearbook 1992*. London: Public Finance Foundation.

Ranson, S. and Thomas, H. (1989) Education reform: consumer democracy or social democracy?, in J. Stewart and G. Stoker (eds) *The Future of Local Government*. London: Macmillan.

Ranson, S. and Travers, T. (1994) Education, in P. Jackson and M. Lavender (eds) *The Public Services Yearbook 1994*. London: Chapman and Hall.

Raynsford, N. (1986) The 1977 Housing (Homeless Persons) Act, in N. Deakin (ed.) *Policy Change in Government: Three Case Studies*. London: Royal Institute of Public Administration.

Redcliffe-Maud, Lord (1969) *Royal Commission on Local Government in England: 1966–1969*, Vol. I: Report, Cmnd 4040. London: HMSO.

Redcliffe-Maud, Lord and Wood, B. (1974) *English Local Government Reformed*. London: Oxford University Press.

Regan, D. (1977) *Local Government and Education*. London: Allen & Unwin.

Rhodes, R.A.W. (1979) Research into central–local relations in Britain: a framework for analysis, Appendix I in *Central–Local Government Relationships*. London: Social Science Research Council.

Rhodes, R.A.W. (1987) Developing the public service orientation, or let's add a *soupcon* of political theory, *Local Government Studies*, 13(3): 63–73.

Rhodes, R.A.W. (1988) *Beyond Westminster and Whitehall: The Sub-Central Governments of Britain*. London: Unwin Hyman.

Rhodes, R.A.W. (1992a) Local government finance, in D. Marsh and R.A.W. Rhodes (eds) *Implementing Thatcherite Policies: Audit of an Era*. Buckingham: Open University Press.

Rhodes, R.A.W. (1992b) Local government, in B. Jones and L. Robins (eds) *Two Decades in British Politics*. Manchester: University of Manchester Press.

Rhodes, R.A.W. (2000) Conclusion: understanding the British governmental tradition: an anti-foundational approach, in R.A.W. Rhodes (ed.) *Transforming British Government: Vol. 2, Changing Roles and Relationships*. London: Macmillan.

Rhodes, R.A.W. (2001) The civil service, in A. Seldon (ed.) *The Blair Effect: The Blair Government 1997–2001*. London: Little, Brown.

Richards, P.G. (1972) *The Backbenchers*. London: Faber and Faber.

Richardson, A. (1983) *Participation*. London: Routledge & Kegan Paul.

Ridley, F. (1995) Towards a skeleton state? Changes to public sector management, in J. Wilson (ed.) *Managing Public Services: Dealing with Dogma*. Eastham: Tudor.

Ridley, N. (1973) Efficiency begins at home, in W.A. Niskanen, *Bureaucracy: Servant or Master?* London: Institute of Economic Affairs.

Ridley, N. (1988a) *The Local Right: Enabling not Providing*. London: Centre for Policy Studies.

Ridley, N. (1988b) Speech to Institute of Housing Conference, 17 June 1988. Department of Environment News Release.

Robinson, R. (1988) *Efficiency and the NHS: A Case for Internal Markets*. London: Institute of Economic Affairs.

Robson, W.A. (1935) The public utilities services, in H. Laski, W.I. Jennings and W.A. Robson (eds) *A Century of Municipal Progress*. London: Allen & Unwin.

Robson, W.A. (1966) *Local Government in Crisis*. London: Allen & Unwin.

Rose, R. (1989) *Politics in England*, 5th edn. London: Macmillan.

Rouse, J. (1999) Performance management, quality management and contracts, in S. Horton and D. Farnham (eds) *Public Management in Britain*. London: Macmillan.

Sargeant, T. (1979) Joint care planning in the health and personal social services, in T. Booth (ed.) *Planning for Welfare*. Oxford: Blackwell/Martin Robertson.

Scrivens, E. (1988) Consumers, accountabilty and quality of service, in R. Maxwell (ed.) *Reshaping the National Health Service*. Hermitage: Policy Journals.

Seebohm, F. (1968) *Report of the Committee on Local Authority and Personal Allied Social Services*, Cmnd 3703. London: HMSO.

Seneviratne, M. (2000) 'Joining up' the ombudsmen – the review of the Public Sector Ombudsmen, *Public Law*, winter: 582–91.

Sharp, E. (1969) *The Ministry of Housing and Local Government*. London: Allen & Unwin.

Sharpe, L.J. (1970) Theories and values of local government, *Political Studies*, 18(2): 153–74.

Skelcher, C. (1998) *The Appointed State: Quasi-governmental Organizations and Democracy*. Buckingham: Open University Press.

Smith, B.C. (1981) Control in British government: a problem of accountability, *Policy Studies Journal*, 9(8): 1163–74.

Smith, B.C. and Stanyer, J. (1976) *Administering Britain*. London: Martin Robertson.

Smith, D. and Cracknell, D. (2001) Fraud and waste cost NHS £7b a year, *Sunday Times*, 2 December.

Social Services Committee (1980) *Third Report 1979–80. The Government's White Papers on Public Expenditure: The Social Services*, HC 702-1. London: HMSO.

Social Services Inspectorate (2002) *A Guide to Social Services Performance 'Star' Ratings*. London: Department of Health.

Spencer, K.M. (1989) Local government and the housing reforms, in J. Stewart and G. Stoker (eds) *The Future of Local Government*. London: Macmillan.

Stanyer, J. (1976) *Understanding Local Government*. London: Fontana.

Stewart, J. (1986) *The New Management of Local Government*. London: Allen & Unwin.

Stewart, J. (1987) Has decentralisation failed?, *Local Government Policy Making*, 14(2): 49–53.

Stewart, J. (1989) The changing organisation and management of local authorities, in J. Stewart and G. Stoker (eds) *The Future of Local Government*. London: Macmillan.

Stewart, J. (1992) The rebuilding of public accountability, in J. Stewart, N. Lewis and D. Longley, *Accountability and the Public*. London: European Policy Forum.

Stewart, J. (1993) The limitations of management by contract, *Public Money and Management*, 13(3): 1–6.

Stewart, J. (2000) *The Nature of British Local Government*. London: Macmillan.

Stewart, J. and Clarke, M. (1987) The public service orientation: issues and dilemmas, *Public Administration*, 69(2): 161–77.

Stewart, J. and Stoker, G. (eds) (1989) Introduction, in *The Future of Local Government*. London: Macmillan.

Stewart, J. and Walsh, K. (1992) Change in the management of public services, *Public Administration*, 70(4): 499–518.

Stoker, G. (1988) *The Politics of Local Government*. London: Macmillan.

Stoker, G. (1990) Government beyond Whitehall, in P. Dunleavy, A. Gamble and G. Peele (eds) *Developments in British Politics 3*. London: Macmillan.

Stoker, G. (1991) *The Politics of Local Government*, 2nd edn. London: Macmillan.

Stott, T. (1994) Market testing and beyond: privatisation and contracting out in British central government, *Teaching Public Administration*, 14(1): 36–48.

Strong, P. and Robinson, J. (1990) *The NHS under New Management*. Buckingham: Open University Press.

Sugden, R. (1984) Voluntary organisations and the welfare state, in J. Le Grand and R. Robinson (eds) *Privatisation and the Welfare State*. London: Allen & Unwin.

Taylor, I. (1999) Raising the expectation interest: New Labour and the Citizen's Charter, *Public Policy and Administration*, 14(4): 29–38.

Taylor, M. (1992) The changing role of the nonprofit sector in Britain: moving toward the market, in B. Gidron, R.M. Kramer and L.M. Sulaman (eds) *Government and the Third Sector*. San Francisco, CA: Jossey-Bass.

Taylor-Gooby, P. and Dale, J. (1981) *Social Theory and Social Welfare*. London: Edward Arnold.

Taylor-Gooby, P. and Lawson, R. (1993) Where do we go from here: the new order in welfare, in P. Taylor-Gooby and R. Lawson (eds) *Markets and Managers: New Issues in the Delivery of Welfare*. Buckingham: Open University Press.

Thorpe-Tracey, S.F. (1987) Financial management initiative in practice: Newcastle Central Office, *Public Administration*, 65(3): 331–7.

Titmuss, R.M. (1974) *Social Policy*. London: Allen & Unwin.

Townsend, P., Davidson, N. and Whitehead, M. (1988) Introduction, in P. Townsend, N. Davidson and M. Whitehead, *Inequalities in Health*. Harmondsworth: Penguin.

Travers, T. (1986) *The Politics of Local Government Finance*. London: Allen & Unwin.

Travers, T. (2001) Reach for the stars, *Public Finance*, 16–22 November.

Travis, T. (1993) DSS hive-off 'could lead to blackmail', *The Guardian*, 21 June.

Treasury and Civil Service Committee (1989) *Fifth Report 1988–89: Developments in the Next Steps Programme*, HC 348. London: HMSO.

Treasury and Civil Service Committee (1990) *Eighth Report 1989–90: Progress in the Next Steps Initiative*, HC 481. London: HMSO.

Trippier, D. (1989) Speech reported in *Voluntary Housing*, 22(2): 10–11, 30.

Waldegrave, W. (1987) Some Reflections on Housing Policy, Conservative Party News Service, 19 May.

Waldegrave, W. (1993) *Public Services and the Future: Reforming Britain's Bureaucracy*. London: Conservative Political Centre.

Walker, A. (1989) Community care, in M. McCarthy (ed.) *The New Politics of Welfare: An Agenda for the Nineties?* London: Macmillan.

Walsh, K. (1989) Competition and service in local government, in J. Stewart and G. Stoker (eds) *The Future of Local Government*. London: Macmillan.

Walsh, K. and Davis, H. (1993) *Competition and Service: The Impact of the Local Government Act 1988*. London: HMSO.

Warner, N. (1984) Raynerism in practice: anatomy of a Rayner scrutiny, *Public Administration*, 62(1): 7–22.

Weaver, M. (2000) Going fast, *The Guardian*, 2 February.

Webb, A. (1991) Coordination: a problem in public sector management, *Policy and Politics*, 19(4): 229–40.

Webb, A. and Wistow, G. (1982) *Whither State Welfare? Policy and Implementation in the Personal Social Services: 1979–80*. London: Royal Institute of Public Administration.

Webb, A. and Wistow, G. (1987) *Social Work, Social Care and Social Planning: The Personal Social Services since Seebohm*. London: Longman.

Webb, A., Day, L. and Weller, D. (1976) *Voluntary Social Service Manpower Resources*. London: Personal Social Services Council.

Weber, M. (1964) *The Theory of Social and Economic Organization*, translated by A.M. Henderson and T. Parsons. New York: Free Press.

Webster, B. (1991) *Customer Service in the Counties*. London: Association of County Councils.

Weir, S. and Hall, S. (1994) *Extra-Governmental Organisations in the United Kingdom and their Accountability*. London: Charter 88 Trust.

Wheatley, Lord (1969) *Royal Commission on Local Government in Scotland*, Report, Cmnd 4150. London: HMSO.

Whitehead, P. (1985) *The Writing on the Wall: Britain in the Seventies*. London: Michael Joseph.

Whitty, G. (1990) The politics of the 1988 Education Reform Act, in P. Dunleavy, A. Gamble and G. Peele (eds) *Developments in British Politics 3*. London: Macmillan.

Wicks, M. (1983) Joint approach to social policy, letter to the editor, *The Times*, 8 July.

Wicks, M. (1987) *A Future for All? Do We Need a Welfare State?* Harmondsworth: Penguin.

Widdicombe, D. (1986) *The Conduct of Local Authority Business: Report of the Committee of Inquiry into the Conduct of Local Authority Business*, Cmnd 9797. London: HMSO.

Wikeley, N. and Young, R. (1992) The administration of benefits in Britain: adjudication officers and the influence of social security appeal tribunals, *Public Law*, summer: 238–62.

Wilcox, B. (1989) The Education Reform Act (1988): implications for schools and local education authorities, in M. Brenton and C. Ungerson (eds) *Social Policy Review 1988–9*. London: Longman.

Wilding, P. (1982) *Professional Power and Social Welfare*. London: Routledge and Kegan Paul.

Willcocks, A.J. (1967) *The Creation of the National Health Service*. London: Routledge and Kegan Paul.

Willmore, N. (1992) The Citizen's Charter brings out the cynics, *The Times*, 20 October.

Wilson, D. (2000a) Towards local governance: rhetoric and reality, *Public Policy and Administration*, 15(1): 43–57.

Wilson, D. (2000b) New Labour, new local governance?, in R. Pyper and L. Robins (eds) *United Kingdom Governance*. London: Macmillan.

Wilson, D. (2001) Local government: balancing diversity and uniformity, *Parliamentary Affairs*, 54(2): 289–307.

Wilson, D. and Game, C. (1998) *Local Government in the United Kingdom*, 2nd edn. London: Macmillan.

Wilson, D. and Game, C. with Leach, S. and Stoker, G. (1994) *Local Government in the United Kingdom*. London: Macmillan.

Winkler, F. (1987) Consumerism in health care: beyond the supermarket model, *Policy and Politics*, 15(1): 1–8.

Wintour, P. (2002) The 'hotline to the nation' goes cold, *The Guardian*, 9 January.

Wistow, G. (1992a) The National Health Service, in D. Marsh and R.A.W. Rhodes (eds) *Implementing Thatcherite Policies: Audit of an Era*. Buckingham: Open University Press.

Wistow, G. (1992b) The health service policy community: professionals pre-eminent or under challenge?, in D. Marsh and R.A.W. Rhodes (eds) *Policy Networks in British Government*. Oxford: Clarendon Press.

Wistow, G. and Barnes, M. (1993) User involvement in community care: origins, purposes and applications, *Public Administration*, 71(3): 279–99.

Wistow, G., Knapp, M., Hardy, B. and Allen, C. (1992) From providing to enabling: local authorities and the mixed economy of care, *Public Administration*, 70(1): 25–45.

Wolfenden, Lord (1978) *The Future of Voluntary Organisations*. London: Croom Helm.

Wood, B. (1988) Privatisation: local government and the health service, in C. Graham and T. Prosser (eds) *Waiving the Rules: The Constitution under Thatcherism*. Milton Keynes: Open University Press.

Woodward, W. (2001a) Profit-making private company takes over running of school, *The Guardian*, 24 May.

Woodward, W. (2001b) Education zones dubbed a flop, *The Guardian*, 27 November.

Wright, M.W. (1977) Public expenditure in Britain: the crisis of control, *Public Administration*, 55(2): 143–69.

Young, S. (1986) The nature of privatisation in Britain 1979–85, *West European Politics*, 9(2): 235–52.

Younghusband, E. (1978) *Social Work in Britain, 1950–1975, Vol. I*. London: Allen & Unwin.

Index

PERSPECTIVES ON WELFARE
IDEAS, IDEOLOGIES AND POLICY DEBATES

Alan Deacon

Of the several discussions of the American poverty theorists I have read, this is easily the best. Anyone interested in that debate should begin here.
> *Professor Lawrence M. Mead, New York University*

a compelling guide to the ideas that have shaped and seek to re-shape welfare provision. This is a student text that teachers will want to read first.
> *Professor Robert Walker, University of Nottingham*

- How do welfare benefits and services shape the attitudes, behaviour and character of claimants? Should entitlement be dependent upon good behaviour?

- What are the major intellectual influences upon current welfare reforms in the UK and the US?

- Is it possible to reform welfare in ways which tackle both social inequality and welfare dependency?

This lucid and engaging book provides an introduction to the current debates about the future direction of welfare reform on both sides of the Atlantic. The first part outlines a range of different perspectives on welfare, and shows how each of these perspectives rests upon a different assumption about the role and purpose of welfare policy and a different understanding of human nature and motivation. Some of these perspectives see the primary role of welfare as to reduce inequalities, while others see the central objective as the reduction of welfare dependency. The second part shows how the current debates in Britain and the United States are informed by these perspectives, and argues that debates about inequality and dependency are not mutually exclusive but address different dimensions of the same problem. In all, this illuminating and forward-looking text is essential reading for courses in social policy, health, and social welfare, as well as those with a political and wider interest in welfare reform.

Contents
Introduction – Part 1 The perspectives – Welfare and equality – Welfare and self-interest – Welfare and paternalism – Welfare and obligation – Welfare as temporary support – Part 2 Policy debates – Ending dependency? Welfare reform in the United States – A new deal for welfare? New Labour and the reform of welfare in Britain – Conclusion – Glossary – Bibliography – Index.

c.160pp   0 335 20320 5 (Paperback)   0 335 20321 3 (Hardback)

POLICY TRANSFER AND BRITISH SOCIAL POLICY
LEARNING FROM THE USA?

David P. Dolowitz with Rob Hulme, Mike Nellis and Fiona O'Neill

Over the past twenty years the British State has undergone fundamental transformations in most areas of public policy, particularly those associated with social policy – welfare, health, education, and law and order. The purpose of this book is to develop and use a model of policy transfer to illustrate how many of the recent changes in British public policy can be traced directly to the process of policy transfer, particularly that between the United States and Britain.

It introduces and illustrates the concept of policy transfer through a selection of case studies, demonstrating its role in the development of particular policy areas, each of which involve different processes, actors and implications. At the same time, each case study also reveals the serious problems in adapting 'foreign' models to their new settings.

Policy Transfer and British Social Policy argues the wider usefulness of the concept of policy transfer in the analysis of policy and institutional development; its analysis and case studies will be invaluable to students and scholars in the fields of public policy, social policy, comparative politics and developmental studies.

Contents
Introduction: a new face to British public policy – Policy transfer: a new framework of policy analysis – Welfare: the Child Support Agency – Health: the 'internal market' and reform of the National Health Service – Education: post-compulsory education in England and Wales – Law and order: the electronic monitoring of offenders – Conclusion: where to we go from here? – Notes – References – Index.

160pp   0 335 19991 7 (Paperback)   0 335 19992 5 (Hardback)

openup

ideas and understanding
in social science

www.**openup**.co.uk

 **Browse, search and
order online**

 **Download detailed
title information and
sample chapters***

*for selected titles

www.**openup**.co.uk

Learning Resources
Centre